SCOTT FORESMAN

Art

Rebecca Brooks, Ph.D.
Program Author

Editorial Offices: Glenview, Illinois • Parsippany, New Jersey • New York, New York

Sales Offices: Boston, Massachusetts • Duluth, Georgia • Glenview, Illinois • Coppell, Texas • Sacramento, California • Mesa, Arizona

9 10 V063 09 08 07 06

Program *Consultants*

Christopher Adejumo, Ph.D.
Associate Professor
Visual Art Studies
University of Texas
Austin, Texas

Doug Blandy, Ph.D.
Professor and Director
Arts and Administration Program
Institute for Community Arts
and Studies
University of Oregon
Eugene, Oregon

Georgia Collins, Ph.D.
Professor Emeritus
College of Fine Arts
University of Kentucky
Lexington, Kentucky

Deborah Cooper, M.Ed.
Coordinating Director of Arts Education
Curriculum and Instruction
Charlotte-Mecklenburg Schools
Charlotte, North Carolina

Sandra M. Epps, Ph.D.
Multicultural Art Education Consultant
New York, New York

Mary Jo Gardere
Multi-Arts Specialist
Eladio Martinez Learning Center
Dallas, Texas

Carlos G. Gómez, M.F.A.
Professor of Fine Art
University of Texas at Brownsville
and Texas Southmost College
Brownsville, Texas

Kristina Lamour, M.F.A.
Assistant Professor
The Art Institute of Boston
at Lesley University
Boston, Massachusetts

Melinda M. Mayer, Ph.D.
Assistant Professor
School of Visual Arts
University of North Texas
Denton, Texas

Robyn Montana Turner, Ph.D.
Author and University Teacher
Austin, Texas

Contributing Authors

Sara A. Chapman, M,Ed.
Coordinator, Visual Arts Program
Alief Independent School District, Houston, TX

James M. Clarke, M,Ed.
Executive Director, Texas Coalition for Quality Arts
Education, Houston, TX

Reviewers

Studio Reviewers

Judy Abbott, *Art Educator*
Allison Elementary School
Austin Independent
School District
Austin, Texas

Lin Altman, *Art Educator*
Cedar Creek
Elementary School
Eanes Independent
School District
Austin, Texas

Geral T. Butler,
Art Educator (Retired)
Heritage High School
Lynchburg City Schools
Lynchburg, Virginia

Dale Case,
Elementary Principal
Fox Meadow Elementary
School
Nettleton School District
Jonesboro, Arkansas

Deborah McLouth,
Art Educator
Zavala Elementary School
Austin Independent
School District
Austin, Texas

Patricia Newman,
Art Educator
Saint Francis Xavier School
Archdiocese of Chicago
La Grange, Illinois

Nancy Sass, *Art Educator*
Cambridge Elementary
School
Alamo Heights Independent
School District
San Antonio, Texas

Sue Spiva Telle, *Art Educator*
Woodridge Elementary
School
Alamo Heights Independent
School District
San Antonio, Texas

Cari Washburn, *Art Educator*
Great Oaks Elementary School
Round Rock Independent
School District
Round Rock, Texas

Critic Readers

Celeste Anderson
Roosevelt Elementary School
Nampa, Idaho

Mary Jo Birkholz
Wilson Elementary School
Janesville, Wisconsin

Mary Jane Cahalan
Mitzi Bond Elementary
School
El Paso, Texas

Cindy Collar
Cloverleaf Elementary School
Cartersville, Georgia

Yvonne Days
St. Louis Public Schools
St. Louis, Missouri

Shirley Dickey
Creative Art Magnet School
Houston, Texas

Ray Durkee
Charlotte Performing
Arts Center
Punta Gorda, Florida

Sue Flores-Minick
Bryker Woods
Elementary School
Austin, Texas

Denise Jennings
Fulton County Schools
Atlanta, Georgia

Alicia Lewis
Stevens Elementary School
Houston, Texas

James Miller
Margo Elementary School
Weslaco, Texas

Marta Olson
Seattle Public Schools
Seattle, Washington

Judy Preble
Florence Avenue School
Irvington, New Jersey

Tonya Roberson
Oleson Elementary School
Houston, Texas

Andrew Southwick
Edgewood Independent
School District
San Antonio, Texas

Nita Ulaszek
Audelia Creek
Elementary School
Dallas, Texas

Tessie Varthas
Office of Creative and
Public Art
Philadelphia, Pennsylvania

Penelope Venola
Spurgeon Intermediate School
Santa Ana, California

Elizabeth Willett
Art Specialist
Fort Worth. Texas

Contents

Unit 1

The Elements of Art 14

M. C. Escher. *Sun and Moon,* 1948.

Alessandro Maganza. *Study for an Angel,*
16th century.

Unit 2
The Principles of Design....................62

Claes Oldenburg. *Clothespin*, 1976.

Artist unknown, Aztec. *Pendant representing the sun.*

Unit 3
Art Media and Techniques 102

Ando Hiroshige. *The Whirlpools at Awa: Naruto Rapido.*

Frédéric-Auguste Bartholdi. *Liberty Enlightening the World (Statue of Liberty),* 1884–1886.

Unit 4
The Creative Process.......................154

Gilbert Stuart. *George Washington,* 1796.

Artist unknown. *Mochica Portrait Stirrup Spout Bottle of a Chief Wearing a Bird Helmet,* A.D. 200–700.

Unit 5

Art Through the Ages 198

Architect unknown. *Neak Pean Shrine,*
A.D. 1181–1219.

Unit 6

Careers in Art 250

Calvin Southwell. *Fashion Design #4.*

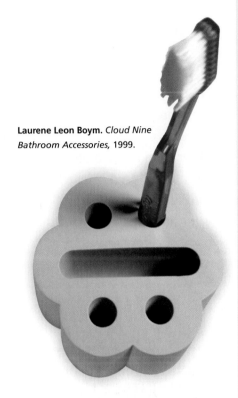

Laurene Leon Boym. *Cloud Nine Bathroom Accessories,* 1999.

Dan Flavin. *Greens Crossing Greens (to Piet Mondrian who lacked green),* 1966.

Introduction to Visual Art

Human beings have been using **visual art** as a method of communication for more than thirty thousand years. In fact, the use of images for communication is older than the use of words. Part of learning about visual art is learning to use it as a tool for communication. You can improve your ability to interpret the visual world by observing and creating a wide variety of artworks.

You may already be familiar with some forms of visual art such as painting, ceramics, weaving, and photography, but have you ever considered other images you see in your daily life as art? Everyday objects such as neon signs, automobiles, and billboard advertisements are all designed by career artists. Like other artworks, these images and objects express a range of emotions, moods, and ideas. The artists who create them rely on the same basic visual arts concepts that you will read about in this book.

You will discover visual art in all parts of your natural and human-made environments. A painting in a museum, the design on a cereal box, and a traffic sign are all part of your **visual culture.** Observing these and other objects will help you explore and understand the visual culture that is all around you. It will foster a greater appreciation and communication with the visual world that fills your environment.

Betsy Graves Reyneau. *William Campbell,* ca. 1944. Oil on canvas, 42 by 31 inches. National Portrait Gallery, Smithsonian Institution, Washington, D.C.

Art Criticism

Works of art would have little meaning without the communication between artist and viewer. The role of the viewer is as important as the artwork itself, and the artist who made it. It is the viewer that gives the art experience purpose and life. Just as individuals practice with materials, tools, and techniques to become skilled artists, viewers use skills in observing and understanding works of art.

Art criticism is the process of looking at works of art in a guided and logical way. Study the artwork on this page as you read about the four levels of art criticism and answer the questions.

Describe asks you to notice the visual qualities of an artwork, such as the materials and tools the artist used, where the artist used elements such as color, shape, and texture, and what the artwork is about.

- What medium did the artist use?
- Where do you see repeated shapes?
- What do you notice about the texture?

Lucy Lewis. *Native North American Vase*, 1959.

Analyze is a tool for studying the way the artist used and applied the qualities described in the first stage. This may include how colors, shapes, and textures are arranged and how they interact with one another in an artwork.

- How did the artist use lines and shapes?
- How does contrast contribute to the design?
- What helps unify the artwork?

Interpret is your idea of an artwork's meaning and the message of the artist. This may include how the previous steps relate to the artist's message, culture, and the period in which an artwork was made.

- How might a vessel of this type have been used by Native Americans?
- Does its form reveal its function? Explain.
- What does this artwork tell you about the artist's culture?

Judge is your opportunity to express your opinion about an artwork. You may discuss how successful the artist was in communicating his or her ideas, the value of the artwork, or compare it to similar works of art.

- What do you like best about this artwork? Why?
- How does this vessel compare to other similar forms you have seen?
- If you were to make a similar vessel, what changes, if any, would you make? Why?

You will have opportunities to apply these four stages of art criticism in each lesson of this book. This process will help you evaluate and appreciate the artworks of others and your own works of art.

Visit a Museum

Art museums can be found in many communities throughout the United States and the world. An **art museum** is designed to house and protect works of art for viewing and appreciating. The artworks are displayed for viewers to learn about the art created by artists from various cultures throughout history. Viewers can gain information about the artist, the process used to create each artwork, as well as the period and culture in which it was made. Observing the size and details of an artwork firsthand can touch your intellect, imagination, and inspire your own creativity.

Art museums are often designed to reflect the type of artworks they exhibit. Some museums, such as the Art Institute of Chicago, house extensive permanent collections, as well as studio and classroom space for up and coming artists. Other art museums may feature a particular art form or medium, such as The Museum of Glass in Tacoma, Washington, or the Eric Carle Museum of Picture Book Art in Amherst, Massachusetts.

The Museum of Glass features glass artworks from artists worldwide.

The Art Institute of Chicago, located on Lake Michigan, has more than 300,000 works of art in its permanent collection.

Art museums employ many people who work behind the scenes. These workers interpret, purchase and display, and preserve the artworks. Many museums also provide staff for education, communication, and research. Some workers volunteer their time.

A **docent** greets the museum's visitors and conducts tours through the exhibitions. The docent's job is to provide information and to answer questions. Many docents are trained volunteers.

A **curator** selects the artworks for an exhibition and decides where and how they should be displayed. Curators often travel the world looking for artworks for a museum's permanent collection. They often work with community members for special exhibitions. For temporary exhibitions, they sometimes borrow artworks from other museums.

A **conservator** works to protect artworks from loss, damage, or neglect. She or he studies the museum's environment and the effects it may have on the artworks. Conservators make every effort to preserve the museum's artistic treasures for future generations to enjoy and appreciate.

Museum Etiquette

When visiting an art museum, remember to:
- Obey all posted signs.
- Talk softly so that you do not disturb others. Loud voices carry in museum galleries.
- Never touch an artwork. Stay at least an arm's length away from artwork.
- Do not walk in front of someone who is viewing an artwork.
- Do not bring food and drink near the artworks.
- Do not take photographs. Flash photography can damage works of art.
- Do not carry backpacks or book bags. Bulky objects can swing and bump into works of art.

Make a Sketchbook Journal

Artists fill the blank pages of their sketchbooks with drawings and words that reflect their observations, imaginations, experiences, and ideas. It is the place where artists experiment, make changes, and practice techniques. It is also the perfect place to take notes and plan art projects.

Follow these steps to make your own Sketchbook Journal.

Materials

- ✓ cardboard (two 10" × 13" sheets)
- ✓ construction paper
- ✓ drawing paper (9" × 12" sheets)
- ✓ fabric (two 12" × 15" pieces)
- ✓ hammer and nail ⚠
- ✓ scissors, tape, glue ⚠
- ✓ raffia, yarn, or twine

1 Use scissors to score one of the pieces of cardboard one inch from the left to make a front cover that will fold. Repeat for back cover.

2 Cut two pieces of fabric one inch larger than your cardboard. Pull the fabric tight and wrap it around the cardboard. Tape the edges to the backside. Glue construction paper over the taped edges to cover them.

3 Use a hammer and nail to punch holes in a zigzag pattern along the spine of the sketchbook. Use your cover as a guide to punch holes through a stack of drawing paper.

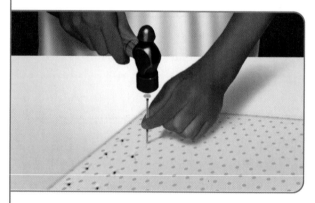

4 Weave raffia, yarn, or twine in and out of the holes to bind the pages together.

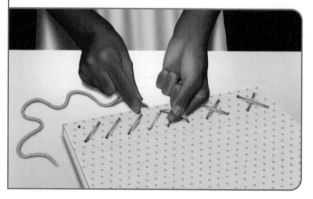

Make a Portfolio

Many artists keep their artworks in a portfolio. This allows them to protect and transport the artworks.

Follow these steps to make your own portfolio.

Materials

- ✓ posterboard
- ✓ tape
- ✓ scissors ⚠
- ✓ yarn or twine
- ✓ stapler ⚠
- ✓ markers or oil pastels

1 Staple or tape two sheets of posterboard along three sides.

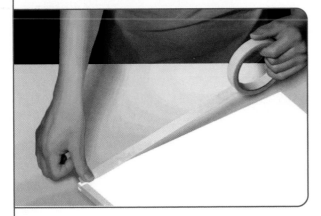

2 Cut a six-inch piece of posterboard the width of the open side. Tape the piece to the back of the open side, fold over the top, and crease it to create a flap.

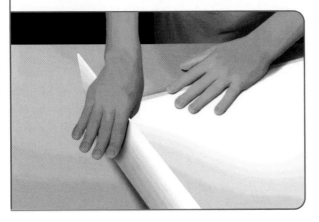

3 Staple a five-inch piece of yarn or twine to the flap as a wraparound tie closure.

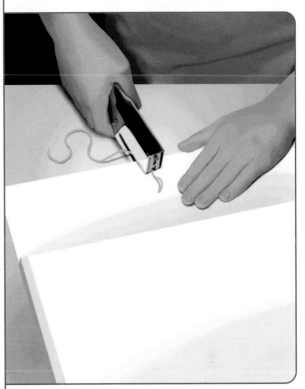

4 Design your portfolio using markers, oil pastels, or a collage technique. Use your imagination! Remember to write your name on your portfolio.

Frida Kahlo. *The Chicken,* 1945. Oil on masonite. Fundacion Dolores Olmedo, Mexico City, Mexico.

The Elements of Art

For more than 30,000 years, humans have created works of art. Even before they had written language, people understood the language of art. They painted on cave walls and carved figures in stone. They used art to understand the world around them.

Art is a form of communication. Each painting, sculpture, and photograph you see represents an idea or a feeling that the artist wants the viewer to understand. Just as a writer uses nouns, verbs, and adjectives to create a sentence, an artist uses **line**, **shape**, **form**, **space**, **value**, **color**, and **texture** to create a work of art. These **elements of art** help the artist express an idea, convey a feeling, or describe a subject. Each artist uses these elements in a different way to create a unique and personal language.

In this unit, you will learn how artists use each of the basic elements of art to convey information to a viewer, and you will explore these elements in your own works of art.

About *the Artist*

Mexican artist **Frida Kahlo** became known for her startling imagery. She twisted perspective and condensed space to describe her own personal view of the world. Read more about Kahlo's life and art on pages 36–39.

Line

A **line** is a mark made by a point moving across a surface. Line is an element of art that you can draw in the sand with a stick. Lines are what you leave behind you when you swipe a fork across wet clay.

You can make a thick line with a marker or a thin one with a pen. When you write your signature, you use a line to form your name. Artists use lines to communicate information, too. Different types of lines can convey different messages.

Vertical lines go up and down. They can convey height or strength.

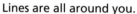

Horizontal lines are parallel to the horizon. They often suggest solid objects.

Diagonal lines slant. They can indicate movement or convey distance.

Parallel lines travel side-by-side but never touch. They are often used to suggest order.

Lines can have different qualities. They can be thick, thin, broken, continuous, zigzag, straight, or curved.

Lines are all around you.

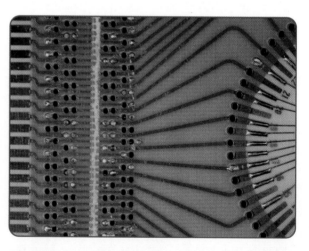

What types of lines do you see in this photograph?

Ando Hiroshige. *Fuji from Sagami River,* 19th century. Colored print, 13 ¼ by 8 ¾ inches. Newark Museum, Newark, NJ.

Lines Express Feelings

Lines can help an artist convey a certain mood or feeling. Thick lines feel bold or aggressive. Thin lines feel delicate. Zigzag or jagged lines feel chaotic or exciting.

Look at the print of Mount Fuji. What types of lines did Hiroshige use? Notice how the lines give the artwork a feeling of calm. Now look at Van Gogh's painting. Even though the colors are similar to those in Hiroshige's print, the mood is much different. It is turbulent. What types of lines does Van Gogh use to create this mood?

Van Gogh created this painting while living in Saint-Rémy, France. He enjoyed painting scenes outdoors, but he painted *The Starry Night* from memory. It has inspired poems and songs about the art and artist.

Vincent van Gogh. *The Starry Night,* 1889. Oil on canvas, 29 by 36 ¼ inches. The Museum of Modern Art, New York.

Sketchbook Journal

Choose an object in your classroom. What types of lines does it have? Sketch the object and label the lines. Then make another sketch of the object, changing the lines. Make them thicker, or curve them more. How do different lines alter the mood of your sketch?

Alessandro Maganza. *Study for an Angel,* 16th century. Pen and ink drawing. Musée Bonnat, Bayonne, France.

What motions does this drawing show?

Visualize players in a basketball game. The players move quickly and may hold one position for just a fleeting moment. How can an artist capture this kind of movement? One technique artists use is the **gesture drawing,** a drawing made rapidly to record a figure's movement or actions. Artists often use this type of drawing in preparation for a finished artwork.

Alessandro Maganza (1556–1640) used lines to capture this figure in motion. Look for these details:

- Details are omitted. In a gesture drawing, the idea is to work rapidly.
- The artist showed the figure's front leg in two positions. Artists often use gesture drawings to show more than one movement in the same drawing.

Actual and Implied Lines

In his drawing, Maganza used **actual lines,** lines that you can see, and **implied lines,** lines that seem to be there because of actual lines, shapes, or colors. Notice that no one line defines the figure's back; it is implied through the use of several actual lines.

Technique Tip

Holding Your Pencil

As you make a gesture drawing, hold your pencil or crayon in this manner: Put the tip between your thumb and first finger and the length of it in your palm. Hold your hand as if you held a remote control. Then draw with large, fluid motions. This position will take some getting used to, but it will help you keep your drawings loose.

Studio 1

Gesture Drawing with Line

Use what you have learned about lines to make a series of gesture drawings that capture a figure's movement.

Materials

✓ 12" × 18" newsprint, two sheets
✓ soft-lead pencil or black crayon

1 Ask a classmate to hold a series of ten action poses for thirty seconds each. Poses can include motions like twisting or throwing.

2 On your first sheet of paper, make a gesture drawing of each of the first five poses. Keep your lines loose and work quickly.

3 On the second sheet, draw the next five poses. This time, vary your lines. For example, use heavier lines for the leg that bears weight.

Review and Reflect

- Describe the types of lines you used in your gesture drawings.
- What areas did you focus on most when trying to capture the pose?
- How do the different types of lines change the drawings?
- Point out the drawing that best conveys a gesture. Why does it work?

Shape

You can tell a duck is a duck without hearing it quack. How? You recognize its shape. **Shape,** an element of art, is an area that has height and width. You can make shapes by cutting them out, by drawing their edges, or by coloring their insides.

Artists use two types of shapes. Precise, mathematical shapes like circles, squares, rectangles, and triangles are called **geometric shapes.** Irregular shapes like those found in nature are called **organic shapes.**

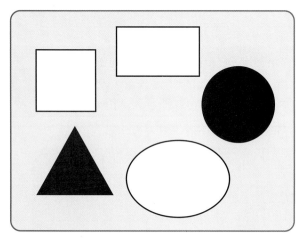

You can identify these geometric shapes easily.

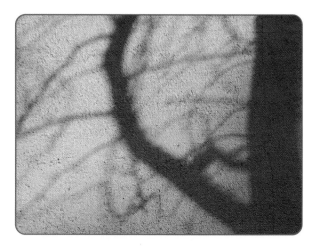

This shadow is a shape because it is two-dimensional. Is it organic or geometric?

What do these organic shapes represent?

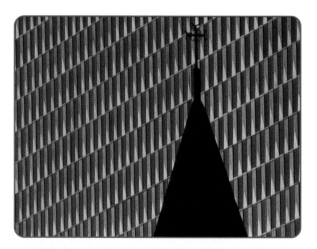

The building casts a shadow that has a geometric shape.

Fernand Léger. *Disks,* 1918.
Oil on canvas, 94 by 71 inches.
Musée d'Art de la Ville de Paris.
Paris, France.

Shapes in Art

The parents of French artist Fernand Léger (1881–1955) wanted him to become an architect. But he became interested in art and showing the workings of a city in his paintings.

Léger used clearly defined shapes in solid colors to create bold patterns on his canvases. He got ideas for shapes from the world around him. Because he was inspired by the buildings and machines of the industrial age, simplified architectural and mechanical shapes often appear in his paintings. Did Léger use organic or geometric shapes in this painting? What objects might have inspired the shapes he used?

Sketchbook Journal

Draw at least ten shapes from the world around you. Label each shape to identify where it came from and what type of shape it is. Choose three or four of the shapes you have drawn. Create a small composition with them by drawing a rectangle and filling it with the shapes you have chosen.

M. C. Escher. *Sun and Moon,* 1948. Woodcut in green, red, gold and black, printed from four blocks, 9 7/8 by 10 5/8 inches. © 1996 Board of Trustees, National Gallery of Art, Washington, D.C., Cornelius Van S. Roosevelt Collection.

What is in this image besides birds?

Dutch artist M. C. Escher (1898–1972) is famous for his interlocking designs. He had a mathematical talent for fitting shapes together in a way that left no space between them, a technique called **tessellation.**

This work of art is a woodcut. To make it, Escher carved shapes into four blocks of wood and then rolled ink onto the blocks and pressed them onto paper to make an impression. Notice these details:

- While each object has the shape of a bird, each bird is slightly different.
- Escher alternated the shapes within the birds. Some have radiating lines projected by the sun, and others have the shapes of the sky, the moon, and the stars.

When you first view this artwork, some birds seem to come forward while others seem to recede, even though they are all on the same two-dimensional surface. Where do you notice actual and implied lines?

Technique Tip

Combine Colors
Experiment with the colors you can create by combining two or more colored pencils, markers, or crayons. Try layering a light color over a darker color. Try a darker color over a lighter one. Add a third color to see what combinations you can make.

Studio 2

Make a Tessellation

Use what you have learned about shape to make a tessellation.

Materials

- ✓ 3" square of poster board
- ✓ pencil
- ✓ scissors ⚠
- ✓ tape
- ✓ 12" × 18" white drawing paper
- ✓ colored pencils, non-toxic markers, or crayons

1 Cut out an unusual organic shape from the left side of the 3" poster board square. Tape the shape to the square's right edge.

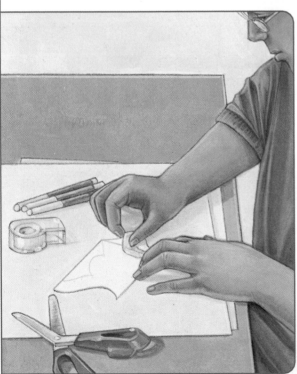

2 Cut another complex organic shape from the top of the poster board and tape it to the bottom edge of the square.

3 Transfer the shape onto white paper several times, fitting the shapes together like puzzle pieces and filling the page. Add color and detail to your tessellation.

Review and Reflect

- Describe the shape you have created. Does it look like anything real?
- How do the colors you added enhance your tessellation?
- Does your tessellation evoke a certain mood or feeling?
- If you were doing it over, what would you change in your tessellation? Why?

Lesson 3

Form

While a shape has only two dimensions, a **form** has three. It has height, width, and depth. A form is something you can hold or go around. Basketballs, snow cones, and alligators are all forms. Like shapes, forms can be geometric or organic.

Geometric forms include objects such as spheres, cylinders, cubes, cones, and pyramids. **Organic forms** are irregular, like the natural forms of pinecones and armadillos.

This dramatic form was not made by humans. What kind of form is it?

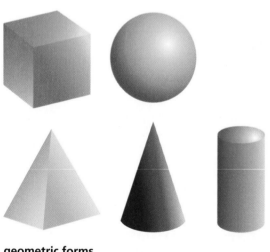

geometric forms

organic forms

The ancient Egyptian pyramid of Khufu is an example of a geometric form.

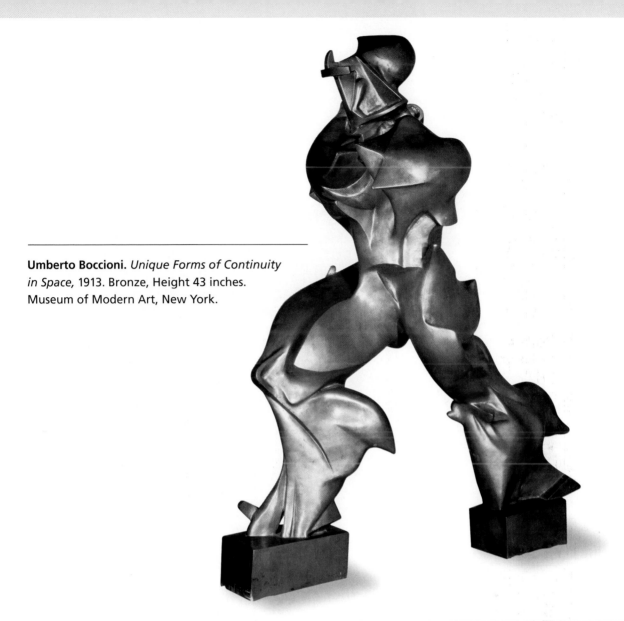

Umberto Boccioni. *Unique Forms of Continuity in Space,* 1913. Bronze, Height 43 inches. Museum of Modern Art, New York.

Motion and Emotion

This artwork is a **sculpture,** an artwork made by modeling, carving, or joining materials into a three-dimensional form. What does this sculpture remind you of? The form is distorted and exaggerated to express an emotion or evoke a feeling.

In this sculpture, Umberto Boccioni (1882–1916) wanted to depict motion as well as emotion. He captured movement in form by showing the figure striding and by sculpting the limbs to look as if garments were blowing in the wind. What feeling do you think Boccioni was trying to convey?

Sketchbook Journal

Because drawing is two-dimensional, artists must create the illusion of form to show a three-dimensional object. Use lines, light, and shadow to draw the illusion of several three-dimensional forms, such as spheres or cubes. Keep one side of the object light, and darken the opposite side.

Sculpted *Form*

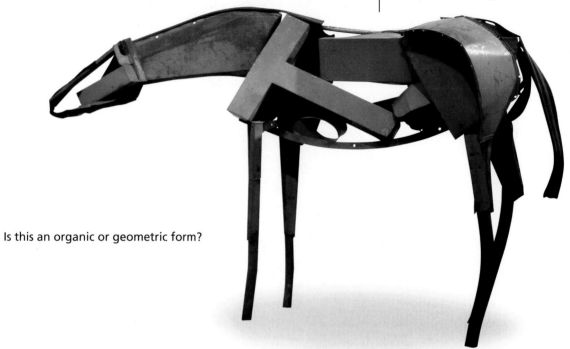

Deborah Butterfield. *Riot,* 1990. Steel, 81 ½ by 120 by 34 inches. Delaware Art Museum, Wilmington, DE.

Is this an organic or geometric form?

In this sculpture, American artist Deborah Butterfield (1949–) combined a variety of shapes in steel to create an organic form. Notice that even though details are left out or simplified, the viewer can still tell what kind of animal the sculpture represents. Look for these details:

- The combined shapes and colors help create actual and implied lines.
- The forms and shapes of the metal pieces help distinguish parts of the horse, though some parts are hollow.

Assemblage

Butterfield often creates her sculptures out of objects that she finds on her Montana ranch or at the dump. She creates sculptures out of pipes, barbed wire, pieces of wood, and scraps of metal. These sculptures are called **assemblages,** artworks made from recycled objects that gain new meaning from the way they are combined. What message do you think Butterfield wanted to convey with her choice of subject and materials?

Technique Tip

Assembling

Glue often takes a good deal of time to dry. When gluing several objects together at the same time, use masking tape to help hold the objects together until the glue is dry. Apply the tape as gently as possible to avoid interfering with the glue. Once the glue has dried, the tape should remove easily.

Studio 3

Assemble a Form

Use what you have learned about form to create an assemblage.

Materials

- ✓ drawing paper
- ✓ pencil and eraser
- ✓ found objects
- ✓ poster board or cardboard
- ✓ scissors ⚠
- ✓ glue
- ✓ tempera or acrylic paint and brushes

1 Draw the form of an animal from memory, or use photographs as a guide. Use your sketch as a reference to create your assemblage.

2 Glue together found objects and shapes cut from poster board or cardboard to create a three-dimensional form of the animal.

3 When the glue has dried, use tempera or acrylic paint to add color to your assemblage.

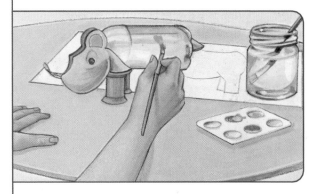

Review and Reflect

- What materials did you use in your assemblage?
- Why did you choose these particular objects for this sculpture?
- How do the materials you chose affect how you think about the animal you created?
- What do you like best about your assemblage? Explain.

Space

As an element of art, **space** is the area in and around an object. It can be empty or full, nearby or far away. Both painters and sculptors manipulate space in their work. A painter might create an artwork that appears flat, showing objects in two-dimensional space. Or a painter might create the illusion of deep space, making objects appear miles away. A sculptor is concerned with space within an artwork as well as the space around it.

Artists deal with two kinds of space, positive and negative. **Positive space** is the area occupied by an object. The area around the object, and that defines the object's edges, is called **negative space.**

The rock formations in the photograph below are the positive space. The opening in the rock creates negative space. Artists who work in two dimensions, such as painters, often create depth in their artworks. **Depth** is the use of perspective to give the illusion of deep space on a two-dimensional plane.

Another way artists create depth is to use **overlapping,** the process of putting one object, color, or line in front of another. This makes the object on top appear closer than the one behind it. Artists also can show space and depth by making objects that are nearby appear larger than objects that are far away.

Identify the positive and negative space in this photograph.

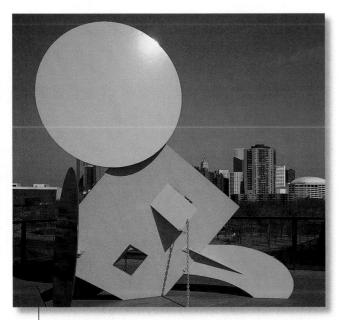

Claes Oldenburg. *Geometric Mouse—Scale A,* 1969–1971. Aluminum, steel, and paint, approximately 12 by 12 by 6 feet. Collection Walker Art Center, Minneapolis. Gift of Mr. and Mrs. Miles Q. Fiterman, 1991.

Artist Unknown. *Turkish Saraband Dance,* ca. 1853. Engraving. Private collection.

Manipulating Space

In this sculpture, Claes Oldenburg (1929–) used geometric shapes to create a representation of a mouse's head. What shapes form the positive space?

By tipping the mouse's head, Oldenburg created negative space between the head and the ground. He also created negative space within the sculpture with openings in the large square of the mouse's face. What might the openings represent?

The engraving below shows dancers and musicians in front of a palace. Notice how the lines and shapes created by the dancers are similar to those of the fountain, the tree, and the palace. Now look at the objects between the palace and the dancers. Closer objects and figures are larger than those that appear farther away. Which objects occupy positive space? How does the artist's placement of these objects help show space and depth?

Sketchbook Journal

Choose an object from your classroom, from nature, or from home. Draw the object multiple times in a single composition, making it seem close, far, and very far away. Use overlapping and diminishing size to give your drawing the illusion of depth.

Space *and Distance*

Grant Wood. *Stone City, Iowa,* 1930. Oil on wood panel, 30 ¼ by 40 inches. Joslyn Art Museum, Omaha, Nebraska.

What details give this painting a sense of depth?

American artist Grant Wood (1892–1942) often used his native Iowa as the subject for his paintings. He used several techniques for depicting space. In this painting, the rolling countryside seems to stretch on for miles. Look for these details:

- Wood overlapped objects to make the ones on top appear closer to the viewer.
- Objects, like trees and buildings, appear smaller the farther away they are.
- The objects that are near are darker and more detailed than the objects that are far away, drawing the viewer's eye to the objects that are closer.

Areas in Space

The objects that are closest to the viewer are in the **foreground,** the part of the painting that is at the very front, and often near the bottom. Most artworks show the most detail in the foreground. In the **background,** farthest from the viewer, are more fields and rolling hills. The town and the river are in the **middle ground,** the area between the foreground and the background. What emotion or feeling does this sense of deep space evoke?

Technique Tip

Find a View

Make a view-finder to help you draw your outdoor scene. Cut a rectangle two inches wide by two and one-half inches long in the center of an index card. Look through the hole in the card as you scan your environment for a suitable view to draw. Using the view-finder will help you concentrate on only what you would see in your composition.

Studio 4

Draw to Show Space

Use what you have learned about showing space to draw an outdoor scene.

Materials

✓ 12" × 18" drawing paper
✓ pencil
✓ colored pencils
  or water-based markers

1 Use a variety of organic shapes, geometric shapes, and lines to draw an outdoor scene that shows space.

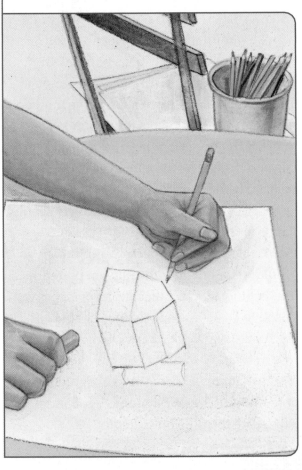

2 Use the techniques you have learned about space to show the foreground, middle ground, and background.

3 Increase the illusion of space by adding details to shapes in the foreground with markers or colored pencils.

Review and Reflect

- What objects did you place in the foreground, middle ground, and background of your drawing?
- How did you make some objects seem closer than others?
- Does your drawing successfully convey the illusion of space?
- How has depicting depth changed the way you look at nature?

Lesson 5

Space and Perspective

Carlo Crivelli. *The Annunciation with Saint Emidius,* 1486. Egg tempera and oil on canvas, approximately 7 by 5 feet. National Gallery of Art, London.

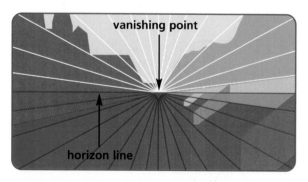

Lines converge at the vanishing point in linear perspective.

When you stand near the corner of a building and look along one wall, the front corner of the building seems bigger than the back corner. Lines on the building that are actually parallel seem to get closer together the farther they are from you. And far down the road, over the hill, objects seem to get fuzzier and lighter. These are tricks of human perception, which artists use to convey depth in their work.

Linear perspective is a technique in which artists use actual and implied lines to create an illusion of space and depth on a two-dimensional surface. In linear perspective, the **horizon line,** the name given to the viewer's eye level, is the implied line where the sky meets the ground. The point on the horizon where lines in a painting or drawing converge, or come together is the **vanishing point.** Linear perspective helps artists make objects seem to recede into the distance.

Atmospheric perspective is another technique for creating the illusion of depth. This technique, also called aerial perspective, is used to create the appearance of atmosphere and space in a work of art. Objects that are close are darker in order to draw the eye; objects that are farther away are lighter and more muted. These changes in light and dark help create the illusion of depth.

Thomas Moran. *A Miracle of Nature*, 1913. Oil on canvas, 20 ⅛ by 30 ⅛ inches. Private collection.

Linear and Atmospheric Perspective

Look at the painting on page 32 by Venetian artist Carlo Crivelli (ca. 1430–ca. 1493). Notice that on the buildings and the ground, the diagonal lines above eye-level angle down and those below eye-level angle up. They all point to the horizon and would meet if they were extended. Where would that point be, relative to the objects in the painting? Why is this technique effective for showing depth?

English painter Thomas Moran (1837–1926) portrayed depth and space in a different way. He used atmospheric perspective. How did Moran make the foreground seem closer than the background? What mood or feeling does this give his painting?

Sketchbook Journal

Make three or four sketches that show linear perspective in outdoor and indoor scenes. Choose objects with strong linear qualities, like buildings and tables. Make notes about what you find difficult in representing these scenes. Describe different ways to solve the difficulties you encountered.

Interior *Perspective*

Josephine Trotter. *French Interior,* 20th century. Private Collection.

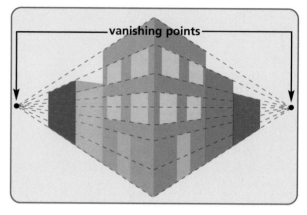

Two-point perspective shows two vanishing points.

In *French Interior,* Josephine Trotter (1940–) used linear and atmospheric perspective to show depth and space. Notice these details:

- Diagonal lines in the hallway would converge at a point outside the door, while diagonal lines in the side room would converge at a different point, behind the wall.
- The colors of objects indoors are brighter and darker than the colors of objects outside.

One- and Two-Point Perspective

One-point perspective is the technique of using a single vanishing point to show space and depth on a two-dimensional plane. The illustration on page 32 shows the guidelines for one-point perspective. **Two-point perspective** employs two

vanishing points to show space and depth on a two-dimensional surface. For example, a building might seem to recede into the distance along two different roads. Notice how Trotter's use of two-point perspective in an indoor scene shows two different vanishing points, much like an outdoor scene.

Technique Tip

Use a Ruler

A ruler or straightedge can be very helpful when rendering one- and two-point perspective. Use a ruler to draw light lines that radiate from the vanishing point. These lines can guide you as you determine the angle of the diagonal lines in your composition. Make sure lines are light enough to erase later.

Studio 5

Paint to Show Perspective

Use what you have learned about linear and atmospheric perspective to create a painting of an interior scene.

Materials

- ✓ 12" × 18" white paper
- ✓ pencil
- ✓ ruler (optional)
- ✓ tempera paints
- ✓ water-based markers

1 Sketch an interior scene using one-point perspective. Draw your scene from memory or by observing a room.

2 Add objects to your drawing that are not in the original scene. Use the techniques of one-point perspective to make the objects fit in.

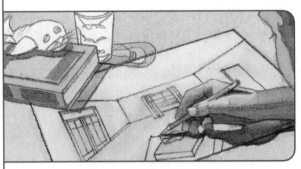

3 Use paint and markers to increase the illusion of perspective. Make foreground objects brighter or darker than background objects.

Review and Reflect

- Describe the interior scene you chose to paint. What additional objects did you include?
- What techniques did you use to make the objects fit in?
- What effect did the inclusion of color have on the illusion of depth?
- How could you improve the illusion of depth in your painting?

Meet *the Artist*

Frida Kahlo

Frida Kahlo never intended to become an artist. But when an accident confined her to bed, she picked up a brush and began to create the images that would launch her into art history. Over her short lifetime Kahlo made about two hundred works of art that tell the often-painful story of her life and love.

Photograph of Frida Kahlo in 1944

"I paint self-portraits because I am so often alone, because I am the person I know best."

—FRIDA KAHLO

Picking Up a Brush

As a child, Frida Kahlo was stricken with polio, permanently leaving her right leg shorter than the left. At about age eighteen, Kahlo was seriously injured in a tragic bus accident. She suffered numerous crushed, broken, and fractured bones. For an entire month, Kahlo remained in a full-body cast. Confined to bed and feeling bored, Kahlo started painting to pass the time. André Breton, a founder of the Surrealist movement, likened her explosive artwork to "a ribbon around a bomb."

Fantasy and Reality

"They thought I was a Surrealist but I wasn't," Kahlo once said. She used her art to express her strong political views and the often painful aspects of her life, including her marriage to muralist Diego Rivera. "I never painted dreams. I painted my own reality."

As a result of her accident, Kahlo underwent thirty different surgeries. She attended her first solo exhibition in Mexico City by being carried in on a stretcher. She died approximately one year later. Today, collectors pay millions of dollars for the paintings she struggled to sell during her lifetime.

Talk About It

- Surrealism often combines realistic and fantasy images. Why do you think Kahlo disliked being called a Surrealist?

- About how old was Kahlo when she attended her first solo exhibition in Mexico City?

The Life of Frida Kahlo

Frida Kahlo

1905

1907
Frida Kahlo born in Coyoacàn, Mexico (July 6)

1915

Kahlo crippled in bus accident
1925 — **1925**

Diego Rivera

Kahlo marries Diego Rivera
1929

Kahlo has solo exhibition at Julien Levy Gallery, New York; Kahlo meets Surrealist artist André Breton **1935**
1938

Frida and Diego

Kahlo divorces Rivera
1939
1940
Kahlo and Rivera remarry

1943
Kahlo becomes painting professor
1945

Kahlo's first solo exhibition held at Galauna de Arte Contemporaneo in Mexico City; Kahlo's right leg is amputated
1953
1954
Kahlo dies, Coyoacàn, Mexico (July 13) **1955**

Look *and Compare*

The World of Frida Kahlo

Frida Kahlo combined personal experiences with imagery from her native Mexico to create artworks that are known for their drama and story-telling power. She is well known for her many self-portraits. But Kahlo also painted imagined scenes that mingle fantasy and reality, as well as more traditional portraits of her friends and family.

The Paintings

Kahlo painted the self-portrait on page 39 during her most productive period as an artist. She is never shown smiling in her many self-portraits. *My Dress Hangs Here* was painted during Kahlo's separation from her husband, Mexican muralist Diego Rivera. It was during this time that she was living in New York and longed to return to Mexico.

Creating Space

Notice Kahlo's use of the elements of art in each artwork. In the self-portrait, the shapes of the leaves crowd around Kahlo and create a flat space without depth. The repeated fine lines add to this feeling of closeness. Even the forms of Kahlo's face and neck are flattened.

In *My Dress Hangs Here,* Kahlo created a foreground, middleground, and background, giving the painting a sense of depth and space. Notice how Kahlo made the objects representing New York City appear smaller and less detailed than objects in the foreground. Consider why she might have placed the objects as she did.

Think about how each artwork reflects the artist's pride in her Mexican heritage.

Frida Kahlo. *Self-Portrait with Monkey,* 1938.
Oil on masonite, 16 by 12 inches.
Albright-Knox Art Gallery, Buffalo, NY.

Frida Kahlo. *My Dress Hangs Here,* 1933–1938.
Oil and collage on masonite, 18 1/8 by 19 3/4 inches.
Estate of Dr. Leo Eloesser.

Compare & Contrast

- What elements of art do the two paintings share?

- Many people admire the story-telling power of Kahlo's artworks. What stories do these paintings seem to tell?

Value

Value, an element of art, is the degree of lightness or darkness of a color. An artist can use different values to define an object or feature in an artwork. For example, in a portrait an artist might use light values to indicate an area where sunlight hits the bridge of the nose and dark values to define the shadow under the chin. A gradual change from light to dark values is called shading. Artists employ many different shading techniques.

blending: gradually changing the value

stippling: a pattern of dots

hatching: thin parallel lines

cross-hatching: lines that cross one another

Notice how changes in value help create the illusion of distance.

Mary Williamson. *Stick Pond*, 1993. Pencil. Gallery Contemporanea, Jacksonville, FL.

Gonzalo Cienfuegos Browne. *Landscape with Large Plants and People,* 1996. Pastel on paper. Private collection.

Value and Mood

Latvian artist Vija Celmins (1939–) used the blending technique in her artwork on page 40 to show value in ocean waves. This artwork conveys both the peace and the energy of the ocean at calm.

In the pastel drawing above, Chilean artist Gonzalo Cienfuegos Browne (1949–) used hatching and cross-hatching to create differences in value. What effect does the artist's use of shading have on each object?

There does not seem to be a single source of light. If there were, darker values would fall on the same side of each object. How does this non-naturalistic use of dark values affect the mood of the artwork?

Research

Discover other artworks by Gonzalo Cienfuegos Browne and other Latino artists online or in your local library. Use *Gonzalo Cienfuegos Browne* and *Latin American art museums* as keywords in your online search. Make notes about the artists' styles and how they used the elements of art.

Studio 6 Setup
Value *and Contrast*

Andy Warhol. *Portrait of Mao.*
Pencil on paper.

Where does the light in this portrait seem to be coming from?

Some artists use value to show the way light falls on a form. They create **contrast,** a difference between light and dark values. In this portrait, Andy Warhol (1928–1987) kept the areas where light falls on the figure free of any lines. But he used loose, hatched lines to define the shadows. Look for these details:

- Shadows fall to the viewer's right: the right side of the nose, the right cheek, and the right eye all are darker.
- The shadow beneath the collar in front makes the collar look as if it stands out from the shirt.

High and Low Contrast

In a high-contrast artwork, the darks are black or very dark, and the lights are nearly white. In a low-contrast artwork, the difference between values is not very big. If you were to squint your eyes at a low-contrast work, the details would seem to disappear and the picture would appear gray. Is this portrait a high- or low-contrast artwork?

Technique Tip

Paper Choices

Some papers are very smooth, and others are rough. Each type of paper produces a different effect. A charcoal line drawn on smooth paper will be continuous, whereas rough paper will produce a line that is more uneven. Choose your paper to take advantage of these effects.

Studio 6

Show Value in a Monument Design

Use what you have learned about value to design a monument honoring a historical figure. Choose a person from your history or social studies textbook.

Materials

- ✓ 12" × 18" white drawing paper
- ✓ pencil
- ✓ black crayon, charcoal, felt-tip marker, or fine-lined pen

1 Sketch your monument design in pencil on your paper, filling the page. Then select a shading technique to show value and contrast.

2 Use the shading technique to add the illusion of form and depth. Include details that help identify the person you are honoring.

3 Consider where you would like to see your monument design constructed. Use lighter values to add objects in the backgound and middle ground.

Review and Reflect

- What techniques did you use to create values in your monument design?
- How did you decide where to concentrate the light and dark values you used?
- What kind of mood have you created by using light and dark values?
- Why did you choose the setting you drew for your monument?

Lesson 7

Color

Sunlight seems white, or perhaps clear. But it is actually composed of a range of colors. When light shines on an object, the object absorbs some of the colors, or hues, and reflects others. So a red ball seems red because it reflects red and absorbs the other colors. **Color,** then, is the visual quality of the object caused by the amount of light it reflects or absorbs. Color is one of the elements of art.

The **primary colors,** red, yellow, and blue, are the colors from which all other colors are mixed. Primary colors cannot be mixed from other colors. Mixing two primary colors makes a **secondary color.**

Secondary colors include orange, green, and violet. **Intermediate colors** are mixed from a primary color and one of the secondary colors closest to it on the color wheel. For example, mixing yellow and green makes yellow-green. All of these kinds of colors can have a variety of values: pink, for example, is a value of red. The color wheel shows the relationship between primary, secondary, and intermediate colors.

Wassily Kandinsky. *Fragment of Composition II*, 1910. Oil on cardboard, 22 7/8 by 18 7/8 inches. Private collection.

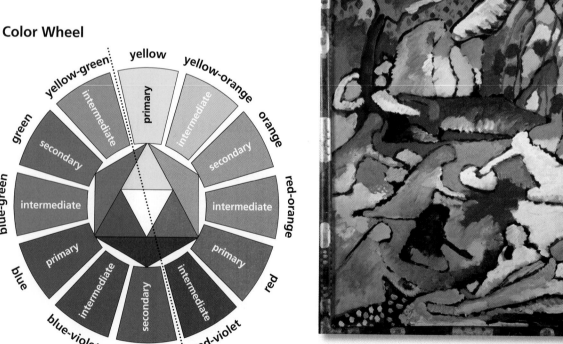

Locate primary, secondary, and intermediate colors in this painting.

Color Wheel

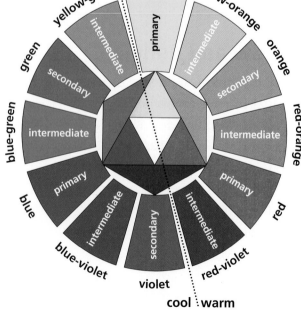

Georgia O'Keeffe. *From the Plains 1,* 1953. Oil on canvas. The McNay Art Museum, San Antonio, TX.

Color and Emotion

American artist Georgia O'Keeffe (1887–1986) painted this artwork at a time in her career when her paintings often celebrated the landscape of her adopted state of New Mexico. Look at the title. What do you think the subject of this painting is?

Two primary colors dominate this painting: yellow and red. O'Keeffe mixed these two colors to create different hues of orange, also. Look for light and dark values in this artwork. Even though she used only a few colors, O'Keeffe created a dramatic effect. What kind of emotion does this bright, limited palette of colors evoke?

Edgar Degas. *Two Blue Dancers,* ca. 1900. Pastel, 29 ¼ by 19 ¹/₁₀ inches. Von der Heydt Museum, Wuppertal, Germany.

How does Degas's use of color create implied lines in this artwork?

Artists choose their colors deliberately, to affect mood, for example, or to draw the viewer's eye to specific areas. In this work of art, Edgar Degas (1834–1917) used color to focus the viewer's attention on the two dancers. Look for these details:

- Degas used blue primarily on the figures of the dancers.

- Some of the red-orange color of the background is repeated in the dancer's torsos, helping to unify the composition.
- The artist's placement of color creates implied lines that show the forms of the dancers.
- The lighter and darker values of the hues give the illusion of form to the figures.

Warm and Cool Colors

Degas created contrast in this composition by using **warm colors,** such as reds, yellows, and oranges, and **cool colors,** such as greens, blues, and violets. Artists use these color families to achieve different effects. For example, they might use cool colors in shadow and warm colors in light. Artists also use color to evoke different moods. Cool colors can evoke a sense of calm or even loneliness. Warm colors can create a sunny, cheerful feeling. What mood do the colors evoke in *Two Blue Dancers*?

Technique Tip

Mix It Up

Keep your colors pure as you mix paints by keeping your brush clean. Rinse it in water between colors, and dry the bristles with a paper towel. It's a good idea to have more than one brush available, too. That way you can use a separate brush for each primary color and its related hues.

Studio 7

Experiment with Colors

Use what you have learned about color to paint an outdoor scene.

Materials

- ✓ tempera or acrylic paints
- ✓ mixing containers or trays
- ✓ 12" × 18" white paper
- ✓ pencil
- ✓ paintbrush

1 Use tempera or acrylic paints to mix several secondary and intermediate colors. Choose the warm and cool colors you like best.

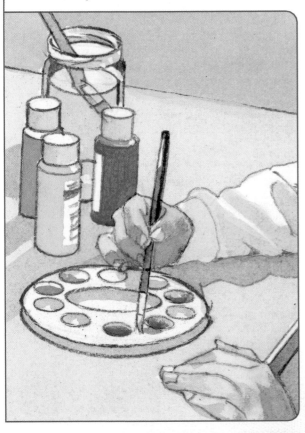

2 Sketch an outdoor scene. Decide which areas should have warm colors and which should have cool colors.

3 Apply the warm and cool colors you chose to your outdoor scene. Be sure to fill all areas of the scene with color.

Review and Reflect

- Where did you use warm colors, and where did you use cool colors?
- Why did you apply warm and cool colors to the areas you did?
- Does the addition of colors create a particular mood in your artwork?
- What do you like best about your finished artwork? Why?

Lesson 8

Color Schemes

When you get dressed for school, do you choose a color scheme for your clothes? A **color scheme** is a plan for combining colors in what you wear and in a work of art. Artists often choose a color scheme before they ever put paint to canvas. They pick their colors carefully to affect the way a viewer feels about the artwork or to reflect the way they feel about their subject.

A **monochromatic** color scheme uses many different values of a single hue, which are created by adding different amounts of white or black. *Monochromatic* comes from the prefix *mono*, which means "one," and the base word *chrome*, which means "color." An artist might use a monochromatic color scheme to unify a composition.

Hues in an **analogous** color scheme are beside one another on the color wheel, and they share a common hue. For example, yellow-green, green, and blue-green are side-by-side on the color wheel and share the hue green.

A **complementary** color scheme employs colors that are across from each other on the color wheel. For example, violet and yellow are complementary colors.

Neutral colors include black, white, and shades of gray. Some artists also consider shades of brown to be neutral colors.

As you experiment with color schemes, notice how the colors affect the mood or tone of your artworks and how they might make the viewer feel.

monochromatic

analogous

complementary

Pablo Picasso. *Two Sisters (The Meeting),* 1902.
Oil on canvas pasted on panel, 59 ¼ by 39 inches.
Hermitage, St. Petersburg, Russia.

Monochromatic Color

Spanish artist Pablo Picasso (1881–1973) used a mostly monochromatic color scheme for this painting. The areas that diverge from the blue hues create contrast. Notice how Picasso used values of blue to show depth and form.

During one period of his life, from 1901 to 1904, Picasso painted mostly in blue. For two years after that, he painted mostly in values of red or pink. What reasons could an artist have for using a monochromatic color scheme for so long?

What feeling or mood does the artist seem to be expressing in this artwork?

Sketchbook Journal

Make three quick sketches of the same scene. Use colored pencils to give each sketch a different color scheme. Make one sketch's color scheme monochromatic, one analogous, and one complementary. Make notes about how each color scheme changes the mood of the drawing.

Vincent van Gogh. *The Red Vineyard*, 1888. Oil on canvas, 29 ¼ by 36 ¼ inches. Pushkin Museum of Fine Arts, Moscow, Russia.

There are only twelve colors on the color wheel, but artists can create many more colors by mixing to create light and dark values. **Tints** are made by mixing a hue with white; **shades** are made by mixing black with a hue. The **intensity** of a hue refers to its brightness or dullness. Pure, unmixed colors are most intense. The intensity of a color declines the more it is mixed with its complement or with white or black.

Vincent van Gogh (1853–1890) conveyed a feeling of energy in this painting by using a complementary color scheme, strong contrast in values, and intense colors. Look for these details:

- Lighter tints of the warm yellow of the sky are used closer to the cool blue trees.

- Many colors are so intense that they seem to have been applied in their purest form, rather than mixed.

Notice how Van Gogh's use of complementary colors makes the blue clothing of the figures stand out against the orange of the plants. The intensity of the colors adds to the color scheme's effect.

Technique Tip

Mixing Tints and Shades

To mix a tint, begin with white paint on your palette. Add a small amount of color and mix the paints. Add color in small amounts to reach the tint you want. To mix a shade, add a little black. Add black in small dots, because it can darken color very fast!

Studio 8

Create Mood with Complementary Colors

Use what you have learned about color schemes to express a mood in a painting using complementary colors.

Materials

✓ tempera or acrylic paints
✓ mixing containers or trays
✓ paintbrushes
✓ newsprint
✓ pencil
✓ 12" × 18" white paper

1 Mix three pairs of complementary colors. Make a chart of their tints and shades.

2 Draw a picture of yourself in a favorite activity. Pick two complementary colors that convey the mood of the activity.

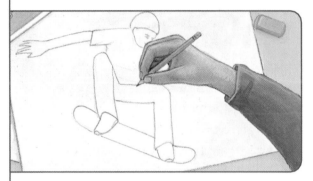

3 Use various tints and shades of the colors you chose to paint your drawing and to express the mood you want to convey.

Review and Reflect

- What activity did you depict, and what colors did you choose?
- How do the colors affect each other in the painting?
- What difficulties did you encounter using tints and shades of only two complementary colors?
- Would you change the color scheme you selected? Why or why not?

Lesson 9

Texture

Run your hand across velvet and you can feel its soft texture. **Texture** is the way an object feels to the touch, or the way it may look. Artists show texture in different ways. A photographer might take a close-up picture of an alligator's rough skin. A painter might use brushstrokes to capture that texture in a painting, and a sculptor might reproduce it in clay. Even though the object is the same, these artists would show different types of texture.

Tactile texture, or actual texture, is the way a surface feels to the touch. An alligator sculpted in clay is an example of tactile texture. If you touched the sculpture, you would feel the rough skin of the alligator.

Visual texture is the way a surface looks like it would feel. Visual texture is also known as simulated texture. A painting of an alligator's skin might appear rough, but if you were to touch the painting, it would not actually feel like an alligator.

In both two- and three-dimensional artworks, texture is an important element of art. It can help make the objects in a painting look realistic, while adding interest to the artwork. Words like *rough* and *smooth* describe tactile texture. *Shiny* and *dull* are words that describe visual texture. Think of ways that you might use these types of texture in your artworks.

How might it feel to touch the skin of this snake?

Describe the tactile and visual textures in this image.

Artist unknown, Inca. *Fez-style hat with alternating step-volute design,* ca. 1530–1570. Decorated with white and tan feathers, diameter 7 inches. David Bernstein Fine Art, New York, NY.

Barbara Benedetti Newton. *Fancy,* 2002. Colored pencil with watercolor, 16 ½ by 21 inches. Private Collection.

Visual and Tactile Texture

Artists often combine textures in their artworks to add interest. Look at the textures used by the artists of these two artworks. Imagine how it might feel to pick up the hat, touch it, and put it on. What kind of textures would you feel?

In the drawing, the apples look so real that it seems like you could pick one up and eat it! Artist Barbara Benedetti Newton used visual texture to show the smooth, shiny surfaces of the apples and the silver plate. Notice how the ribbon appears soft, silky, and shiny. How do these textures contrast with those of the lace?

Visual Culture

Some Web pages use simulated texture as a background for words, pictures, and icons. For example, a Web site that sells paper products might use a simulated paper texture as a background. What other textures can you find on Web pages? How do they relate to the content of the page?

53

Meret Oppenheim.
Object (Luncheon in Fur), 1936. Fur-covered cup, saucer, and spoon, approximately 9 3/8 by 3 inches. Museum of Modern Art, NY.

How does texture create surprise in this artwork?

Tactile texture is the main focus of this artwork by Swiss artist Meret Oppenheim (1913–1985). Ordinary objects become extraordinary because of the unexpected texture. Look for these details:

- Every surface is covered in fur.
- The fur on the outside of the cup is lighter than the fur anywhere else, creating a contrast that makes the cup stand out.

More Than Reality

Oppenheim was twenty-two years old when she created this furry combination. The sculpture caused a sensation when it was exhibited in 1936. It quickly became an international symbol of the Surrealists, a group of artists who tried to create startling images by mixing reality with dream and fantasy. The sculpture gets its power from the combination of materials, and the use of unexpected texture on common objects. What type of texture does this artwork show? Why do you think Oppenheim chose to combine these materials?

Technique Tip

One Person's Trash
Keep an eye on the ground as you go to and from school every day and as you travel around your neighborhood. Pick up usable objects that catch your attention. Be sure to collect only the items with no sharp edges and that will not decay. Keep a container handy so you can store your found objects until you are ready to use them in an artwork.

Studio 9

Make Textured Dinnerware

Use what you have learned about texture to create a sculpture of textured dinnerware.

Materials

✓ newsprint and pencils
✓ heavy-duty paper plates or bowls
✓ white glue
✓ found objects, such as beads, buttons, shells, and bottle caps
✓ papier mâché paste or wheat paste
✓ tempera paint and brush
✓ scissors Ⓢ

1 Make a drawing of a natural texture you want to imitate. Glue found objects to the dinnerware to simulate that texture. Allow the glue to dry.

2 Cover the texture with newspaper dampened with papier mâché paste.

3 When the paste dries, apply color to your dinnerware to emphasize the texture you have created.

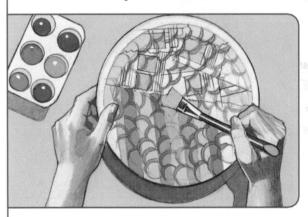

Review and Reflect

- What texture did you choose for your dinnerware?
- How do the materials you used reflect your chosen texture?
- How might someone using your dinnerware feel? Why do you think so?
- What is the best feature of your dinnerware? Why?

Portfolio *Project*

Say It with Painted Flowers

Christian Pierre. *Purple Irises,* 1995.
Mixed media. Private collection.

Plan

In this unit, you read how artists use lines, shapes, color schemes, and textures to create a particular mood or feeling. In this artwork, Christian Pierre (1962–) used a variety of color values in the background. The flowers are organic shapes that fill the canvas. The swirling strokes on the tabletop create a sense of energy.

- What colors do you see in this painting? Are they warm or cool colors? What color scheme did the artist use?
- Describe the shading in the background and on the tabletop. What techniques did Pierre employ? What mood do these techniques create?
- What kind of mood do you associate with a vase of flowers? How could you use the elements of art to create such a mood in your own artwork?

Use what you have learned about the elements of art to express a mood or feeling with a still life of sunflowers in a vase on a table.

Sketchbook Journal

Experiment with drawing organic and geometric flower shapes. First, draw the flower in its recognizable organic shape. Then, draw it using various geometric shapes. Keep in mind the mood the flowers convey and try to create that mood using organic and geometric shapes.

Materials

- ✓ a vase with flowers
- ✓ white chalk
- ✓ heavy black paper
- ✓ oil pastels
- ✓ newsprint

Create

1 Lightly sketch your composition in white chalk on the black paper. Allow the still life to reach the edge of the paper on all four sides.

2 Use a color scheme to reflect colors found in your still life by practicing with oil pastels on newsprint. Choose light, medium, and dark values.

3 Add value and texture with cross-hatching. Layer one color on top of another without blending or smearing.

4 Show depth in your drawing by emphasizing the way flowers and leaves overlap. Use value to increase depth.

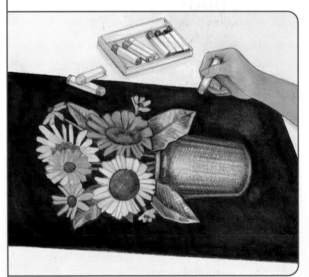

Reflect

- How does the color scheme you chose compare to the colors in the vase and flowers you drew?
- How did you use value to show depth in your artwork?
- What mood does your artwork evoke?
- Where will you display your artwork?

57

Unit 1 *Review*

Vocabulary Review

A Match each art term below with its definition.

> form   tessellation
> vanishing point   value
> stippling   assemblage
> gesture drawing   shape
> shading   intensity

1. sculpture made of found objects and recycled materials
2. the lightness or darkness of a color
3. a series of shapes that fit together with no space in between
4. an object with height, width, and depth
5. a quick drawing made to capture a figure's form and action
6. a two-dimensional area
7. the point at which converging lines meet in an artwork
8. a series of dots used to create values
9. a gradual change from light to dark values
10. brightness or dullness of a color

Artists and Their Art

B Each work of art listed in the box appears in this unit. Use the titles to finish the sentences below.

> *Disks*
> *The Annunciation with Saint Emidius*
> *Fuji from Sagami River*
> *Stone City*
> *French Interior*
> *Unique Forms of Continuity in Space*

1. Grant Wood used overlapping to show depth in ___.
2. ___ by Josephine Trotter highlights the use of two-point perspective.
3. Fernand Léger used geometric shapes inspired by machines in ___.
4. ___ by Umberto Boccioni shows motion through exaggerated form.
5. Ando Hiroshige's use of thin, delicate lines evokes a sense of calm in ___.
6. Carlo Crivelli shows depth using one-point perspective in ___.

Grant Wood

B. F. Dolbin, *Portrait of Fernand Léger.*

Respond to Art

C Look at David Hockney's photographic collage, *Pearblossom Highway, 11–18 April 1986.* In a class discussion or on a sheet of paper, match each art term below with examples from the artwork.

David Hockney. *Pearblossom Hwy., 11–18 April 1986, No. 2,* 1986. Photographic collage of chromogenic prints, 78 by 111 inches. The J. Paul Getty Museum, Los Angeles, CA.

Art Terms

1. geometric shape
2. diagonal line
3. tint
4. neutral color
5. overlapping
6. primary color
7. texture
8. horizon line

Unit 1 *Review*

Write About Art

Descriptive Paragraph

D Look back at the artworks in this unit. Choose one to describe in a paragraph. Copy the chart below and use it for prewriting. Fill in the seven elements of art in the first column. In the second column, write details about how each element is used in the artwork you have chosen. Use the completed chart to help you organize your writing. Revise your draft for organization, supporting sentences, transitions, correct spelling, capitalization, punctuation, and usage errors.

Elements of Art	How They Are Used
1.	
2.	
3.	
4.	
5.	
6.	
7.	

Your Studio Work

E Answer these questions in your Sketchbook Journal or on a separate sheet of paper.

1. Which work of art inspired you most to create artwork of your own? Why?
2. What medium from this unit did you most enjoy working with? Why? What technique suits that medium best?
3. What problems did you encounter as you experimented with new media and techniques? How did you solve the problems you encountered?
4. Of the artwork you created in this unit, which was most successful? What made it a success?

Put It All Together

Carmen Lomas Garza. *Empanadas (Pastries),* 1991. Gouache painting, 20 by 28 inches. Collection of Romeo Montalvo, M.D., Brownsville, TX. © 1991 Carmen Lomas Garza. Photograph by Judy Reed.

F **Discuss or write about Carmen Lomas Garza's painting *Empanadas,* using the questions below to view the artwork critically.**

1. **Describe** What is the subject of this work of art? Identify as many objects in the painting as you can. Describe the artist's use of color and value in the painting.
2. **Analyze** How do the colors work together to show the scene? How and why did the artist use them? How did Lomas Garza show space?
3. **Interpret** What is the mood of this artwork? What elements of art contribute to this mood? What do you think the artist wanted to say?

4. **Judge** American artist Carmen Lomas Garza (1948–) grew up in a Mexican American community in South Texas. Her artworks include scenes from her childhood, and she has said that she wants them to show her pride in her heritage. How do you think this painting fits with that goal? Why do you think the title of this painting is in both Spanish and English?

Carmen Lomas Garza's artworks encourage the viewer to understand Mexican American culture.

> *"I make my art not only for Chicanos, but also for others to see who we are as a people."* —CARMEN LOMAS GARZA

Georges Braque. *The Round Table,* 1929. Oil on canvas, 57 by 44 inches.
The Phillips Collection, Washington, D.C.

Unit 2

The Principles of Design

A guitar, a book, a table, and a knife. There are an infinite number of ways to depict and combine these items in a work of art. How does an artist decide? By using the **principles of design.** Understanding the principles of **balance, emphasis, proportion, rhythm, pattern, unity,** and **variety** can help an artist decide how to use the elements of line and shape to express a particular idea.

French painter Georges Braque (1882–1963) understood these principles well. His intense interest in pattern, unity, and rhythm prompted one art critic to accuse Braque of despising form. "Braque," he said, "reduces everything . . . to geometrical patterns, to cubes." By focusing on the principles of design, Braque introduced not only a new way of painting, but also a new way of seeing.

In this unit you will learn how artists use the principles of design as a guide for combining the elements of art, like line and shape, into a work of art. You will also learn how to use these principles in your own artworks.

About *the Artist*

Georges Braque was one of the founders of the influential art movement called Cubism. Braque and Picasso used Cubism to show objects in a fragmented and abstract style. Read more about Braque's contributions to art on page 84.

Georges Braque continued creating art until his death at age eighty-one.

63

Balance

Visualize a scale. To balance a scale, you must put equal weight on each side. Artists face a similar task. They must make sure one part of an artwork does not carry more visual weight than another. They achieve **balance** in their artwork by arranging the parts to create a sense that the visual weight is equal overall. Artists have three ways to balance a work of art.

A work of art has **symmetrical balance** when one half matches the other half. The features or visual properties are similar or identical on either side of a dividing line. The line can be horizontal, vertical, or diagonal, as long as it travels through the center of the artwork. This type of balance is also called formal balance.

An artwork has **asymmetrical balance** when the two halves are not identical but carry similar visual weight. For example, one side of a painting might show a huge, gray boulder while the other side shows a small, bright red boat. The bright color of the boat would balance the large size of the boulder.

When lines or shapes spread out in a regular pattern from a center point, a work of art has **radial balance.** A bicycle wheel is an example of an object with radial balance. What other type of balance does *South Rose Window* show?

Burleson and Grylls. *South Rose Window.* Westminster Abbey, 1902.

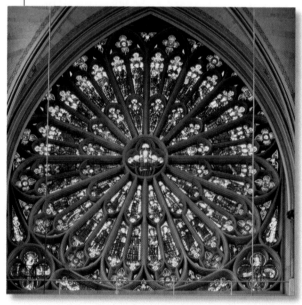

This window shows radial balance.

Artist unknown, Tlingit culture. *Chilkat weaving.* Wool and caribou hide. Field Museum of Natural History, Chicago, IL.

What type of balance does this weaving show?

Helen Turner. *Morning News,* 1915.
Oil on canvas, 16 by 14 inches. Jersey
City Museum, Jersey City, NJ.

Asymmetrical Balance

Although this painting is not the same
on both sides, it still appears balanced. The
images on each half are not identical, yet
each side seems to have a similar visual
weight. American artist Helen Turner
(1858–1958) used color and shape to give the
artwork asymmetrical balance. Notice how
the long spill of red fabric on the right is
balanced by smaller touches of red on the
left. The red forms a diagonal line on the
canvas from top left to bottom right. How
did Turner use shapes to reinforce the
painting's asymmetrical balance?

Sketchbook Journal

**Look for balance in the world
around you. Find objects or
scenes that display symmetrical,
asymmetrical, and radial
balance. Draw each object or
scene and label it with the kind
of balance it displays. List other
objects from memory that
reflect each type of balance.**

Artist unknown, Aztec. *Pendant representing the sun.* Gold, height 3 ³/₄ inches. Museo Nacional de Antropologia, Mexico City, Mexico.

What types of balance does this pendant show?

If you could bend gold, you could fold this pendant in half along its vertical axis and both sides would match. It is symmetrically balanced. It also shows elements of radial balance. Look for these details:

- The triangular shapes are spaced evenly around the outside disk.
- The double lines between the triangles on the outside disk seem to continue outward from a single central point.

Mesoamerican Art

The radial disk represents the sun in this pendant, which was created by an artist from ancient Mesoamerica. The image of the sun was important to the people of Mexico and Central America, and it often appears in works of art created before the Spanish exploration and conquest of the sixteenth century. Why might Mesoamerican artists single out the image of the sun by including it in works of art? Who do you think might have been allowed to wear this pendant?

Technique Tip

Measure Up

Your paper beads will look much more professional if your triangles are measured precisely, so be sure to look closely at your ruler as you measure out your triangles. You will not have to re-cut your paper if you measure carefully the first time.

Studio 1

Make a Pendant

Use what you have learned to create a pendant of paper beads that displays two types of balance.

Materials

- ✓ sheets of 8 ½" × 11" colored wallpaper
- ✓ felt-tip pen
- ✓ ruler
- ✓ scissors ⚠
- ✓ cotton swab, cotton removed
- ✓ fishing line or string
- ✓ wire
- ✓ needle-nose pliers ⚠
- ✓ glue

1 Divide the wallpaper into triangles, and cut them out. Create beads by wrapping each triangle around the swab. Glue the tip.

2 Create a pendant by making a circle with the wire. Cut three equal lengths of wire to cross in the middle. Add beads before attaching.

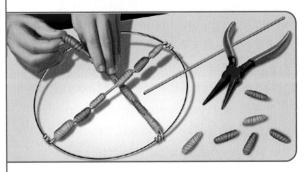

3 Put the pendant on the string. Then add beads on either side of the pendant to show symmetrical or asymmetrical balance.

Review and Reflect

- What colors of wallpaper did you choose to make your beads? Why?
- What kinds of balance does your finished pendant show? How did you achieve those kinds of balance?
- How does your choice of balance affect the finished product?
- What do you like best about your pendant? What do you like least? Explain.

Emphasis

When you are making a point in a conversation, you might stress certain words to emphasize them. Artists do this too. They create **emphasis** by stressing an area of a composition to draw the viewer's attention, or focus. Artists can create this focal point by giving an object dominance, for example making it larger than other objects, or by using contrast, such as in color or in texture.

A portrait is a work of art that emphasizes a person's face. When you look at the portrait to the right, where is your eye drawn to first? French painter Gustave Courbet (1819–1877) emphasized his subject's face by creating a contrast between light and dark values. He emphasized the model's eyes by contrasting their darkness with the paleness of the face. Courbet also emphasized his subject's shirt, making it white against the dark jacket. Why might Courbet emphasize the shirt? Even though the artist has created two areas of emphasis, he manipulated color and contrast to give the face dominance over the rest of the painting.

Courbet was a leader in the French art movement toward realism. Most artists of the time glorified their subjects, but Courbet painted people and places as they actually appeared. Notice how emphasis helps reveal the look of melancholy on the model's face.

Gustave Courbet. *Portrait of H.J. van Wisselingh*, 1846. Oil on panel, 22 by 18 1/8 inches. Kimbell Art Museum, Fort Worth, TX.

Marc Chagall. *The Farm, the Village,* 1954–1962. Oil on canvas, 24 by 29 inches. Private collection.

A Big Yellow Cow

You can tell what painter Marc Chagall (1887–1985) wanted the viewer to see first in this painting. Chagall emphasized the big yellow cow in the center of the composition, making it the focal point of the artwork. He created a dramatic contrast between the warm yellow of the animal and the cool greens and blues of the background. As a painter, printmaker, and designer, Chagall was skillful at using the principles of design to express his ideas in works of art. What other elements of the composition draw the viewer's attention?

Visual Culture

To be successful, a billboard must grab your attention and communicate information quickly. Effective billboards have a clear focal point. Draw three or four billboards from your community. Note how the designer has used dominance, focal point, and contrast to convey information and persuade viewers.

Charles Demuth. *Figure Five in Gold,* 1928. Oil on board, 36 by 30 inches. Metropolitan Museum of Art, New York.

What is this painting about?

A Portrait Without a Face

This painting is the most famous of Demuth's "poster portraits" of friends. Demuth arranged symbols to reflect the interests and personalities of people he knew. This painting is a portrait of the influential American poet William Carlos Williams. The title and the 5 refer to Williams' poem, "The Great Figure":

> *Among the rain*
> *and lights*
> *I saw the figure 5*
> *in gold*
> *on a red*
> *fire truck*
> *moving*
> *tense*
> *unheeded*
> *to gong clangs,*
> *siren howls*
> *and wheels rumbling*
> *through the dark city.*

Would you be surprised to learn that this artwork is a portrait? By using both images and the words in the painting's title, American artist Charles Demuth (1883–1935) emphasized a number rather than a person's face. Look for these details:

- The number 5 is repeated three times.
- The radiating lines and colors at the bottom of the composition point inward, toward the 5 in the center.
- The sizes, placement, and color of the numbers make them stand out against the red and neutral background colors.

Technique Tip

Glue and Paper

Some types of glue can make paper pucker as it dries. Try using different types of glue when you create a collage. Liquid starch, flour and water, or a commercial product may work better. You can also try different types of paper. Thicker paper will pucker less than thin paper.

Emphasize to Show Meaning

Use what you have learned about emphasis to create a collage with meaning.

Materials

- ✓ pencil
- ✓ cardboard
- ✓ scissors ⚠
- ✓ two sheets of dark-colored construction paper
- ✓ 12" × 18" sheet of white paper
- ✓ glue
- ✓ various types and colors of paper, such as wrapping, tissue, metallic
- ✓ felt-tip pen

1 Draw an outline of a musical instrument in three sizes on the cardboard. Cut out the shapes to use as stencils.

2 Use the stencils to cut multiple images from the construction paper. Arrange the images on the white paper and glue them down.

3 Cut shapes from the other types of paper and glue them to fill the space between the instruments. Accent with a felt-tip pen.

Review and Reflect

- What instrument did you choose as your main image?
- How did you arrange your shapes to create emphasis?
- How does the arrangement you chose affect the meaning of the finished work of art?
- What do you find most interesting about the artwork you have created? Why?

Lesson 3

Proportion

An artist can create interesting compositions by manipulating proportion. **Proportion** in artworks is the relationship of the parts to each other and to the whole work. **Standard proportion** describes a person or an object that seems to have appropriate height, width, and depth compared to its surroundings. **Altered proportion** describes objects or people whose proportions have been changed or altered.

As a principle of design, proportion has to do with one part compared to another within a work of art. An artist must also consider the scale of the objects and people within the artwork. For example, a furniture designer must build desks and chairs to fit people, so the furniture is built on a human scale. Look at the seated figures in the photograph of the temple. Are they built on a human scale? How can you tell?

Artists sometimes highlight unusual size relationships by their placement of objects in a composition. As you read in Unit 1, placing an object in the foreground, middle ground, or background is a clue to its size and its distance from the viewer. By manipulating the placement of an object, an artist can create unusual size relationships.

Artist unknown. *Funerary Temple of Ramesses II at Abu Simbel, Egypt,* 1260 B.C.

William Karp. *Electric Production and Direction,*
ca. 1933–1934. Mural study (two panels).
Smithsonian American Art Museum, Washington, D.C.

Altering Proportions

Study the way the artist has manipulated proportion in this composition. In the top panel, a seated human figure is smaller than the human hand behind it, which is about the same size as the human eyeball in the background. These altered proportions give an eerie sense of unreality to the artwork.

Now look at the bottom panel. How has the artist altered the proportions? What do you think the artist is trying to say by changing the proportions of the objects in this artwork so dramatically?

Sketchbook Journal

Make one sketch showing three objects and a setting in normal proportion. Make a second sketch of the same objects and setting using altered proportion. Then label each drawing. How does proportion affect the meaning of the objects and setting in each sketch?

In this sculpture, Claes Oldenburg (1929–) has made an object that usually is very small and overlooked—the humble clothespin—into the focal point of a busy intersection between office buildings. Notice these details:

- The size of the artwork makes it impossible to overlook.
- Even though the clothespin towers over the cars and trees beneath it, the proportions of the clothespin's parts are normal in relationship to each other.

Proportion and Emphasis

Works of art are called exaggerated when they have objects with distorted or exaggerated proportions to show emphasis. Artworks that have smaller-than-life proportions are called miniature artworks. This sculpture is monumental; its proportions are much larger than life. Why do you think Oldenburg chose to create a monumental sculpture of a clothespin?

Claes Oldenburg. *Clothespin*, 1976. Cor-ten and stainless steel, 45 by 12 ½ by 4 ½ feet. Centre Square Plaza, Philadelphia, PA.

How has the artist exaggerated proportion in this sculpture?

Technique Tip

Let There Be Light
Remember to use a good source of light when drawing. Sit near a window or turn on all the lights in the room. Bring a lamp to your workstation to increase the available light. You want to be able to convey your ideas as accurately as possible, so keep your area well lit.

Studio 3

Design a Sculpture

Use what you have learned about proportion to design a monumental sculpture for your community.

Materials

✓ magazines or a camera
✓ pencil with soft lead, pen, or felt-tip marker
✓ white drawing paper
✓ paper for photocopying

1 Take pictures of a local area or find magazine photographs that show an area where you could add a monumental artwork.

2 Plan the sculpture you would create for the space and make sketches of your ideas. Keep in mind its final proportions.

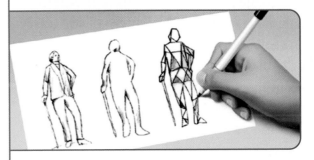

3 Photocopy the picture of the location you chose. Draw your proposed sculpture on the photocopy in the position it would take.

Review and Reflect

- Describe the elements in your monumental sculpture design.
- How does your sculpture relate to the area around it? How does it compare to the scale of the people and buildings?
- What are you trying to say with the sculpture you have designed?
- Would your sculpture work on all sides, or does it work best from only one view? Explain.

Lesson 4

Rhythm

Language and music both have rhythm. In language, rhythm is the pattern of stressed and unstressed elements in the sound of your words. In music, it is the pattern of the notes in the melody. Rhythm gives speech and music a sense of motion. Works of art have this sort of pattern too. In art, **rhythm** is the repetition of visual elements, such as lines, shapes, or colors, that creates a feeling of motion.

An artist can harness different types of rhythm to make an artwork seem active.

Regular rhythm is the repetition of an element without any variation.

Alternating rhythm is the repetition of two or more elements in an even pattern.

Progressive rhythm is created by showing regular changes in a repeated element.

Look at the painting below by Piet Mondrian (1872–1944). Notice how your eye jumps from square to square and from color to color. This movement of your eye across the canvas is caused by the rhythm of the elements repeated throughout the composition. The pattern of the repetition is not regular or predictable, so it is called random rhythm. What kind of music does the rhythm of this painting remind you of?

Piet Mondrian. *Victory Boogie Woogie (unfinished)*, 1944. Oil and Paper on Canvas, 49 5/8 by 49 5/8 inches. Diagonal Measurement 70 1/4 inches. © 2005 Mondrian/Holtzman Trust c/o HCR International, Warrenton, VA.

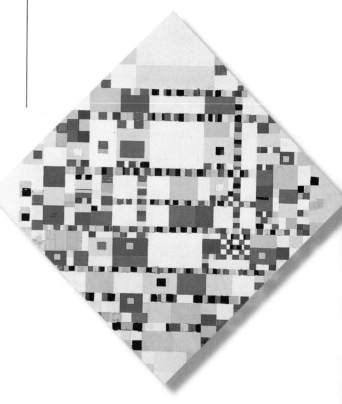

José Cuneo. *Ranchos Orilleros,* 1932. Oil on burlap, 24 ¼ by 36 inches. Private collection.

Rhythm and Movement

Notice how Uruguayan artist José Cuneo (1887–1977) repeats elements in this composition to give the painting a sense of movement. Cuneo repeats the houses, varying their colors slightly and tilting most of them in the same direction. He echoes this movement with the lines of the earth in the foreground, as well as with one figure and one tree. He creates movement in the opposite direction with the other figure, two other trees, and one of the houses. This gives the composition a kind of woozy, rolling feeling. What type of rhythm has Cuneo used with the clouds?

Sketchbook Journal

Listen to your favorite song and isolate its rhythm. For example, pick out the bass line from a rock and roll song. Create a simple sketch that shows the rhythm of the song visually. Label the composition as having regular, alternating, progressive, or random rhythm.

Sonia Terk Delaunay.
Composition, 1955. Oil on canvas,
62 ½ by 84 inches. Musée
National d'Art Moderne, Centre
Georges Pompidou, Paris, France.

What kind of visual rhythm does
this painting have?

Russian painter Sonia Terk Delaunay (1885–1979) created this painting when she was about seventy years of age. The painting is an example of how she used shape and color to show progressive rhythm. Look for these details:

- The color and size of the solid semicircles change as they move from right to left.
- The curved yellow and blue lines become progressively larger in diameter as they radiate from a center point.

Forging a Style

Delaunay and her husband, French painter Robert Delaunay, painted in a style called Orphism, in which they employed bright colors and bold, repeating patterns. To create her patterns and colors, Delaunay drew inspiration from the folk art of her childhood in Russia. She used the principles of Orphism to create bold designs on fabrics and pottery too. Her work with textiles influenced international fashions in the 1920s. Why might designs with progressive rhythm be interesting to someone who designs clothing?

Technique Tip

Tear It Up

When tearing paper, place your index finger on the paper and slowly tear right next to it for better control. Try to tear with the grain of the paper. To make straight tears, fold the sheet back and forth along a crease before tearing, or put the sheet over the sharp edge of a table. Hold the paper to the table with one hand and tear downward with the other.

Create Rhythmic Shapes

Use what you have learned about rhythm to create colorful shapes that show rhythm.

Materials

✓ variety of colored construction paper
✓ 12" × 18" white paper
✓ glue
✓ colored pencils

1 Think of one or more shapes in nature that you can repeat rhythmically. Tear multiples of the shapes from construction paper.

2 Arrange your torn shapes on the white paper, creating a regular, alternating, or progressive rhythm. Glue the shapes down.

3 Use colored pencils to accentuate the rhythm you have created, or use them to add a different rhythm to the composition.

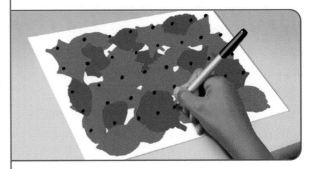

Review and Reflect

• Describe the shapes and colors you chose to show rhythm.
• What kind of rhythm did you create and how did you use shape and color to create it?
• If the rhythm you created were turned into music, how would it sound?
• What do you like least about your artwork? How would you change it?

Pattern

You have seen patterns; they are around you everywhere. There are patterns on fabrics and wallpaper. The waves make patterns of ripples in the sand at the beach. The leaves of a tree create a pattern against the sky behind it. You can find patterns in art too. As a principle of design, **pattern** is the repeated colors, lines, shapes, forms, or textures in an artwork. Artists use pattern to help them express their ideas or feelings.

Look how the lines and curves repeat in the photograph of Slot Canyon. The repetition emphasizes the pattern and feeling of the land's undulating movement.

Patterns create a different feeling in *Daffodils and Lemon.* The artist has incorporated many different patterns in this work of art. On the plate, dots form spirals around the outside edge and short lines march around the rim. Longer lines create stripes around the top of the jug. Lines of varying width and color form a pattern on the blankets in the background of the composition and draw the viewer's eye to the center. Notice also how the patterns give the artwork a sense of visual movement and rhythm. All the patterns contribute to a feeling of joy and exuberance in the painting.

As you go through each day, identify patterns you see around you, such as in the floors of your school, the windows of a building, or the plants in a garden. Observe which elements of art create the patterns.

Photograph of Slot Canyon, Paria Canyon Wilderness Area, Utah, USA. © Henry Lehn/SuperStock.

Isy Ochoa. *Daffodils and Lemon,* 1999. Oil on canvas, 35 9/10 by 28 1/2 inches. Private collection.

Artist unknown, Asante People, Ghana. *Woman's Kente Cloth,* mid-20th century. Rayon, 64 ½ by 33 ¾ inches. The Newark Museum, Newark, NJ.

Patterns in Cloth

The Asante weavers of Ghana, West Africa, are known around the world for their skill at weaving patterns into cloth. Patterns are particularly important to the Asante. They incorporate certain patterns to indicate specific things, such as a wealthy person or a person about to be married, or ideas, such as the unity in diversity. Until relatively recently, most cloth made in both Eastern and Western Africa was woven from locally grown, hand-spun cotton. Although most fibers are now spun in factories, some Asante weavers still weave vibrant patterns into hand-spun cotton cloth.

Research

The Industrial Revolution brought an end in many countries to the wide-scale production of cloth by hand. But many artists still use these ancient skills to express their ideas. Research how cloth is woven. In your Sketchbook Journal, write down the steps involved in the traditional method of weaving cloth and how it has changed over the last one hundred years.

81

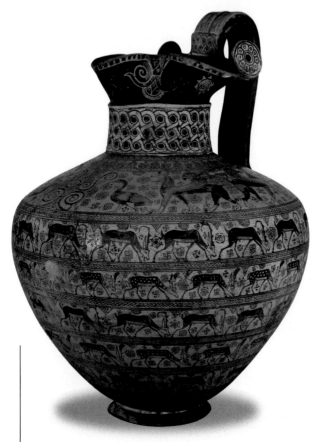

Artist unknown, Greek. *Oenochoe, called Levy Oenochoe,* 650 B.C. Terra cotta. Musée du Louvre, Paris, France.

What patterns do you see in this Greek vessel?

The ancient Greeks are well known for their skill in making patterned pottery. Examine the patterns on this Greek vessel. Look for these details:

- The interlocking circular pattern repeats three times on the neck of the vessel.
- The body of the vessel features repeating horizontal bands that contain a repeating animal pattern.

Painting on Pots

The Greeks gradually changed their style of pottery painting. At first, Greek artists used only geometric shapes. They would cover a pot in patterns of arcs and circles. Gradually animals, and later people, began to appear on the pots, and artists began to use the vessels as a canvas on which to tell a story. Much of what we know today about Greek life and thought comes from the paintings on their pottery.

The ancient Greeks used different shapes of vessels to hold different liquids. This vessel is called an oenochoe. It was most likely used to hold wine.

Technique Tip

Avoid Mud Pies

Even though you may be tempted to wet your hands before you start to work with clay, avoid the temptation. It actually works better to have dry hands as you work. You don't need to add any water unless the clay starts to dry out severely. If it does, use a mister to dampen the object, and then cover it with a plastic bag overnight. It will be more workable the next day.

Make a Patterned Clay Pot

Use what you have learned about pattern to create a patterned, functional clay pot.

Materials

- ✓ plastic mat to cover the table
- ✓ lump of wedged clay
- ✓ implements you can use to make patterns, such as a plastic fork, a pencil, or an interesting drawer pull
- ✓ slip
- ✓ clay glazes or watercolors
- ✓ brushes

1 Roll a piece of clay to about the size of a tennis ball. Make a pinch pot by pressing your thumb into the center and pinching the clay evenly.

2 Score the top edge and add slip. Roll several clay coils and add them to the top, scoring and using slip each time.

3 Cut a slab of clay to form a lid for your pot. Then carve or press patterns into the pot and lid. Let them dry. Add color with glazes or watercolor.

Review and Reflect

- Describe the pattern you created on your pottery.
- How does the use of a pattern affect your appreciation of the pot?
- Did the pattern you chose have any special meaning for you? Explain.
- What did you like most about working with clay? Why?

Meet *the Artist*

Georges Braque

While some artists paint from their heart, French artist Georges Braque painted from his head. Braque used his canvases to promote an idea: that a painting is not an illusion of nature and should not look like one. So while Braque took his subject matter from nature, he distorted it, fragmented it, and abstracted it. And in doing so, he helped create an entirely new style of painting, one which unified seemingly disjointed images into soothing, reflective works of art.

Georges Braque painting in his studio.

"Painting is a nail to which I fasten my ideas."

—GEORGES BRAQUE

Developing Cubism

In 1907, Braque met Pablo Picasso. They rejected the idea that art should imitate nature. They used few colors and broke shapes into their basic geometric forms. Then they fragmented those forms, or offered multiple views of an object on a two-dimensional surface. At first, the subjects of their artworks were not as significant as their methods; later, both artists gave more importance to their subject matter. Viewing a Cubist painting is like looking at an image in broken glass. No one before them had ever painted anything like it.

War Interferes

Less than ten years after Braque and Picasso met, World War I compelled Braque to put down his brushes and join the war. He served until 1915, when he was seriously wounded. Braque continued to explore the ideas of Cubism after the war, but he never worked with Picasso again.

By the 1920s Braque began to venture into other media, including stage sets and some forms of sculpture. In 1961 he became the first living artist to have work in the prestigious Louvre Museum.

Talk About It

- Why do you think Braque never collaborated with Picasso after the war?

- According to the timeline, about how old was Braque when he had his first solo show?

The Life of Georges Braque

1880

1882
Georges Braque born on May 13

Braque has first solo show **1900**

1908

Braque marries Marcelle Lapré
1912

WWI begins in Europe, breaking up partnership between Braque and Picasso; Braque joins the French army
1914

WWI armistice celebraton

1918
WWI ends; Braque, wounded, had left the war in 1915 **1920**

1923
French ballet impresario Sergey Diaghilev commissions Braque to design stage sets

Braque wins first prize at the *Carnegie International*, Pittsburgh
1937

Americans in WWII

1939
WWII begins; Braque turns to Greek themes **1940**

1945
WWII ends; Braque returns to creating groups of paintings focusing on a single subject

1948
Braque wins main painting prize at Venice Biennale

Biennale Exhibition

1960

1963
Braque dies August 31 in Paris

Look *and Compare*

One Subject, Two Styles

These two paintings have a lot in common. Their subjects are the same. They both feature the breakdown of form into colored shapes that create patterns across the canvas. Both artists were born in the same year, and they made both paintings in the same year. Even the titles are almost the same. But the works themselves are very different from each other. Why?

Braque and Lentulov were both inspired by the paintings of French artist Paul Cézanne. Though they took inspiration from the same artist, they used this inspiration in different ways to develop their own style of expression. Does one of these two paintings inspire you more than the other? Explain.

Painters such as Braque and Lentulov use a variety of brushes and tools to create bold shapes and delicate lines.

Braque

Georges Braque and Aristarkh Lentulov (1882–1943) were born on opposite sides of Europe. Braque was from France at a time when the soft, colorful paintings of the Impressionists were popular. Braque first worked in this style. After moving to Paris, however, Braque and fellow artist Pablo Picasso developed a new style of painting. Called **Cubism,** the artworks featured objects and figures that were fractured into geometric planes.

Lentulov

Born in Russia, Aristarkh Lentulov (1882–1943) first saw the revolutionary Cubist paintings when he moved to Paris. In what ways does Lentulov's painting incorporate the ideas developed by Braque? How do the two paintings differ? Lentulov did not just duplicate the Cubist style. Instead, his artwork often draws on imagery from his Russian childhood. He and a group of Russian avant-garde painters were also inspired by traditional Russian folk art and deliberately incorporated folk art imagery and colors into their artwork.

Both Braque and Lentulov were influenced by the time and culture in which they lived. The color palette in each artwork reflects the artist's personal style and expression of these influences. Do you think these artworks would be different if the artists had lived in the United States? Explain.

Aristarkh Lentulov. *Portrait: Woman with a Guitar,* 1913. Oil on canvas, 39 by 37 ⁴/₅ inches. Museum of Art, Kazan, Russia.

Georges Braque. *Woman Playing a Guitar,* 1913. Oil on canvas, 50 ³/₄ by 28 ¹/₂ inches. Musée National d' Art Moderne, Paris, France.

Compare & Contrast

- What kind of rhythm did each artist establish in his painting? What kind of music does each remind you of?

- Braque once said, "Art is made to disturb." How do these paintings reflect Braque's statement?

Unity

If all the parts of a work of art look right together, the artwork is unified. **Unity** is the quality of seeming whole, complete, or harmonious. Artists can achieve unity in several ways. For example, a painter might repeat a color or a shape in several areas of the composition or use a color scheme, such as analogous or monochromatic, to create a unified work of art.

Notice how French painter Henri Matisse (1869–1954) used pattern and color to unify this composition. Most of the colors are tints and shades of the primary colors red, blue, and yellow.

Matisse used red as the background color to tie the whole composition together.

He balanced that vast area of red with the small red building in the distance. Matisse used shades of blue to emphasize the progressive plant patterns on the tablecloth; then he echoed the pattern on the wallpaper. Where has Matisse used other shades of blue to unify his composition? Matisse introduced yellow with the geometric shape of the lemons sitting on the table and on the plate. He repeated the shape and color in the flowers visible through the window as well as those in the vase on the table. What kind of balance did he employ in this artwork? How do these elements provide unity to the painting?

Henri Matisse. *Harmony in Red (The Red Room),* 1908. Oil on canvas, 70 ¼ by 85 ¾ inches. The Hermitage Museum, St. Petersburg, Russia.

Marilee Whitehouse-Holm. *Purple Perca Plus Pals,* 1996. © Marilee Whitehouse-Holm.

Unity With Shapes and Colors

Notice how Marilee Whitehouse-Holm (1949–) used balance, proportion, rhythm, and pattern to create a unified composition. Because the visual properties are very similar on each side of the centerline, the viewer can describe this composition as being symmetrically balanced. All the fish have similar proportions, and they are painted with similar patterns of dots and color. This repetition creates a regular rhythm that is restful yet interesting to the eye. What other techniques or elements of art did Whitehouse-Holm use to achieve unity in this painting?

Sketchbook Journal

Find a view of the outside environment that features repeated elements. Make a sketch of the view, emphasizing the elements that repeat. As you draw, simplify objects in the environment to reinforce their similarities. Make notes about colors and shapes you might use to help unify your drawing.

Unity *in Assemblage*

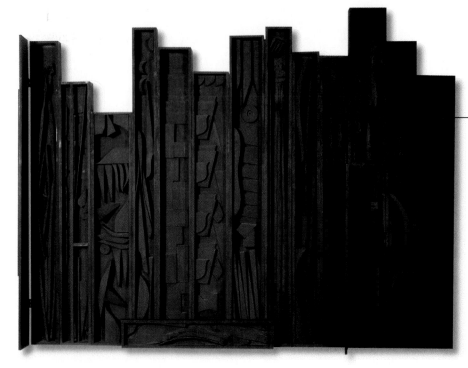

Louise Nevelson. *Tropical Garden II*, 1959. Painted wood, 89 ⅓ by 113 ½ by 12 inches. Musée National d'Art Moderne, Centre Georges Pompidou, Paris, France.

What unifies this composition?

An assemblage, as you discovered in Unit 1, is a sculpture made with found objects. In this assemblage, American sculptor Louise Nevelson (ca. 1900–1988) used shape and color to achieve unity. Look for these details:

- The artwork is composed of a series of rectangular boxes with similar proportions, each of which contains a different pattern of shapes.
- Everything in the composition is painted the same color.

Unifying Found Objects

Nevelson often used a single color to unify a sculpture. She is best known for her monochromatic artworks created around the time she made this assemblage. Most of her artworks from this period feature open wooden boxes stacked to make walls. In the boxes, Nevelson would arrange pieces of broken furniture and bits of wood to create interesting patterns. Nevelson once said that she worked with found objects like these because, at the time, she could not afford to work with anything else.

Technique Tip

Carry the Weight

If you want to hang a heavy artwork, such as an assemblage, be sure to use the right equipment. Commercial picture-hangers are good because their packages state the weight the hangers can hold. You may need to use two hangers to distribute the weight evenly. Another option is to install a small shelf, and then display the assemblage on top.

Studio 6

Assemble a Unified Composition

Use what you have learned to create an assemblage that displays unity.

Materials

- ✓ wood scraps and shapes
- ✓ tempera paint
- ✓ mixing tray or plate
- ✓ paintbrushes
- ✓ wood glue
- ✓ container of water for rinsing
- ✓ six or more medium binder clips
- ✓ three small, sturdy cardboard boxes of different sizes, none larger than a shoebox

1 Collect a variety of small wooden objects, such as spools, toothpicks, and scraps. Paint them all one color or in one color scheme.

2 Glue the three boxes together and clip them with binder clips until they dry. Remove the clips and paint the boxes a single color.

3 Arrange the painted wooden objects in the boxes. When you have found a pleasing composition, glue the objects in place.

Review and Reflect

- What shapes did you use in your assemblage?
- What techniques, objects, or colors did you use to unify your work of art?
- What kind of mood does your assemblage convey?
- What title would you give your assemblage? Where would you display it? Why?

Variety

If a composition is unified but has no variety, it can appear visually boring. **Variety,** the use of different elements to add interest to a work of art, is the final principle of design. It works hand in hand with unity to create a pleasing composition. In an artwork with many repeated elements, an artist can introduce variety to add emphasis and meaning.

This is one of Belgian artist René Magritte's early works of art. Magritte (1898–1967) created it soon after finishing art school, when he worked as a designer for a wallpaper factory. While the designs he would have created for wallpaper would focus on repetition to achieve unity, this composition introduces variety, yet remains unified.

In a composition dominated by geometric shapes, the natural shapes stand out and add variety. For example, notice how each human figure is different from the others in both color and shape. On the other hand, the houses in the background have a similar color and shape. Where else can you detect the principle of variety in this artwork?

René Magritte. *Untitled (The Horsewoman),* 1922. Oil on cardboard on wood, approximately 24 ½ by 35 inches. Private collection.

Magritte introduced variety using shapes and colors.

Judith Leyster.
Boy Playing the Flute,
1635. Oil on canvas,
28 ¹⁄₂ by 24 ¹⁄₄ inches.
National Museum,
Stockholm, Sweden.

Variety Using Lines and Color

This painting is one of the best-known works of art by Dutch painter Judith Leyster (1609–1660). At first glance, the painting looks so unified that it is difficult to see the variety Leyster has introduced. She uses lines and color to achieve subtle variations. For example, look at the lines made by the flute on the wall, the violin bow, and the flute in the boy's hands. The lines form an arc from right to left, drawing the viewer's attention to the boy's face, where Leyster captures the play of light by using variations in hue. Where else has Leyster used color to introduce variety?

Research

At age twenty-four, Judith Leyster became the first woman ever admitted to the Haarlem painter's guild. She was also among the first Dutch artists to depict domestic scenes in her paintings. Using your library or the Web, find out more about Leyster. Record what you learn in your Sketchbook Journal.

Artist unknown. *Untitled.* Tempera on fabric. Private collection.

How did the artist create variety?

Variety is as important in textiles as it is in all other types of art, such as paintings and sculptures. The artist's use of a limited colors in this textile helps provide unity. With so many repeating patterns and colors, variety is essential to the success of this work of art. Look for these details:

- Each of the two animals in the composition is unique: it appears only once in the design.
- The figures, though very similar, are facing in different directions and performing a variety of tasks.

- The patterns of shapes at the top and bottom are different.
- The black color of the horse adds interest to the limited color palette.

Art in South Asia

This work of art was created by an artist in India, which is in South Asia, where artists traditionally have been held in great esteem. All forms of art, including dance, visual art, literature, and music, are thought to be linked, so it is important that an artist in one discipline know the other disciplines well. In the South Asian tradition, painters rank just behind sculptors in importance. Painters consider line to be the most important part of a composition, and work hard to say as much as possible with each artwork they create.

Technique Tip

Stay Sharp with Scissors

When cutting fabric you must use very sharp scissors so the cuts are not ragged. Be careful to cut with the points of your scissors away from your body. After each use, clean your scissors to help them stay sharp. Never let scissors stay wet, though. They will rust quickly.

Studio 7

Make a Fabric Hanging

Use what you have learned to create a textile wall hanging that shows variety.

Materials

- ✓ variety of patterned fabrics
- ✓ large piece of fabric, approximately 18" × 22"
- ✓ scissors ⚠
- ✓ glue
- ✓ small tree branch or dowel
- ✓ raffia, twine, rope, or strip of fabric

1 Choose a group of fabrics whose dominant color is the same. Choose another group whose dominant color is the complement of the first group.

2 Cut identical triangles from each fabric. Arrange the triangles of one color group like a puzzle on the large piece of fabric. Create a border around the arrangement with the complementary pieces.

3 Wrap the top edge of the hanging over a stick or dowel and glue. Let dry. Tie on a hanger of raffia or other fiber.

Review and Reflect

- Describe the color scheme and arrangement you chose.
- What elements introduce variety into your textile?
- What elements help to unify the artwork?
- How successful is your textile at showing variety? Explain.

Portfolio *Project*

Homescape

Jane Wooster Scott. *The City by the Golden Gate*, 1988. Oil on canvas, 24 by 30 inches. © Jane Wooster Scott.

Plan

Twentieth-century American artist Jane Wooster Scott represents scenes from across the American landscape in her artworks. Scott uses a technique called serigraph, which requires her to create a separate screen stencil to layer each color onto her canvas. Look at how using the principles of design helped the artist in both her technique and the creation of a lively and intricate depiction of the San Francisco skyline.

- The bay creates a dividing line that gives the artwork asymmetrical balance. How does the artist's use of balance relate to the scene of the city and the neighborhood?

- Rhythm is created by the repetition of similar shapes of the neighborhood houses, the city buildings, and the clouds. What types of rhythm did the artist show and how do they affect the painting?
- Notice the artist's use of line and color. How did she use these elements to achieve unity and variety?

Using what you have learned about the principles of design, paint a street scene of an unusual sight in your own neighborhood.

Sketchbook Journal

Draw a sketch of the houses or buildings in your neighborhood. Look at the background as well as the foreground. Is your scene best depicted using flowing curves or strong vertical and horizontal lines? Incorporate rhythm in your sketch. Also, include elements to unify your scene as well as to create variety.

Materials

- ✓ neighborhood sketch from Sketchbook Journal activity (optional)
- ✓ pencil
- ✓ 11" × 17" heavy drawing paper and newsprint
- ✓ tempera paint and mixing tray or plate
- ✓ brushes and water container
- ✓ black or colored markers

Create

1 Choose three or four houses from the sketches in your Sketchbook Journal. Make preparatory drawings, experimenting with proportion.

2 Lightly sketch your composition on drawing paper. Include balance, pattern, and rhythm with your placement of objects in the scene.

3 Experiment with a color scheme for your painting. Choose colors that help you show both unity and variety.

4 Apply the paints you chose to your composition. Use color to reinforce the mood you are trying to convey. Add details and texture using black or colored markers.

Reflect

- Use words to explain the scene you painted. What kind of neighborhood is it? Who would live there?
- What principles of design did you incorporate into your scene? How did they affect your depiction of the scene?
- How would your painting be different if the houses or buildings were in a different setting? How would a person who lived in that neighborhood feel about your painting?
- What does your painting say about the neighborhood that you depicted? Do you think others would like to live in this neighborhood? Explain.

Unit 2 *Review*

Vocabulary Review

A Match each art term below with its definition.

pattern	unity
scale	miniature
balance	emphasis
focal point	proportion
variety	rhythm

1. the use of different elements to add interest to a work of art
2. an element that is the center of interest
3. the sense of importance that an artist gives to an area of an artwork
4. regular repetition in an artwork
5. a sense of movement achieved through repetition
6. artworks that are smaller than life
7. the size of a part in relation to the size of the whole
8. a sense of wholeness and completion
9. proportional relationship between a real object and the object rendered as an artwork
10. a sense of equality in visual weight

Artists and Their Art

B Each work of art listed in the box appears in this unit. Use the titles to finish the sentences below.

I Saw the Figure Five in Gold
Tropical Garden II
Portrait of H.J. van Wisselingh
Boy Playing the Flute
South Rose Window
Morning News

1. Gustave Courbet used a contrast between light and shadow to emphasize the face of the subject of ___.
2. ___ at Westminster Abbey shows radial balance with its flower-like shape.
3. Helen Turner used splashes of red to help balance the composition of ___.
4. ___ by Charles Demuth was inspired by a poem by William Carlos Williams and features a number repeated three times for emphasis.
5. Louise Nevelson achieved unity by using one color of paint on the boxes and shapes that comprise ___.
6. ___ is one of the most famous paintings by seventeenth-century Dutch artist Judith Leyster.

Gustave Courbet

Judith Leyster. (Detail)
Self-Portrait, ca. 1630.

Respond to Art

C Look at *The Boating Party* by Mary Cassatt. Then match the letters in the line drawing of the artwork to the art terms.

Mary Cassatt. *The Boating Party,* 1893–1894. Oil on canvas, 35 7/16 by 46 1/8 inches. National Gallery of Art, Washington, D.C.

Art Terms

1. pattern
2. emphasis
3. asymmetrical balance
4. variety

Unit 2 *Review*

Write About Art

Persuasive Paragraphs

D Look back at the artworks you saw in this unit. Choose one that you think successfully reflects the elements of art and principles of design. Write a persuasive composition to convince an art museum why the artwork is a good choice to include in its collection. Include why the artist's use of the elements and principles make it worthy of being part of the museum's collection. Copy the chart below and use it to develop your thoughts and ideas before writing.

Name of Artwork
_____

1. Concluding Statement
_____

2. Supporting Facts
_____

3. Conclusion Checklist

Your Studio Work

E Answer these questions in your Sketchbook Journal or on a separate sheet of paper.

1. Which artist from this unit would you most like to learn more about? Why?
2. What principle of design inspired you most to create your own works of art? Why?
3. What problems did you encounter as you applied the principles of design to your own artworks? How did you solve the problems you encountered?
4. Of the artworks you created in this unit, which was most successful? Why?

Put It All Together

Jennifer Bartlett. *Boats,* 1987. Oil on canvas, approximately 10 by 14 feet, with two wooden boats, each 66 by 47 by 46 inches. © Jennifer Bartlett/Charles Street Artist Studio.

F **Discuss or write about Jennifer Bartlett's work of art *Boats* using the four steps below for viewing artwork critically.**

1. **Describe** What is the subject of this artwork? What object or objects did the artist show? What colors did the artist use and where did she use them?
2. **Analyze** How did the artist create unity in this work of art? How did the artist introduce variety? What kind of rhythm has she set up?
3. **Interpret** What do you think the artist is trying to say with this artwork? What mood has she created? What elements contribute to this mood? Why do you think the artist has used both sculpture and painting in this one composition?
4. **Judge** American artist Jennifer Bartlett (1941–) is a sculptor, painter, and installation artist. An installation is an artwork assembled in a specific place. Many of Bartlett's installations explore the relationship between an object and a painted image of the object. How successful do you think this installation is, and why?

Jennifer Bartlett's artwork portrays common items repeated in a variety of perspectives. Water and light are common subjects in her artworks.

At the young age of five, Jennifer Bartlett proclaimed, "I am going to be an artist."

Louise Nevelson. *Atmosphere and Environment V,* 1966. Enamel on aluminum, 96 by 102 by 324 inches. Corning Tower Plaza, Albany, NY.

Unit 3

Art Media and Techniques

For centuries, artists have been using a variety of materials to create works of art. Some art media, such as charcoal and paint, are used today as they were thousands of years ago. Today's materials and technology provide artists with a host of media for creating art.

Artists use different techniques, or methods of working with specific media, to create artworks. Painters, sculptors, and weavers often experiment with their media in different ways to discover new techniques. They use these techniques to achieve special results and express their ideas in their art.

In this unit you will read about a variety of media and techniques. You will also use combinations of media to express a wide range of images, thoughts, and feelings.

About *the Artist*

Louise Nevelson never doubted that she would become a professional artist. Through decades of poverty and challenges, she never wavered from the path. Read more about how Nevelson established herself as a contemporary sculptor on page 120.

Drawing

People have communicated through drawings since humans first drew with charcoal on a cave wall. Charcoal, graphite and colored pencils, crayons, markers, ink, and oil and chalk pastels are only a few of the media, or materials, that an artist can use to draw. An artist can use a single **medium,** or combine it with other media. A drawing can be a work of art in itself, or an artist can use it to develop an idea for another artwork.

Many artists draw or sketch every day to keep their skills sharp and to improve their perception. Drawing forces an artist to pay attention to what he or she is seeing, to examine every detail. Because drawing requires such intense concentration, it helps an artist become more aware of the elements in his or her environment.

Look at the drawing to the right. The artist has used a single medium to capture the details that make the woman distinctive. Notice the artist's use of line and value. Identify the shading technique the artist used. Does this look like a finished work of art, or do you think it is a preparatory drawing? How long do you think it took the artist to draw this portrait?

Robert McIntosh. *Portrait Class,* 1934. Charcoal on paper. © Robert McIntosh.

Barbara Benedetti Newton. *Patience,* 2001. Colored pencil on paper,
8 ¾ by 9 ¾ inches. Private collection.

Control and Precision

Barbara Benedetti Newton (1943–) began her art career as an illustrator in the 1960s, using pen and ink. She began working with colored pencils in 1990 because she liked the way she could control the medium. With colored pencils, she can establish and deepen color slowly and carefully. Her control of the medium is evident in the artwork above. Notice how she captures precise and subtle tints and shades of the blue of the bowl, and the flush of pink on the eggs. Look at the glass bowl and the shadows it casts. Then notice how the artist created the shiny texture on the bowl as well as its transparent quality.

Sketchbook Journal

Choose a drawing medium, such as pencil or ink pen, and an object to draw, such as a plant or a car. Practice your drawing skills by making a detailed drawing of the object you chose. Spend as much time as you can on the drawing and record every detail you see.

Edgar Degas. *Blue Dancers,* 1897. Pastel. Hermitage Museum, St. Petersburg, Russia.

Which direction is the light coming from in this artwork?

In many works of art, the artist chooses a **light source,** or a point of illumination for emphasis, contrast, unity, or dramatic effect. Degas chose to place his light source above the dancers, out of the frame of his canvas. Notice these details:

- Shadows fall on the dancers' backs or below their arms.
- Light seems to shine on the front of the dancers and on the tops of their arms.

What It's About

Degas used his light source to create a contrast for dramatic effect. This contrast highlights the artwork's subject. The **subject** of an artwork is its topic or main idea. You may recall that artists use shading techniques such as blending, stippling, hatching, and cross-hatching to show light and shadow in

a work of art. What techniques has Degas used to show light and shadow in this artwork? Degas also used color to depict shadows. Notice on the dresses how the artist used different values of blue to indicate the direction of the light.

Technique Tip

First Draft

When you begin to block out a drawing, keep your lines light until you have the shapes and proportions the way you want them. Then go back and reinforce the lines that best reflect what you want to depict. You can erase the early lines later, but consider leaving your first sketchy lines in your finished drawing.

Studio 1

Show Light

Use what you have learned to create an oil pastel drawing that uses shading and value to reflect a light source.

Materials

✓ sections of white plastic pipe
✓ newsprint
✓ heavy white drawing paper
✓ charcoal
✓ oil pastels
✓ lamp or other strong light source

1 Arrange the pipe in a symmetrical or asymmetrical composition. Draw several sketches on newsprint to work out details.

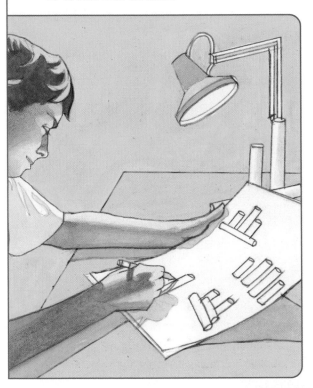

2 Use charcoal to transfer your composition to white paper. Use oil pastels to show light and shadow in your drawing.

3 Use charcoal to complete the background, making the brilliant colors of the pipes stand out.

Review and Reflect

- What colors did you use on the sections of pipe? What objects did you include in the background?
- How do the colors you chose affect the mood and the overall composition?
- What part of your composition was the most difficult to draw?
- Are you satisfied with your completed drawing? Why or why not?

Painting

Painters use a powerful expressive tool, color. Paint and painting media derive their color from pigment, a fine powder made from plants, minerals, or chemicals. The pigment is held together with a binder, such as wax, egg, glue, resin, or oil. To thin the paint, an artist can add a solvent, like water or turpentine, to the pigment-binder mix.

Artists have used oil-based paint for more than five hundred years. The binder in **oil-based paint** is linseed oil and the solvent is turpentine. Oil paints dry slowly, which gives an artist time to adjust the painting if necessary.

Water-based paints, such as acrylic, watercolor, and tempera, dry more quickly than oil paints. Artists first used acrylic paint in the 1940s. The binder in acrylic paint is a type of plastic, and as long as it is wet, acrylic is water-solvent. Though it dries more quickly, acrylic paint can often achieve results similar to oils. Watercolor paints have gum arabic as a binder, which is relatively weak. This allows artists to remove color by blotting but also makes the finished painting rather delicate. Before the invention of oil and acrylic paints, artists used **tempera paint.** Traditionally, the binder for tempera was egg yolk. Some modern artists still work in this traditional method.

Robin Shepherd. *Red Saxophone,* 20th century. Acrylic on canvas. © Robin Shepard.

What type of paint has the artist used to create this artwork?

Heliette Wzgarda. *The Irises of Guemappe*, 1993. Oil on canvas. The Grand Design, Leeds, England.

Flowers in Oil

Heliette Wzgarda (1943–) used oil paint to create the vibrant colors in this artwork. She likely painted from a **palette,** a flat surface used as a mixing tray. Wzgarda mixed tints and shades of the different colors to make the flowers in the foreground very crisp and detailed. She used these color values to define the ridges and ruffles in the petals, and the curve in the stems. The values also give the painting a sense of space and depth. The flowers in the background are mere smudges suggesting petals and stems. How would you describe the rhythm that the artist created by altering and repeating the shapes of petals, flowers, and stems?

Sketchbook Journal

Create notes for a painting you want to start. Begin making a sketch of an indoor or outdoor scene. Label each element with detailed notes about the colors you will use. Be sure to be specific about color, tint, and shade.

Tempera *and Other Media*

What media has the artist used?

André Masson. *Meditation on an Oak Leaf,* 1942.
Tempera, pastel, and sand on canvas, 40 by 33 inches.
The Museum of Modern Art, New York.

Automatic Drawing

André Masson was a leading figure in the Surrealist Movement and pioneered the use of **automatic drawing,** a technique in which drawings are made by free-association or randomly. Masson hoped this method would free his creative process from the control of reason. Masson made this painting during World War II. Many of his paintings from this period were inspired by the natural environment. What elements of art and principles of design can you identify in this painting?

An artist can apply paint in a way that makes it either **transparent,** so you can see what is behind it, or **opaque,** where nothing can be seen through the paint. French Surrealist André Masson (1896–1987) applied paint both opaquely and transparently in this artwork. Look for these details:

- The red on the lower left is applied so that the background color shows through at the edges.
- The bottom white shape is painted so you cannot see the background through it.

Technique Tip

Mix It Up
When mixing secondary colors, use magenta instead of red and turquoise instead of blue. Add white and black to achieve different values. Experiment by adding soap, coffee grounds, or liquid starch.

Studio 2

Combine Tempera with Other Media

Use what you have learned to create an artwork with chalk, ink, and water-based paint as your media.

Materials

✓ watercolor paper
✓ chalk
✓ tempera paint and brush
✓ tissue
✓ India ink and brush

1 Choose a subject, such as leaves or shells. Use chalk to draw a composition that features your subject in a repeated pattern.

2 Apply tempera paint heavily inside the chalk lines. After your painting has dried, use a tissue to wipe away the chalk lines.

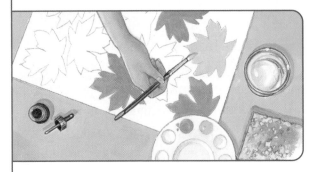

3 Use a brush to gently cover the painting with a coat of India ink. Let it dry for ten minutes, and then rinse under running water.

Review and Reflect

- What shape did you use to create a pattern? What colors did you choose?
- What kind of balance did you achieve in your composition?
- How would you describe the rhythm you created with pattern and color?
- What do you like best about your composition? What do you like least? Explain.

111

Printmaking

When artists want more than one copy of an artwork, they make prints. A print is a mark or shape made on a flat surface by an inked **block,** a piece of carved wood or linoleum, or by a **plate,** a thin sheet of material like metal. **Printmaking** is the process by which the different types of prints are made. When the image is printed from the raised carving on a block, it is called a **relief print.** If it is printed from an image scratched into a metal plate, it is called an **intaglio print.**

A **lithograph** is a method of printing from a flat stone. A lithographer sometimes uses a metal or plastic plate instead of a stone. The artist makes a drawing on the flat surface with a greasy crayon and then rinses the surface with water. Printing ink, which is thicker than writing ink, is applied to the surface with a brayer, a tool with a handle and a roller. The ink will stick to the greasy drawing but will run off the wet surface. When the printing plate is applied to the paper or other flat surface, only the lines of the drawing will transfer. In color lithography, a separate drawing is made for each color. Four drawings were needed to print Smith's lithograph—one for each of the colors.

Jaune Quick-to-See Smith. *Untitled, from the portfolio of Indian Self-Rule,* 1983. Color lithograph on paper, 27 ¼ by 19 ¼ inches. Smithsonian American Art Museum, Washington, D.C.

Ando Hiroshige. *The Whirlpools at Awa: Naruto Rapido,* 19th century. Japanese colored woodblock print. Victoria and Albert Museum, London.

Whirlpool in a Woodcut

Japanese artist Ando Hiroshige (1797–1858) created this asymmetrically balanced woodblock print. A woodblock print, or woodcut, is made from a design carved out of a block of wood. What parts of the artwork help make the visual weight equal on both sides of the composition? Notice how Hiroshige created rhythm and movement with the pattern of swirling lines in the whirlpool and the staggered lines of the crashing waves. How did he show depth and distance?

Hiroshige created more than five thousand prints in his career as an artist. As you study this print, consider which parts of the paper received the printing ink and which did not.

Sketchbook Journal

Make several sketches of objects, figures, or scenes. Include natural and human-made objects in your sketches. Next to each sketch, make notes about the kind of print that would work best. Include the printmaking techniques and colors you would use to create each print.

Tadek Beutlich. *Fish.* Color Woodcut, linocut print, (CT29823). Victoria and Albert Museum, London.

What two types of printing has the artist used?

British artist Tadek Beutlich (1922–) has combined woodcuts and linocut to create this work of art. Look for these details:

- The work is composed of only two colors, red and black. This limited palette gives the composition unity.
- The black ink that defines the shape of the fish is applied transparently over parts of the background. This allows the red background to show through.
- The shape of the fish is roughly symmetrical. The line through the middle of the fish divides it into two more or less equal shapes.
- The artist created progressive rhythm with the repeated diagonal lines that form the ribs of the fish.

Beyond Printmaking

Beutlich is also known for his complex tapestries and wall hangings. Consider how the elements of art and principles of design apply to printmaking and other art forms.

Technique Tip

On Blocks

When preparing linoleum block or other block printing material, remember that what you cut away will remain white and what you leave will print black. If words or letters are used, reverse the letters so the image will print correctly. Some tool marks will show, so carve in the same direction in any one area. Be very careful when using any cutting tool.

Studio 3

Print in Combinations

Use what you have learned to combine two types of printmaking to create a work of art.

Materials

✓ unused square pink erasers
✓ tempera paint
✓ 8" × 12" heavy drawing paper
✓ 6" × 10" linoleum block or similar product
✓ linoleum cutter ⑤
✓ brayer and printing ink
✓ inking plate or clean foam meat tray ⑤
✓ spoon

1 Make a stamp print by carving stripes on an eraser. Dip it into tempera paint and stamp a border around your paper.

2 Using a bold, linear design, carefully carve a portrait into a linoleum block. Spread ink evenly on the block with a brayer until the ink is tacky.

3 Center the bordered paper upside down on the printing block and apply pressure by rubbing a spoon over the entire surface. Pull the print.

Review and Reflect

- What two types of printing did you combine for this project?
- How did the media you used affect the final work of art?
- What was most difficult about working with these media?
- What do you like most about your finished work of art? What do you like least? Explain.

Lesson 4

Collage

Empty a wastebasket in any office and you will find everything from candy wrappers to paper clips; plastic bottle caps to newspapers and magazines. This is the trash of modern society. In most cases it would be discarded or recycled, but for some artists, it is the material for a work of art. One way an artist can use these materials is in **collage,** a design created by adhering materials onto a flat surface.

A collage can incorporate traditional artistic media as well. When paint, ink, or pastel is added to a collage, the artwork is described as being **mixed media.** Part of the creative process involves exploring and experimenting with a wide range of media and materials. An object or material with an interesting texture, image, or printed text can be just the element to inspire artistic expression.

Many contemporary artists are especially interested in using the cast-off junk of modern society. This gives them not only fascinating materials with which to express ideas, but a more universal way to communicate those ideas. After all, we usually recognize the source of the materials and have personal ideas about and connections with them. This extends and deepens the meaning of each work of art.

Elizabeth Barakah Hodges.
Sunday at Corky's, 1995.
Mixed media and collage.

Artist unknown. *African American Vaudeville Trunk*, ca. 1920s. Leather, wood, metal, collage, and mixed media. Ricco-Maresca Gallery, New York.

Show Time

Long before TV variety shows, vaudeville brought entertainment to the masses. In the late nineteenth century and early twentieth century, Americans in big cities could go to a theater to watch magicians, acrobats, comedians, and dancers perform live on stage. Performers would travel from town to town, taking their show on the road.

The *African American Vaudeville Trunk* above would have been used, and most likely was even decorated, by one of those performers. Notice the variety of materials used to collage the trunk. What images has the artist chosen to use? Who do you think is the intended audience for this work?

Research

Use your library or go online to discover how Cubist artists Pablo Picasso and Georges Braque modified the technique of collage in the early twentieth century. Write a narrative comparing Picasso's and Braque's artworks.

Collages *with Dimension*

Frank Stella. *The Beggar Woman of Locarno [N#5]*, 1999. Collage on paper on wood, 94 ½ by 200 inches. Collection of the artist.

What is the subject of this artwork?

American artist Frank Stella (1936–) uses shapes and forms that are geometric and organic to create abstract artworks. Look for these details:

- Horizontal, diagonal, and vertical lines seem to suggest overlapping shapes.
- The jagged lines simulate a bristly texture and give the composition a sense of energy.

From Line to Shape to Form

Stella, who was born in Massachusetts, became known in the late 1950s for his paintings that featured black stripes on raw canvas. In the late 1960s, Stella introduced color and geometric shapes into his paintings, and in the 1970s he created mixed-media

reliefs that featured curves and organic shapes. How has the artist's style changed since the 1950s?

Technique Tip

Best-laid Plans

When creating a collage, be organized. If you place your materials carelessly, your picture will look hasty and haphazard. Careful placement will ensure that your composition has balance and rhythm. Stand back from your work and look for a pleasing design and sense of unity. Then glue your collage.

Studio 4

Make a Collage with Dimension

Use what you have learned to make a collage showing dimension.

Materials

✓ scissors ⚠
✓ foam core or posterboard
✓ railroad board or tagboard
✓ cloth, paper, and found objects
✓ glue
✓ water-based markers and paint

1 Decide on a scene or abstract composition, as well as a color scheme. Cut a large shape for your background from foam core.

2 Glue various shapes of tagboard, cloth, paper, and other materials to your background.

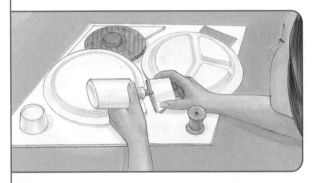

3 Use small squares of foam core pasted to the back of some shapes to make them stand out. Add color with paint or markers.

Review and Reflect

• Did you choose a realistic or abstract composition? What colors, shapes, and textures did you use?
• What idea were you trying to convey in your work of art?
• How do the colors and shapes help convey that idea?
• How did the collage convey your personal expression?

Louise Nevelson

Louise Nevelson spent decades as a struggling, unknown artist. Then she hit on an idea that brought her great respect in the art world. Nevelson began collecting scraps of wood and objects that she found lying around her neighborhood. With society's castoffs, she created some of the most innovative artworks of her time.

Louise Nevelson used her life lessons to create art.

Christopher Felver, photographer. *Sculptor Louise Nevelson*, 1985. New York.

"The very nature of creation is not a performing glory on the outside, it's a painful, difficult search within."

—LOUISE NEVELSON

Getting Her Start

Nevelson was born in Kiev, Russia, and moved to the United States with her family in 1905. A librarian once asked her what she wanted to be when she grew up. She glanced at a nearby plaster sculpture and announced, "I'm going to be an artist." She quickly added, "No, I'm going to be a sculptor. I don't want color to help me."

Nevelson studied art in New York City and Europe. In 1932, she started making figurative sculptures influenced by Central American art. In these artworks she included the found objects that would become her trademark. She held her first individual show in 1941.

Years of Acclaim

By her late fifties, Nevelson had developed her own style. She stacked open-faced boxes into sculptural walls. In each box, Nevelson placed found objects in carefully arranged abstract compositions. Then she painted the entire sculpture one color, usually black.

In 1958, one of Nevelson's new sculptures appeared in a New York exhibition. Critics took notice, and museums started buying her art. In 1967, the Whitney Museum of American Art held a major exhibition covering her entire career.

Talk About It

Look back at *Atmosphere and Environment V* on page 102. What elements contribute to the unity of this sculpture? Discuss the theme of Nevelson's artworks.

The Life of Louise Nevelson

Kiev, Russia

ca.1899
Louise Nevelson born in Kiev, Russia

1900

1905
Nevelson and her family immigrate to the United States

1925

Nevelson has first individual exhibition in New York City
1941

Nevelson makes her first reliefs in shadow boxes and constructs her first wall
1950

1957

1958
Show at Museum of Modern Art brings Nevelson recognition as a major modern artist

Museum of Modern Art, New York

1967
Whitney Museum of American Art hosts Nevelson's first major museum retrospective

1975

1988
Nevelson dies

2000

The Everyday Made into Art

Nevelson's signature style is marked by found objects placed in boxes and stacked into a monochromatic wall. Like Louise Nevelson, German artist and poet Kurt Schwitters (1887–1948) made art out of everyday objects. His relief sculptures and collages include objects like string, newspaper, and train tickets.

Objects Find New Meaning

Nevelson's *Sky Cathedral* is a wall of thirty-eight black boxes containing found objects carefully placed into abstract arrangements. Nevelson often paints her sculptures a single color, usually black, but sometimes white or gold. The coat of black paint unifies the differently shaped objects in this artwork. The objects lose their separate identities and became parts of a new object, the sculpture.

Merz

In 1919, the year he finished *Merzbild IA, The mental doctor*, Schwitters invented the word *Merz*, which he took from the German word for "commerce." Schwitters called his artworks *Merzbilder*, which means "Merz pictures." The everyday objects he used in his collages and sculptures were *Merz*, or the cast-off items of commerce and society, its garbage. Schwitters started to see everything as *Merz*, not just discarded items. He thought that a piece of string had as much artistic value as paint and other art materials.

Merzbild IA, The mental doctor shows Schwitters's idea about *Merz*. It includes found objects as well as fine-art materials. All of these elements work together to create a portrait. The artwork is unified by its subject, but the pieces of it keep their own identities. The overall theme is how all of these objects, including things that have been thrown away, can come together to create something attractive, a work of art.

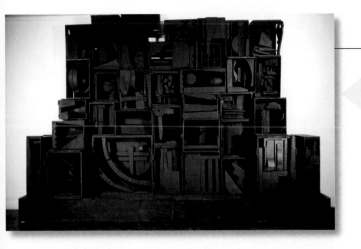

Louise Nevelson. *Sky Cathedral,* 1958. Wood painted black, 98 ½ by 98 ½ inches. Courtesy of The Pace Gallery, New York.

Kurt Schwitters. *Merzbild IA, The mental doctor,* 1919. Assemblage. Fundacion Coleccion Thyssen-Bornemisza, Madrid, Spain.

Compare & Contrast

- What objects can you identify in each of these artworks? How do the two artworks differ?

- How do these artworks reflect Nevelson's statement that "Art is everywhere, except it has to pass through a creative mind"?

Lesson 5

Textiles and Fibers

Many thousands of years ago, humans learned how to create baskets by interlacing reeds. This technique is called **weaving.** Ancient cultures soon adapted this technique to create textiles. **Textiles,** cloth made of yarn or other fibers, brought early humans warmth and a bit of luxury in a hard world. The word *textile* comes from the French "to weave," but textiles have evolved from simple woven cloth into complex works of art.

All cloth, including the clothes you are wearing, is woven on a large frame called a loom. Threads are woven around the loom vertically and then interlaced horizontally to create the fabric. The vertical threads are called the warp, and the horizontal threads are called the weft. Although the cloth you are wearing most likely was woven in a factory on a machine-driven loom, all looms operate basically the same way.

Weaving is one example of **fiber arts,** artworks created from yarn, thread, cloth, and even materials like reeds and grasses. Another example of fiber art is **stitchery,** in which artworks are created with a needle, cloth, and thread or yarn. Examples include fabrics stitched onto a background to form an image, as in the technique of appliqué, or two layers of fabric stitched together around a layer of padding, as in quilting.

Barbara S. Randall. *Pocket Full of Stones,* 2000. Mixed media collage, 13 ½ by 16 ½ inches. Cajun Blues Studios. © Barbara S. Randall.

Bold color, pattern, and visual texture bring a sense of life and movement to this work of fiber art.

Mary Adams. *Wedding Cake Basket,* 1986.
Woven sweet grass and ash splints, 25 ½
by 15 ¾ inches. Smithsonian American Art
Museum, Washington, D.C.

This ornate, intricate weaving represents the
culmination of Adams's work as an artist.

Weaving a Life

As a child of six, Mary Adams (1917–1999)
learned from her mother how to weave
baskets from fragrant sweetgrass leaves.
Only four years later, her mother died and
Adams was forced to support herself with
that skill. Adams, a member of the St. Regis
Mohawk Indian Nation, gained worldwide
recognition for her skill in weaving baskets.
Wedding Cake Basket honors the twenty-
fifth wedding anniversary of one of her
children. Adams mimicked the look of
icing by repeating forms made of curled
sweetgrass. Many baskets are woven in the
same manner as fabrics. Study Adams's
basket to find the warp and weft fibers.

Sketchbook Journal

Sketch a design for a work of
fiber art. Decide which technique
you would use, such as basket
making or appliqué. Draw your
design and indicate color
choices with colored pencils.
Label each part with the kind of
fiber or cloth you would use.
Then label the entire drawing
with the technique you chose.

Faith Ringgold. *Three panels: The Accident, The Fire, and The Homecoming,* 1985. Oil, felt-tipped pen, dyed fabric, and sequins sewn on canvas, sewn to quilted fabrics, 90 by 144 inches overall. The Metropolitan Museum of Art, New York.
© Faith Ringgold.

Why do you think the artist used three panels?

Everyone likes a good story. For some fiber artists, the **quilt** has become the perfect form to explore narrative art, or storytelling through images. American artist Faith Ringgold (1930–) is known for her quilts of narrative art. Notice these details:

- The quilt is in the form of a three-panel composition, called a **triptych.**
- In each of the three panels, the inhabitants of the apartment building look on as the scene changes.

Nontraditional Techniques

Beginning as a painter more than thirty-five years ago, Ringgold is more recently known as a fiber artist. She uses mixed-media quilts to express her thoughts and feelings about modern life. Ringgold's quilts incorporate nontraditional fiber art techniques, such as painting directly on fabric with acrylic paint. Notice that Ringgold also used appliqué in this quilt.

Technique Tip

Watching Paint Dry

The binder for acrylic paint is a kind of plastic, and it hardens when it has been exposed to air for a couple of hours. After you are done painting, squeeze out whatever paint remains in your brushes and wash them with soap and water. Store them with bristles up in a jar.

Make a Mixed-Media Triptych

Use what you have learned about textiles to make a mixed-media triptych.

Materials

- ✓ newsprint and pencil
- ✓ fabric and felt in many colors
- ✓ three 8" × 15" rectangles of fabric
- ✓ scissors ⚠
- ✓ fabric glue
- ✓ acrylic paint
- ✓ brushes and water for cleanup

1 Draw a composition that tells a story in three panels. Make notes about what colors you will use in each of the three panels.

2 Cut shapes from the felt and cloth, and arrange them to reflect the triptych you drew. Glue the shapes to the fabric panels.

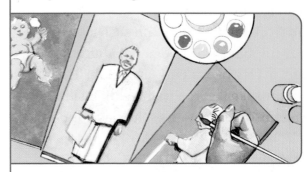

3 Use acrylic paint to add details to your narrative triptych. To hang your artwork, attach fabric loops to the panels with glue.

Review and Reflect

- Describe the shapes and colors you used. What story does your triptych tell?
- How do the shapes and colors you chose help tell your story?
- Would someone who does not know you understand the story? Explain.
- How does the technique you used in your triptych compare with the technique used to create a collage?

Sculpture

In Unit 1 you read about assemblage, sculptures made by **assembling** recycled objects. Artists have used another method of producing sculpture, called **casting,** for centuries. To cast a sculpture, an artist pours a liquid such as molten metal or plaster into a mold. When the liquid hardens, the artist removes the mold to reveal the sculpture.

French sculptor Frédéric-Auguste Bartholdi designed the Statue of Liberty to be assembled in a different manner. It was constructed from large sheets of copper hammered into shape by hand and then assembled around an iron framework.

To work out the details on such a large-scale sculpture, artists sometimes create a model in clay over a wire **armature.** The armature, like the iron framework inside the Statue of Liberty, gives the clay support.

The Statue of Liberty was a gift of friendship from the people of France.

Workers assemble the armature for the Statue of Liberty.

Frédéric-Auguste Bartholdi. *Liberty Enlightening the World (Statue of Liberty),* 1884–1886. Iron frame, copper cladding, height: 151 feet 1 inch (base to tip of torch). Liberty Island, New York, NY.

Nam June Paik. *Global Encoder,* 1994. 6 KEC 9-inch televisions, 1 13-inch television, steel frame, chassis, neon, satellite dish, 2 laser disk players, and 2 original Paik laser disks, 122 by 84 by 55 inches. Courtesy of Carl Solway Gallery, Cincinnati, OH.

Art and Imagery

Nam June Paik (1932–) has been described as the father of video art because of his pioneering use in the 1960s of what was then a brand-new medium. His first work was a video he made while his taxi was stuck in a New York traffic jam caused by the motorcade of Pope Paul VI. Paik now explores the technological revolution by incorporating video into artworks that have been described as playful and inventive. What objects can you recognize in this sculpture? What do you think Paik is trying to say with this artwork?

Sketchbook Journal

Many of the images you see are on a screen: TV shows, movies on the big screen, video games in an arcade, Web pages on the Internet, even email on your computer screen. Make a sketch for an artwork that shows what you think about the power of the onscreen image in American culture.

Artist unknown, Egyptian. *Bas-Relief of Offering Bearers in Tomb of Ti.*

What kinds of symbols do you see on and around the figures?

The sculptures on the previous pages are all three-dimensional forms that can be observed from all sides. These are known as sculpture in the round. Some sculptures are created using similar media and techniques, but they are not three-dimensional. The sculpture above is an example of a **relief sculpture,** an artwork in which a design projects from the background. Study the relief sculpture to notice these details:

• The tints and shades come from the play of light on the sculpted figures.
• The carved lines around each figure cast a shadow that helps define it.

Off the Wall

Relief sculptures were common on the walls of ancient Egypt. In high-relief sculptures, the figures stand out almost completely from the background. Egyptian artists carved low-relief, or bas-relief, sculptures in which the figures and objects stand out only slightly from the background. The ancient Egyptians carved their low-relief sculptures into the stone walls of tombs and temples and then painted them. Artists carved scenes that showed how the deceased might spend an afterlife as well as scenes that depicted offerings for the recently departed. Scenes often included **symbols,** objects that stand for other things as well as for themselves. What might be the symbolic meaning of the offerings in this relief?

Technique Tip

Drying Clay Slabs

When clay dries, it shrinks. This can cause warping and curling if some areas of your project dry faster than others. Dry clay projects on wire racks, or try to rotate your project during the day if possible. At night, cover your clay with wet paper towels and plastic. To keep the edges of your piece from drying too quickly, try keeping scraps of wet clay tucked up against the outside edges.

Studio 6

Create Symbols in Bas-Relief

Use what you have learned about sculpture to create a bas-relief of a symbol that is personally meaningful for you.

Materials

- ✓ low-fire clay and slip
- ✓ rolling pin
- ✓ plastic wrap
- ✓ carving tools
- ✓ glazes and brushes

1 **Use a rolling pin to make two 4-by-6-inch slabs of clay, about a quarter-inch thick. Place one on a sheet of plastic wrap.**

2 **Carve your symbol out of the other slab. Use slip to attach it to the first slab. Add details with small pinches of wet clay.**

3 **Scratch in texture and pattern with a fork or clay tool. Fire your sculpture. Apply glaze and fire again.**

Review and Reflect

- Describe the symbol you chose to represent in your bas-relief sculpture.
- How did you use shape to convey meaning in your sculpture?
- What does your symbol mean to you? What might it mean to others?
- Does your sculpture communicate the meaning you intended? Explain.

Architecture

An **architect** is an artist who designs buildings. **Architecture,** the art and science of planning buildings, is a complex, detailed process. An architect first designs an interior floor plan and an **elevation,** a scale drawing of the outside of the structure. Next, he or she creates an architectural model to show how the finished building will look. The final step is the creation of **blueprints,** large photographic copies of the plans, to show builders how to put the building together.

In the late 1920s, American architect William Van Allen (1883–1954) designed the Chrysler Building, which has been praised as a perfect Art Deco monument to capitalism. The Art Deco style used geometric shapes to create streamlined, sophisticated designs. It celebrated the popularity and rise of commerce, technology, and speed. This building was designed for Walter Chrysler, director of the Chrysler Corporation. Chrysler wanted a building that would not merely scrape the sky but that would "pierce it."

Although it looks somewhat old-fashioned in comparison to some of today's twenty-first-century buildings, the Chrysler Building was the wonder of New York City in its time. At 1,048 feet, it was the tallest building ever built, at least until the following year, when the 1,250-foot Empire State Building was completed. Even today, the Chrysler Building, with its unusual blend of historical styles and automobile themes, attracts the interest of contemporary product designers and architects.

William Van Allen, architect. *Chrysler Building, 1928–1930.* New York.

The sunburst pattern at the top of the Chrysler Building is a classic Art Deco design.

Architect unknown, Japanese. *Himeji Castle,* 1609. Himeji, Japan.

Castle Walls

This stone and tile building sits in humid, subtropical Himeji City in Japan. Built sometime between 1601 and 1614, the building served as a castle and fortress. It was protected by a moat and had a maze-like spiral structure inside to confuse enemies if they ever breached the thick, flared walls. Historians believe the fortress represents the highest achievement in Japanese castle architecture. It is estimated that as many as fifty million people—from supervisors to laborers to farmers to warriors—played a part in its construction.

Research

Builders of the Himeji Castle hid spikes in areas where the enemy might invade and created spaces behind walls for warriors to hide. Go online to learn more about the castle's design. Write a brief description of the castle's architecture and construction and include photos from the Web.

Ornamental Municipal Gardens. Formal ornamental beds with topiary in municipal gardens. Angers, France.

How do these landscapes differ?

Worthy Manor Garden.
Porlock, Somerset, England.

To create a visually interesting landscape, landscape architects use the same elements of art and principles of design that a painter uses to create a vibrant painting. But in **landscape architecture,** the artist's canvas is an outdoor environment. The artist creates texture, color, shape, and form by manipulating nature. Notice these details:

- In the French garden, formal balance is created by trimming the plants into organic and geometric shapes and forms.
- The more informal English garden has been carefully planned to look as if it just happened to grow that way.

Redesigning Nature

Landscape architects design parks, yards, golf courses, theme parks, and the public spaces around buildings. They use trees, rocks, bricks, flowers, fountains, ponds, and fences to create pleasing outdoor environments.

Technique Tip

Templates

Ever wonder how landscape architects draw the perfect tree and bush shapes on their design plans? They use templates. Make your own templates from cardboard. Include a key, or description of what each shape represents, in your design plan.

Design a Public Landscape

Use what you have learned about architecture to design a landscape for a park or public area between buildings.

Materials

- ✓ graph paper
- ✓ pencil
- ✓ ruler
- ✓ cardboard templates (optional)
- ✓ colored pencils

1 Draw the shape of your park or public space on graph paper. Make sure your space is scaled to the grid on the paper.

2 Use the grid lines to draw scale-sized symbols indicating the location of trees, benches, tables, walkways, and so forth.

3 Add a key to your plan. Color your key and symbols appropriately. Use different colors for grassy areas and paved areas.

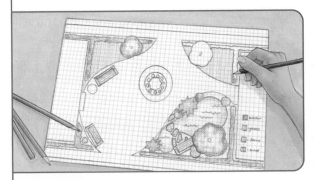

Review and Reflect

- Describe the space you have created. What type of balance did you show?
- How did you create comfortable places for people to use?
- What mood is evoked by the colors you chose for your public space?
- How do you think people spending time in your public space would feel? Why?

Lesson 8

Ceramics and Pottery

Some of the oldest works of art are ceramics, or **pottery,** vessels hand-built of clay and then hardened with intense heat. Virtually every civilization in every time period has made pottery. Archeologists often use the designs on a pot as well as the method and form of its construction as clues to the way people in a certain culture lived. These functional pottery pieces, along with jewelry, textiles, and other useful objects, are called **applied art.**

Decorative art includes functional objects that are designed to be ornamental. For example, they may be part of a home's interior decoration, such as a carved wooden clock or a ceramic vase.

Look at the clay sculpture below. American artist Marian Haigh (1951–) pressed clay into a mold to create the form of deer antlers that clutch this vessel. Notice how the antlers appear almost real. Haigh is inspired by the rhythms and cycles in nature. She uses textures and forms from the environment to express feelings through her art. You can see smooth texture on the antlers and rough texture on the woven pattern between the antlers. Look at the title of this decorative artwork. What kind of feeling or idea do you think Haigh was trying to convey?

Marian Haigh's artwork often reflects the phases of life.

Marian Haigh. *Cradle,* 1992. Glazed and smoked earthenware, 7 ½ by 18 ½ by 11 inches. Private collection. © Marian Haigh.

Artist unknown,
Mogollona/Anasazi.
Chacomy, ca. 1100. Maxwell
Museum of Anthropology,
Albuquerque, NM.

Anasazi Art

This vessel was made almost a thousand years ago, during the Classic Pueblo period of Anasazi culture. At that time, the Anasazi survived the blistering heat of the Southwest in cliff dwellings, multi-storied apartment-like structures built against a mountain face. Although the number of Pueblo villages has dwindled since the Classic period, Anasazi artists continue to produce the distinctive vessels and patterns that potters first mastered hundreds of years ago. The artist of this vessel applied black and white lines and shapes that are repeated, creating a geometric pattern. What might this vessel have been used for?

Sketchbook Journal

Think of a design for a jar with a lid. Make a sketch to work out the details of your idea. As you work on your design, consider what the jar's function will be. Will it be narrow or fat? Will it have handles? Use colored pencils to add designs to your jar or to indicate texture.

Giorgio di Pietro Andreoli. *Vase and cover,* 1500–1510. Tin-glazed earthenware with luster decoration, approximately 10 by 9 ⅓ by 6 ⅘ inches. Victoria and Albert Museum, London.

How did the artist create actual texture on this vessel?

Renaissance artist Giorgio di Pietro Andreoli (ca. 1465–1553) manipulated the clay surface of this vessel to create texture. Notice these details:

- Red objects project from the surface to form two bands around the vase.
- A coil of clay snakes around the bottom of the vase and forms a third band.

Clay Ceramics

Ceramics include pottery and hollow sculptures made of clay. One technique for creating ceramics is hand-building. Artists can pinch and squeeze clay into a desired shape. Or they can make clay slabs or roll clay ropes to create a variety of shapes. To connect different pieces of clay, artists use **slip.** Slip is clay mixed with enough water to make a soupy liquid. It works like cement to bind separate pieces of clay together.

Ceramics are hardened in a special oven called a kiln. Artists can then apply a glaze. **Glazes** are finely ground minerals suspended in water, which, when fired, melt into a glass-like coating. Glazes waterproof the container and can be applied to add color and pattern.

Technique Tip

Slip

Be careful when attaching clay pieces, or your artwork could fall apart in the kiln. Before attaching pieces, make a bowl of slip by adding water to clay and blending it together. Keep adding water until your slip is about as thick as catsup. Use a fork to score each piece where it will connect. Cover the scored parts with slip and then press them firmly together to seal all connecting parts.

Studio 8

Create a Textured Ceramic Jar

Use what you have learned about pottery and ceramics to create a textured ceramic jar and lid.

Materials

- ✓ low-fire clay
- ✓ slip
- ✓ items to score and scratch in texture, such as clay tools, toothpicks, forks, and stiff brushes
- ✓ glazes

1 Roll the clay into long, half-inch ropes. Coil the clay ropes on top of each other to form the jar's shape. Use slip and score to smooth the coils together.

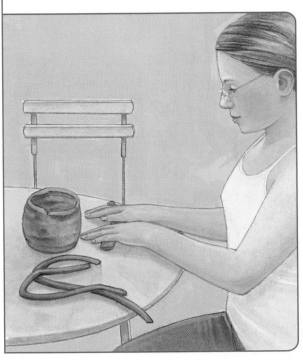

2 Use slip to attach additional pieces. Use forks, toothpicks, and so forth, to add texture to your jar. Make a lid in the same way.

3 Fire the jar. Add different colors of glaze to your pot to emphasize the textures you created. Fire your jar again.

Review and Reflect

- What shape did you choose for your pot? What kinds of texture did you add?
- How well do the textures work with the shape of the jar?
- How do the colors you chose emphasize the textures you added?
- Is your jar functional, decorative, or both? Explain.

Lesson 9

Photography and Videography

The invention of photography around 1830 was an important milestone in history. For the first time, people and events could be recorded with an accuracy never before imagined. The camera neither exaggerated events nor flattered its subjects. All were treated with equal attention and objectivity. Though some viewed photography as a threat to art, many welcomed the freedom photography presented.

Ansel Adams (1902–1984) is one of the most well-known photographers the United States has ever produced. When he began taking photographs, photography was not yet accepted as a fine art. His untiring promotion of it, as well as his widely admired skill at capturing the drama of the Western landscape, helped win photography its place as a fine art.

Still photography has evolved since the early days. Although photographers continue to capture images on light-sensitive paper, they also can capture images electronically with a digital camera, and then manipulate them with a computer graphics program. Photographers can capture moving images as well in works of **video art.**

Ansel Adams. *Grand Canyon,* 1941. Black-and-white photograph. Grand Canyon National Park, AZ.

The framing of this composition highlights the differences in value between foreground, middle ground, and background.

140

Safi wa Nairobi. *I Still Have A Dream,* 2001. Silver gelatin photograph, 16 by 20 inches. © 2001 Safi wa Nairobi.

Still photographers consider the elements of art and principles of design as they capture moments in time on film.

Expressive Photography

American artist Safi wa Nairobi created this artwork in response to the terrorist attacks in New York City and Washington, D.C., on September 11, 2001. This artwork's title refers to a 1963 speech by civil rights leader Martin Luther King, Jr. Almost 250,000 people had gathered in Washington, D.C., to hear King speak. He told the crowd about his own dream for freedom. "I have a dream that one day this nation will rise up and live out the true meaning of its creed: 'We hold these truths to be self-evident, that all men are created equal.' " Why do you think Nairobi refers to this speech in her title?

Research

Music videos used to just show recordings of songs performed in concert. Now many are highly styled short movies. Use the Internet to research the change in music videos. Find out what critics consider to be the first music video. Write a brief report describing the changes from then until now.

Joanne Mariol. *Museum Pink*, 2002. Colorized black-and-white photograph, 8 by 12 inches. Collection of the artist. © 2003 Joanne Mariol.

How do you think the artist chose which parts of the photograph to colorize?

In the early days of photography, photographers added color to their images by hand because color film had not yet been invented. Photographer Joanne Mariol added color to parts of *Museum Pink* to add emphasis and accentuate the focal point. Look for these details:

- The perspective the artist used to shoot the photograph draws attention to the car's smooth, shiny texture.
- Mariol added color only to the upper portion of the car and its taillights. This emphasizes them as the focal point.
- She added only red and a light value, or tint, of red.

Adjusting Reality

Many artists who hand-color photographs apply thin layers of oil paint made especially for this purpose. Some scan the image into a computer and add color digitally. Joanne Mariol uses both media to colorize her photographs. Consider how the techniques for using these two media would create different effects. Why might an artist choose to colorize a black-and-white photograph rather than shooting the subject using color film?

Technique Tip

Tinting Photographs

If you are colorizing a photocopy of a photograph, use colored pencils. Markers will dampen the ink on the photocopy and make your colors muddy. If you are colorizing a photograph on photo paper, use oil paint or oil pastels. Be sure your image is printed on matte paper, however, because oil paint and pastels will not adhere to a glossy finish.

Colorize a Photograph

Use what you have learned about photography to colorize a black-and-white photocopy or digital photograph.

Materials

- ✓ personal photograph from a family collection or a new photograph
- ✓ camera and scanner (optional)
- ✓ photocopier or computer and color printer
- ✓ black-and-white versions of the photograph
- ✓ colored pencils, watercolors, or computer software

1 Look through family albums for a photograph that appeals to you, or take a new photograph of a chosen subject.

2 Make black-and-white photocopies of the image or scan it into a computer. Reframe the picture or zoom in on details as desired.

3 Add color to create emphasis using colored pencils, watercolor, or a computer. Leave some portions uncolored.

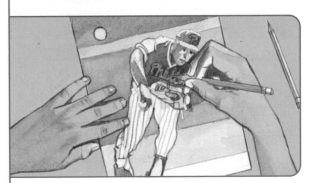

Review and Reflect

- Describe your colorized photograph. Which objects did you emphasize?
- How did the colors you added create emphasis?
- What mood did the color scheme you chose create?
- Did your color scheme effectively establish the mood you wanted? Explain.

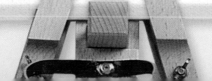

Lesson 10

Computer Art

Richard Taylor. *Optrix Oasis,* 2002.
Computer art, 17 by 11 inches.
Phillips Gallery. Salt Lake City, UT.

Notice how the artist applied the
techniques of perspective to give
the illusion of space and depth.

Once, computers did little more than crunch numbers. Skeptics thought of "computer art" as a contradiction in terms, like "jumbo shrimp." How could a cold, calculating machine make something as intensely human as art? But some visionary artists were excited about the possibilities. Today, digital technology has caught up with these artists' wildest dreams, and computers are important art tools.

Today visual contact with people a world away can take place in seconds. Sounds, images, and ideas are shared at the speed of light. **Digital technology** —whether in the form of cameras, video and audio recorders, or computers—has revolutionized people's lives. It has also revolutionized the art world.

Computer art pioneer Richard Taylor never doubted the effect digital technology would have on art. "I knew from the beginning that it would become the most powerful visual tool ever created by man," he said.

Taylor's *Optrix Oasis* is **computer art,** artwork created with the assistance of a computer. Taylor made this artwork with **software,** computer applications used for various functions, such as creating graphics. Taylor used precise geometric shapes and smooth surfaces to give *Optrix Oasis* a scientific feel.

Leslye Bloom. *Technicolor Daydream: Colorful*, 2001. Computer art encaustic, 27 by 35 inches. Collection of the artist. © Leslye Bloom.

Organic Computer Art

American artist Leslye Bloom calls *Technicolor Daydream: Colorful* a "computage," a mix of *computer* and *collage*. Her creative process often starts with a **scanner,** a device used to transfer text or graphics into a computer.

"I begin with the scanner and digital camera and use the computer to process images and print them," Bloom says. In *Technicolor Daydream: Colorful,* Bloom used digital technology to create an artwork composed almost entirely of organic shapes, colors, and textures. What do you think her original photograph showed?

Sketchbook Journal

Computer Web page design is quite diverse. Some pages might have one photograph and three words. Others pack images, words, and graphics onto a page with flashing advertisements and automatic music. Visit some of your favorite Web sites and take notes in your Sketchbook Journal on their design.

Dorling Kindersley Web site, showing the "Arts and Culture" page:

http://us.dk.com/static/cs/us/11/arts/index.html?11CS

What is the main point of this Web page?

People who run Web sites usually want something from you. The first thing they want is for you to stop and read their Web page. To get you to do this, Web designers use the principles of design to draw your interest and focus your attention on their message. Look for these details:

- Large type and images grab your attention and impart a message quickly. Web designers use a wide variety of fonts, or styles of type, to create interest.
- Navigation tools, such as arrows and buttons, invite you to browse the site or to link to other sites with similar content.

Designing the Web

Web design, the way a Web page looks and operates, requires a variety of sophisticated software. Web design software helps the designers lay out the page and insert common elements like navigation tools and links to related Web pages. Web designers often use animation software to make words or characters move across the page. They also can add digitized art or photographs or digital music, like MP3s.

Technique Tip

Getting Around

Consider including a navigation bar along one side of your Web page designs. A navigation bar is an area of the page that has links to all the other pages on your Web site. It will help readers figure out everything on your site as well as how to get there.

Studio 10

Design a Web Page

Use what you have learned about online art to design a Web page for your artwork.

Materials

- ✓ graph paper
- ✓ pencils, pens, and markers
- ✓ a computer and Web page design program (optional)

1 Select some of your favorite artworks to put on your personal Web site. Sketch out the design of your Web site on graph paper.

2 Use thumbnail sketches of your artworks as icons linked to full-size images of your artworks. Include information about each artwork.

3 Add color to create interest and emphasize certain elements. If possible, use a Web design program to lay out your Web page.

Review and Reflect

- What part of your Web page first catches the viewer's eye?
- How does the use of color affect the path of your eye across the Web page?
- What elements of your Web site create unity with your artworks?
- Does your Web page design effectively persuade viewers to look more closely at your artworks? Explain.

Make a Multimedia Sculpture

Aggie Zed. *Copper Horse,* 1995. Ceramic, copper, found objects, height 8 inches. Private collection. © Aggie Zed.

Plan

American artist Aggie Zed (1952–) is inspired by the animals on her Virginia farm. Horses, rats, dogs, and other animals appear often in her sculpture and painting. In some of her sculpture, Zed creates figures of clay. In other artworks, she combines materials like copper and found objects.

- What media has the artist used in this sculpture? What is the subject of this work of art?
- Why do you think the artist has chosen these materials?
- How has the artist used the media she chose to describe her subject or convey an idea?
- What idea would you like to express in your multimedia sculpture? How could you use your media to convey this idea?

Use found objects, paint, and papier-mâché to create your own multimedia sculpture.

Sketchbook Journal

Think of an animal or another form that you would like to base your sculpture on. Gather photographs to use as reference. Make a series of sketches to work out your ideas. Draw your form from several angles to make sure it looks good from all sides. Make notes about materials you could use.

Materials

✓ wood, such as limbs or 2" × 4"s
✓ wire, nails, or screws ⚠
✓ glue and masking tape
✓ old newspapers
✓ papier-mâché strips and paste
✓ pieces of cloth, paper, and found objects
✓ acrylic paint, varnish, and brushes

Create

1 Make an armature for your sculpture by wiring, nailing, or screwing the wood into the desired shape. Tape wadded-up newspaper to parts of your armature to form the contours of your sculpture.

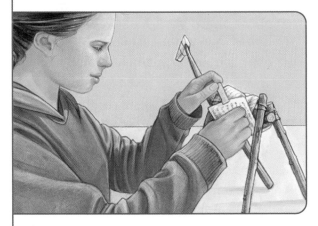

2 Apply papier-mâché over the wadded-up newspaper. Leave parts of your armature showing. Mold details from newspaper softened in paste.

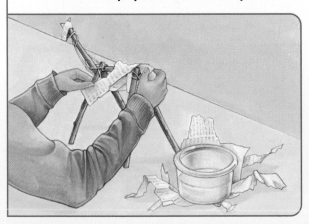

3 When the papier-mâché dries, glue pieces of cloth, paper, and fabric to it. Attach found objects to your sculpture with wire or glue. Add paint to unify all the elements.

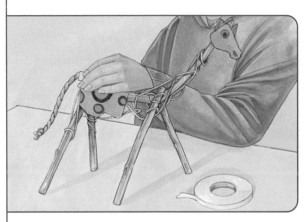

4 Photograph your finished work of art. Choose a background deliberately so it complements your sculpture. Plan your light source to make sure you get the effect you want.

Reflect

- What idea were you trying to convey with your artwork? How did you use the media you chose to convey that idea?
- What mood does your finished artwork convey?
- What did you discover about creating sculpture?
- What problems did you encounter while completing your artwork? How did you solve them?

149

Unit 3 *Review*

Vocabulary Review

A Match each art term below with its definition.

light source	slip
textiles	pottery
relief sculpture	collage
media	triptych
applied art	relief print

1. art that is functional or utilitarian
2. vessels made of clay
3. artwork made by pressing paper to the raised surface of an inked block or plate
4. point of illumination in an artwork
5. artwork made by gluing pieces of paper, fabric, or other material to a flat surface
6. sculpture in which forms project from a flat surface
7. a work of art with three panels
8. artworks made using fiber or fabric
9. materials used to create works of art
10. liquid clay

Artists and Their Art

B Each artwork listed in the box appears in this unit. Use the titles to finish the sentences below.

> *The Whirlpools at Awa: Naruto Rapido*
> *Street Story Quilt #1, 2, 3*
> *Sky Cathedral*
> *Blue Dancers*
> *Fish*
> *Wedding Cake Basket*

1. Louise Nevelson arranged found objects in boxes, painted it all black, and called it ___.
2. ___, by Tadek Beutlich, combines color woodcut and linocut.
3. Mary Adams repeats forms made from curled sweetgrass in ___.
4. ___ is a mixed-media triptych by Faith Ringgold.
5. Edgar Degas placed the light source above his subjects and out of the frame in ___.
6. ___ by Ando Hiroshige is a woodblock print showing rhythm and movement.

Louise Nevelson

Faith Ringgold

Respond to Art

C Look at Sandy Skoglund's *Gathering Paradise.* In a class discussion or on a sheet of paper, match each art term below with examples from the artwork.

Sandy Skoglund. *Gathering Paradise,* 1991. Cibachrome photograph, 48 by 61 inches. Installation with sculpted squirrels, cast in resin, artificial reptile skin upholstery on house exterior, with furniture. © 1991 Sandy Skoglund.

Art Terms

1. pattern
2. mixed media
3. complementary colors
4. photograph
5. texture
6. organic forms

Unit 3 *Review*

Write About Art

Explanatory Paragraphs

D Look back at the artworks you saw in this unit. Choose one that inspired you to try to create a similar work of art in the same medium. Write three paragraphs about the artwork you would make. First explain your idea. Then describe each of the steps you would take to complete your work of art. Copy the chart below and use it to organize your thoughts before you start writing.

Name of Artwork

A. Idea

   1. Subject: _____

   2. Media: _____

   3. Color Scheme: _____

   4. Other: _____

B. Steps to complete

   1. _____

   2. _____

   3. _____

   4. _____

Your Studio Work

E Answer these questions in your Sketchbook Journal or on a separate sheet of paper.

1. Of all the artists' works you learned about in this unit, which did you like the least? Why?
2. What new techniques from this unit did you enjoy using the most? Why?
3. What problems did you encounter as you tried the new techniques?
4. How did you solve those problems?
5. What media most inspired you to create your own works of art?
6. Of all the artworks you created in this unit, which do you think was the most successful? Why?

You are logged in as: ship2

78945011

(Amazon order #109-7794578-7606629)

Date ordered: 2012-11-05 12:32:38 – *Ship via:*Standard

SCOTT FORESMAN ART 2...

Z-QO-00632

0328080381 QTY: 1

Release your orders

Periodicals, newspapers, comic books, food and drink, eBooks and other digital downloads, gift cards, return gift cards, items marked "non-returnable," "final sale" or the like and out-of-print, collectible or pre-owned items cannot be returned or exchanged.

Returns and exchanges to a Borders, Borders Express or Waldenbooks retail store of merchandise purchased from Borders.com may be permitted in certain circumstances. See Borders.com for details.

BORDERS.

Returns

Returns of merchandise purchased from a Borders, Borders Express or Waldenbooks retail store will be permitted only if presented in saleable condition accompanied by the original sales receipt or Borders gift receipt within the time periods specified below. Returns accompanied by the original sales receipt must be made within 30 days of purchase and the purchase price will be refunded in the same form as the original purchase. Returns accompanied by the original Borders gift receipt must be made within 60 days of purchase and the purchase price will be refunded in the form of a return gift card.

Exchanges of opened audio books, music, videos, video games, software and electronics will be permitted subject to the same time periods and receipt requirements as above and can be made for the same item only.

Put It All Together

Willie Bester. *Kakebeen*, 1996. Mixed-media collage.
© Contemporary African Art Collection Limited.

F Discuss or write about Willie Bester's
work of art *Kakebeen* using the four
steps for viewing artwork critically.

1. **Describe** What media has the artist
   used in this work of art? What objects
   can you identify? What colors did the
   artist use, and where did he use them?
   What do you think is the subject of
   this artwork?

2. **Analyze** How did the artist create
   unity in this artwork? How did the
   artist introduce variety? What kind
   of rhythm does the artwork show?

3. **Interpret** What do you think the artist
   was trying to say with this work of
   art? What mood has the artist created?
   What elements contribute to this
   mood? Why do you think the artist
   has used such a wide range of media
   in this one artwork?

4. **Judge** Willie Bester (1956–) uses his
   collages to focus on the realities of
   life in the townships of South Africa.
   How do you think this collage reflects
   his purpose?

Willie Bester is one of South Africa's
foremost artists.

*"I am not a political
painter. I don't want
to be. But in this . . .
country, you can paint
flowers—and it is
political."* —WILLIE BESTER

153

Anne Vallayer-Coster. *Still Life With Coral, Shells, and Lithophytes,* 1769. Oil on canvas, 51 ⅛ by 38 inches. Musée du Louvre, Paris.

Unit 4

The Creative Process

All artists go through the same basic steps, called the **creative process,** to pick a subject and a medium. It begins with an idea. An idea may come from nature, journal notes, the daily news, a remark overheard on the bus—anything that sparks your interest can be inspiration for a work of art. Artists use sketches, notes, and models to develop their ideas, and then bring it to life in a form that adds to their message. As a last step, artists decide if the artwork is successful. In other words, they judge the artwork to see if it expresses the idea in an interesting way.

Some artists choose subjects like people, animals, and landscapes. Other artists create artworks using only the elements of art. These artworks are **non-objective,** meaning there is no recognizable subject. In this unit, you will see how artists use style and subject matter to express ideas, and you will work with a variety of subjects to develop your own style.

About *the Artist*

Still-life painter **Anne Vallayer-Coster** was part of the court of Marie-Antoinette, the queen whose lifestyle helped spark the French Revolution. Read more about this painter to the queen on page 176–179.

Anne Vallayer-Coster. *Self-Portrait,* ca. 1774.

Expressive Portraits

Long before the camera, artists recorded the images of the famous and the unknown in portraits. A portrait is an artwork featuring a person, an animal, or a small group. Artists create a likeness by capturing a subject's **features,** characteristics that stand out, such as the eyes and mouth. Artists use size, proportion, and placement of features to show a realistic subject. Or they may exaggerate some features to create a profound study of their subject's character.

frontal view

Mary Cassatt. *Head of a Young Girl,* ca. 1904. Watercolor on paper, 17 by 13 ½ inches. Marion Koogler McNay Art Museum, San Antonio, TX.

three-quarter view

profile view

Are the proportions of the features in this portrait exaggerated or realistic?

Compare the position of the features in each view of the face.

Gilbert Stuart. *George Washington, unfinished portrait,* 1796. Oil on canvas, 47 by 37 inches. National Portrait Gallery, Smithsonian Institution, Washington, D.C.

Which view has the artist used in this well-known portrait?

Learning to Look at Portraits

Observing and studying portraits in an organized way will help you understand and enjoy them. As you examine the portraits in this lesson and throughout the book, ask yourself these questions:

- What can you read in the eyes of the subject? What is the expression on the subject's face?
- How do the posture and clothes suggest the character of the subject?
- What is shown in the background? What information does it give the viewer about the subject?
- Is any part of the portrait exaggerated or distorted?
- How do you think the artist felt about the subject?

Sketchbook Journal

Make quick portrait sketches in ink. Capture individuals' expressions as they read, talk on the phone, or watch TV. What view seems the easiest to capture—frontal, three-quarter, or profile? Why? Label each portrait with the person's name and the view you chose.

James Whistler. *Arrangement in Grey and Black, No. 1: Portrait of the Artist's Mother,* 1871. Oil on canvas, 56 ¾ by 64 inches. Musée d'Orsay, Paris.

Where is the subject of this painting sitting?

In this well-known portrait, American artist James Whistler (1834–1903) painted his mother in profile against a gray wall. Her image is a bold organic shape within a stark geometric design. Notice these details:

- The dark colors and simple shapes balance the composition asymmetrically.
- This is a full-length portrait—the subject is portrayed from head to foot.
- The geometric shape of the framed art on the wall helps draw the viewer's eye to the subject.
- The artist's neutral color scheme helps to unify the artwork.

It Is No Accident

The setting of this painting seems simple, yet it is an important part of the message Whistler wanted to express. The room reflects a more "modern" and simplistic design than was common for Victorian times. Two simply framed works of art hang on the wall, one only partly visible. A delicately patterned curtain frames the artwork on the left. The woman in the painting is in contrast with these surroundings. She appears solemn and dressed in heavy, subdued clothing, while the room and its furnishings appear clean and modern.

Whistler used the setting of the artwork to help convey a specific idea. The artist's modern tastes contrast with the moral character suggested by the image of his mother. Whistler believed that art should be created for art's sake rather than to convey a moral message.

Technique Tip

Return of the Viewfinder

Use a viewfinder to help you create a portrait. Mark the middle of each inside edge of the viewfinder. Then mark the one-quarter and three-quarter points on each edge. As you look through the viewfinder, the marks will help you easily determine your subject's proportions.

Draw an Expressive Portrait

Use elements and techniques such as color, setting, realism, or exaggeration to create an expressive portrait.

Materials

- ✓ full-sized photograph of a person's face
- ✓ scissors ⓢ
- ✓ non-toxic rubber cement
- ✓ drawing paper
- ✓ drawing pencils
- ✓ colored pencils or pastel crayons

1 Find, or photograph and print, a full-page picture of a person's face. Cut it in half using the nose as the center point.

2 Lightly glue half of the photograph to drawing paper. Draw the missing half, matching the features. Remove the photograph and draw the other half of the face.

3 Add color to the face and the background. Choose colors to enhance the portrait's expressive qualities.

Review and Reflect

- What did you include in your portrait? What kind of background did you show?
- How did you use elements like color to convey an idea or emotion?
- Based on your portrait, what kind of person does your subject seem to be?
- Which of your subject's qualities or features does your portrait capture best?

Faces in Three Dimensions

Not all portraits are on paper or canvas. Artists use a variety of media to recreate the human face in three dimensions. Each medium lends a different quality to a portrait and can add meaning to the artwork beyond the mere identity of the subject. Three-dimensional portraits can stand on their own as works of art, or they can be used to adorn functional pieces, such as the vessel shown here.

This vessel was created by an artist from the ancient Moche culture of Peru. The Moche were skilled and productive farmers. They channeled water from the melting snows of the Andes Mountains into elaborate irrigation systems to water their crops. The vessels they made to hold both water and food were important household items. These containers also represent a quality of pottery made in ancient America that has lasted for thousands of years.

The Moche used realistic three-dimensional portraits to give form to their vessels. One common type is a stirrup spout vessel, so called by modern archeologists because the spout looked like the stirrup on a saddle. The artwork on the right is an example of this kind of vessel. What might be the purpose of having a portrait on a container like this?

Artist unknown, Moche, Peru. *Stirrup Spout Jar With Head of Male Figure,* A.D. 200–700. Burstein Collection.

Does the portrait on this vessel seem realistic or exaggerated?

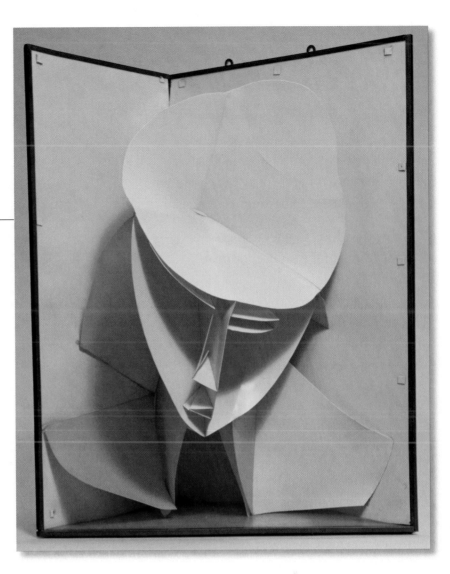

Naum Gabo. *Head of a Woman,*
1917–1920. Construction
in celluloid and metal, 24 1/2
by 19 1/4 by 14 inches. Museum
of Modern Art, New York.

Is this abstract portrait
symmetrical or asymmetrical?

Faces in the Abstract

Throughout the centuries, artists have
represented the unique combination of
shapes, spaces, and textures that make up
the human face. The viewer can usually
recognize the features of the human face in
portraits, even when the portrait shows
abstract features. The sculpture above, for
example, is clearly a human face, yet it is
asymmetrical. Russian American artist
Naum Gabo (1890–1977) used metal and
celluloid, a kind of plastic used for motion-
picture film, to construct this portrait.
How has Gabo used the elements of art
and the principles of design to create unity
in this artwork?

Sketchbook Journal

Make three or four sketches of
portrait containers you might
like to make. Before you begin,
consider what you would use
the containers for, what
materials they would be made
from, and how big they would
be. Label your finished
sketches with this information.

Moche portrait containers are known for their realism. As you study the container on this page, notice these details:

- Two birds adorn the helmet.
- The features of the subject appear symmetrical.
- Though the image shows only the front of the vessel, it is shaped to look like a realistic head all the way around.
- The artist created details in the subject's features. These details add to the portrait's realistic qualities.

A Common Form

The Moche were not the only people to put portraits on their pottery. Ancient and modern cultures from the Americas to Zaire showed men, women, animals, and deities on their ceramic pottery. Portrait pots like these are also called **effigy vessels.** Like portraits, they show a representation of a person.

Because many ancient cultures did not have a written language, much of what we know comes from ceramics like these. Portrait vessels can tell us what people wore, how they looked, and what kinds of plants and animals lived in the area. Archaeologists most often find containers like these in burial sites. They believe the vessels were meant to hold offerings for the dead.

Artist unknown. *Mochica Portrait Stirrup Spout Bottle of a Chief Wearing a Bird Helmet,* A.D. 200–700.

What purpose might this portrait vessel have served?

Technique Tip

Explosive Bubbles

Clay often contains air bubbles. Even tiny bubbles in clay can cause a container to explode when fired in a kiln. Wedging, which is similar to kneading bread dough, removes these bubbles. To see if your clay needs wedging, slice through it with a wire tool. Examine each side. If there are even tiny bubbles, the clay needs to be wedged.

Create Expressions in Clay

Use what you have learned to create a portrait vessel with a ceremonial function and a symbolic meaning.

Materials

✓ newsprint
✓ pencil and eraser
✓ self-hardening or ceramic clay
✓ clay tools and slip

1 Pick one of the portrait-vessel designs from your Sketchbook Journal, or draw a new one using a pencil and newsprint.

2 Build your vessel using the coil or slab method. Use a clay tool to outline the basic facial features on the surface of your vessel.

3 Add clay to model features that convey an expression. Add patterns and textures to suggest the container's ceremonial use.

Review and Reflect

- Describe the expression of the face in your three-dimensional portrait.
- How did you use lines, shapes, and forms to create that expression?
- In what kind of ceremony would your container be used? What symbolic message were you trying to convey?
- Does your container successfully convey its symbolic meaning? Explain.

Lesson 3

People Living and Working

Artists often watch people as they go about their daily lives. Many artists turn these observations into works of art. Their paintings become a window through which we can watch how other people live, work, and play. These paintings from everyday life are often called **genre scenes** or genre art. The term was used as a criticism when it was coined in the 1700s. But it now simply describes art showing how people live and work.

Dutch artist Jan Steen (ca. 1626–1679) was a painter of genre scenes. He is known for his ability to capture emotions with gestures, glances, and expressions. Unlike some Dutch painters of the seventeenth century, Steen often included humor in his scenes. Look at the painting on this page. In the Netherlands, children celebrate this holiday by leaving their shoes out in hopes of receiving gifts in them. Good children get candy and toys. Bad children get lumps of coal or sticks. In the painting, a family has gathered to find out what gifts were received. How do the expressions on the faces of the children reveal who has been good and who has been bad? The gestures and views of the figures' faces help lead the viewer's eye around the composition. Notice where the artist used the techniques of linear perspective, overlapping, and space in this scene.

Jan Steen. *The Feast of St. Nicholas,* 1663-1665. Oil on canvas, 33 by 28 inches. Rijksmuseum, Amsterdam.

What is unusual about the light source in this painting?

Pierre Auguste Renoir. *Luncheon of the Boating Party,* 1881. Oil on canvas, 51 by 68 inches. Phillips Collection, Washington, D.C.

The woman with the dog is Aline Charigot, a seamstress Renoir had just met and would later marry.

The Finer Things

French painter Pierre Auguste Renoir (1841–1919) painted the pleasures of life. Renoir and his friends often took brief trips to Chatou, a small town near Paris on the banks of the River Seine. Renoir became friends with the owner of a small Chatou hotel, and he sometimes traded paintings for food or a night's stay. The painting above shows Renoir's friends on a balcony of the hotel. Notice the different styles of dress. Some of the men are dressed to go rowing, and others are dressed more formally. How would you describe the portrait views the artist used?

Sketchbook Journal

Watch students and teachers as they eat lunch and visit in the school cafeteria. Make quick sketches in your Sketchbook Journal that capture their gestures and expressions. Draw people in different positions, such as standing in line waiting for food or sitting down to eat.

Kelvin W. Henderson. *Rejoice*, 2001. Acrylic on canvas, 36 by 48 inches. Private collection. © Kelvin W. Henderson.

How does the title of the painting reflect the mood of the artwork?

American artist Kelvin W. Henderson uses line, color, and shape, rather than the expressions on people's faces, to show how they feel. Look at the painting above and notice these details:

- The faces on each of the figures in the painting are blank.
- The details of the figures are left out and each block of color is outlined in black.

People in Motion

The figures in this painting do not represent specific people. Instead, they seem to represent people in general. The figures seem to sway away from the central figure in white, as if some unheard music were causing them to dance. The artist balanced the large organic shapes and bright colors asymmetrically. Notice, for example, how the same shade of blue is used on the right, the left, and in the center of the composition. Other colors are treated in the same way, unifying the subjects within the painting.

Technique Tip

Posers

Be considerate of your models. It is difficult to hold one position for a long time. Either choose positions that your models can stay in comfortably for up to fifteen minutes, or give your models frequent breaks. To help your models get into the same positions after a break, use a piece of chalk to outline any body part that comes into contact with a surface.

Studio 3

Paint a Group Portrait

Use what you have learned to create an expressive painting of a group that shows movement and feeling.

Materials

- ✓ white paper
- ✓ vine charcoal
- ✓ tempera paint (several colors plus black and white)

1 Break into groups of five. Take turns with four students posing and one student drawing the poses.

2 Use vine charcoal to capture the group pose on white paper. Emphasize the movement of the pose and ignore detail.

3 Outline the figures in black and fill in the negative spaces with tints and shades of tempera paint.

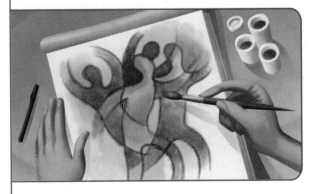

Review and Reflect

- Describe the positions of each of the figures in your painting.
- How do those positions each convey a mood?
- How do the tints and shades you used add to that mood?
- Describe the music that you would select to go with your painting. Why did you select the music you did?

Expressions in Still Life

Just as some people enjoy finding, buying, and collecting objects, artists love to arrange and draw, print, or paint them. An arrangement of inanimate objects and the art that depicts them is known as a **still life.** As a subject for art, the still life has a long history. The first ones appeared more than two thousand years ago on the walls of Roman houses. Still-life paintings were originally visual celebrations of the good life.

Even though ancient artists painted still lifes, these groupings of food and other objects often were part of a larger composition. In the seventeenth century, however, still lifes gained respect in their own right. They became a separate category of painting, as important and expressive as portraits or landscapes. Even sixteenth-century artists used the objects in their paintings as symbols for other things. For example, they might include a skull, a candle, or an hourglass as symbols of death. Or they might include flowers and fruit from all four seasons as a symbol of the cycles of nature.

Look at the painting below. The artist included objects that provide a contrast in textures, which adds interest. The bottom suitcase and the balls appear rough, while the top suitcase and books appear smooth. What do you think the suitcases in the painting might symbolize?

Arnie Fisk. *Well Traveled,* ca. 1995. Oil on canvas, 28 by 24 inches. Courtesy of Art In Motion. © Arnie Fisk. Licensed to Scott Foresman by Art In Motion.

Where do you notice rough and smooth textures in this painting?

Samuel van Hoogstraten. *A Trompe L'Oeil of Objects Attached to a Letter Rack,* 1664. Johnny van Haeften Gallery, London.

Art That Imitates Life

In the painting above, Dutch artist Samuel van Hoogstraten (1627–1678) assembled a collection of objects that reflect an interest in writing and in learning. The feather quill pen, letter opener, sealing wax, powder shaker, and paper all are associated with writing. What objects are associated with learning? Van Hoogstraten used a technique called *trompe l'oeil* (pronounced "tromp loy"), a French term meaning "trick the eye." The objects in the painting look so real that it seems the viewer could pick one of the letters right off the rack.

Research

Go online or to the library to research modern trompe l'oeil artists, such as painter and sculptor Audrey Flack, muralist Richard Haas, and painter Aaron Bohrod. What subjects do these artists paint? What media do they use? Summarize your findings in three to five paragraphs.

Jean-Baptiste Siméon Chardin. *The Attributes of the Arts and Their Rewards Which Are Accorded Them,* 1766. Minneapolis Institute of Arts, MN.

How did the artist decide what objects to include in this collection?

Although this collection of objects looks accidental, French artist Jean-Baptiste Siméon Chardin (1699–1779) took great care in selecting the objects and arranging them on the table. Nothing here appears by chance. Chardin chose each object to represent a different art form. Look for these details:

- Building plans and drafting tools represent architecture.
- Paintbrushes, a palette, and a paint box represent painting.
- The plaster model represents sculpture.
- The red portfolio represents drawing.
- The pitcher represents goldsmithing.

A Tribute to a Friend

The painting carries another layer of meaning too. The plaster model of the god Mercury is a model of an actual sculpture by the artist's friend, J. B. Pigalle. Pigalle was the first sculptor to be awarded the Order of Saint Michael, the highest honor a French artist could receive. That award is shown on the left; it is the starburst medal dangling from a black ribbon.

Technique Tip

Steady as She Goes

If you are trying to achieve a trompe l'oeil effect in your painting, you will need a steady hand. Try a mahlstick. A mahlstick is a long piece of wood that an artist rests the painting hand on to steady it. One end of the stick, which often is wrapped with cloth, is set against the edge of the painting. The artist holds the other end with the non-painting hand.

Paint a Personal Collection Still Life

Use what you have learned to paint a realistic still life of objects that have special meaning to you.

Materials

- ✓ pencil or vine charcoal
- ✓ newsprint
- ✓ 12" × 18" white paper
- ✓ tempera paint and brushes
- ✓ container with rinsing water
- ✓ various objects to arrange in a still life

1 **Arrange several objects on a table or bulletin board. Draw your composition on newsprint to work out the details.**

2 **Transfer your composition to drawing paper. Use tempera paint to begin adding color in a realistic manner.**

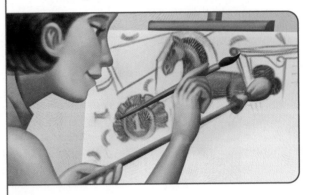

3 **Add details as well as shadows and highlights to add to the illusion of space and form.**

Review and Reflect

- Describe the objects you chose for your still life and how you chose them.
- How did you achieve a realistic effect in your work of art?
- What message would a viewer get from the combination of objects you chose?
- Does your painting look exactly like the objects you arranged? How could you improve your painting?

Lesson 5

Animals As a Form of Expression

Artist unknown. *Chinese Horse*, ca. 15,000–13,000 B.C. Axial Gallery at Lascaux, Dordogne, France.

Why do you think this cave painting found in France is titled *Chinese Horse?*

Animals are recurring subjects throughout the history of art. In every culture and every age, artists have created works of art that feature animals. Artists include animals in their work for different reasons. Sometimes an artist is interested in a creature just because it is interesting to observe and draw. Other times, animals can serve as symbols in an artwork, such as a scene that tells a story about a particular culture or event.

In symbolic artworks, artists may choose to faithfully replicate an animal's anatomy, or may instead make up a creature entirely from their own imaginations. The prehistoric artist of the cave painting above simplified and exaggerated the features of the horse with a black outline. The artist then filled the shape with brownish red and black pigments. This painting is believed to resemble horses found in ancient Chinese paintings. The caves contain images of more than six hundred animals, such as deer, bison, cats, and herds of horses. They were drawn and painted in shades of yellow, red, brown, and black. Archaeologists estimate the drawings were made about fifteen thousand years ago.

The Symbolism of an Antelope

Animals often play an important role in a culture's beliefs and traditions. Artists of these cultures might show animals in a variety of artworks, such as pottery, textiles, and masks. In what other art forms have you seen animals as subjects?

The headdress shown here was made by an artist from Mali in West Africa. For the Bambara tribe of Mali, the antelope symbolizes Tyiwara, the spirit who introduced agriculture. Farmers attach headdresses like this to wicker caps and wear them as they leap and dance to celebrate planting and harvest times. This headdress shows the graceful, arching neck of the antelope as well as its triangular head. What other details remind you of an antelope? How did the artist show patterns?

Artist unknown. *Bambara Chi Wara Antelope Headdress,* late 19th–20th century. Wood, 42 inches high. Burstein Collection.

Visual Culture

Advertisers often use animals to sell products. Tigers promote cereal and gasoline. Dogs endorse bus companies. Look for animals in ads as you watch TV and read magazines. Make a list in your Sketchbook Journal of companies and describe how each one uses an animal to sell its products.

Artist unknown, Egyptian. *Patron-goddess of Bubastis, as a cat,* 713–332 B.C. Bronze figure with inlaid blue glass eyes, height 13 ¼ inches. Musée du Louvre, Paris.

How do these two depictions of cats differ?

Francisco de Goya. *Don Manuel Osorio Manrrique de Zuñiga,* ca. 1784. Oil on canvas, 50 by 40 inches. The Metropolitan Museum of Art, New York.

Each of the artworks on this page features a cat. The sculpture is Egyptian. The painting is by Spanish painter Francisco de Goya (1746–1828). As you examine the artworks, look for these details:

- The Egyptian cat is calm and regal. Its form is streamlined and simplified.
- de Goya's cats are alert and seem ready to pounce on the boy's bird.

Cultural Symbols

Cats were sacred animals in ancient Egypt. They represented the goddess Bast, who had the head of a cat. Archaeologists have discovered thousands of mummified cats in ancient Egyptian tombs. Mummified mice buried with the cats may have been meant as food in an afterlife.

The animals in de Goya's painting symbolize something else entirely. In Baroque art, caged birds, such as those on the right in the painting, represent innocence. In Christian art, birds often represent the soul.

Technique Tip

Water-based Ink

Water-based printing ink dries quickly. Use only enough ink for one print. Clean your work surface between prints. If you are using a glass work surface, use a paint scraper from a hardware store. If you are using foam trays, use a new one for each print.

Studio 5

Create an Animal Print

Use what you have learned about animals in artworks to create an animal print.

Materials

- ✓ newsprint
- ✓ blunt pencil
- ✓ 2 or more clean foam trays ⚠ⓢ
- ✓ water-based black printing ink and brayer
- ✓ 9" × 12" colored construction paper

1 Choose an animal and make several sketches of it on newsprint. Practice exaggerating different features in each sketch.

2 Select your favorite sketch. Transfer it to the outside bottom of a foam tray. Use a blunt pencil to make a groove along the outline.

3 Use the second tray to ink your brayer. Apply ink to the first tray. Press paper against the tray and then lift to see the image.

Review and Reflect

- What animal did you choose for your print? What features did you exaggerate?
- How does your exaggeration change the meaning of the final image?
- If you were using your image for an advertisement, what kind of product could it sell?
- Is your print successful? Why or why not?

Meet *the Artist*

Anne Vallayer-Coster

Unless you are an art critic or art historian, you may never have heard of Anne Vallayer-Coster. Her paintings amazed the art critics of her time and were collected by the aristocracy. Yet, she became almost unknown after the French Revolution. Not until recent years has she regained even a tiny measure of the fame she once had.

An exhibition of thirty-five of her paintings has appeared at the National Gallery of Art, the Dallas Museum of Art, and the Frick Collection. A book published in 2002, *Anne Vallayer-Coster: Painter to the Court of Marie-Antoinette,* accompanied the exhibition.

Anne Vallayer-Coster. *Self-Portrait,* ca. 1774. Musée de Châlons-en-Champagne. Photo by Hervé Maillot.

"The disadvantages of her sex notwithstanding, she has taken the difficult art of rendering nature to a degree of perfection that enchants and surprises us."

—MERCURE DE FRANCE, ABOUT ANNE VALLAYER-COSTER, 1770

Realism

In the late 1700s, Vallayer-Coster was the toast of Paris. At age twenty-six, she was accepted into the prestigious French Royal Academy of Painting and Sculpture in France. She was one of a few women allowed to become a member before the French Revolution. Critics, and more importantly, the queen, were in awe of the realism she achieved in her paintings. The extravagant Queen Marie-Antoinette invited the artist to become her court painter, a rare and profitable opportunity.

Revolution

In 1792, the French Revolution swept Vallayer-Coster's queen off the throne. The Emperor Napoleon and Empress Josephine soon ruled France. Josephine acquired two of the artist's paintings in 1804. However, the pre-Revolution style of art, with its emphasis on luxury, fell quickly out of fashion. In the years that followed, Vallayer-Coster and her realistic art were forgotten. In 1970, more than 150 years later, an art historian rekindled interest in the artist's work with an academic paper. Vallayer-Coster's reputation has slowly been renewed. In 2002, a major showing of her artwork traveled the United States. Now, once again, critics have recognized Vallayer-Coster as one of the best still-life painters of eighteenth-century France.

Talk About It

Look back at *Still Life With Coral, Shells, and Lithophytes* on page 154. How did the artist use color to bring unity to the painting?

The Life of Anne Vallayer-Coster

1740

1744
Anne Vallayer-Coster is born in Paris

1760

Vallayer-Coster is accepted into the French Royal Academy of Painting and Sculpture; her paintings are exhibited at the Louvre
1770

the Louvre, Paris

Moves into the apartment and studio in the Louvre given to her by Queen Marie-Antoinette; marries Jean-Pierre Silvestre Coster
1780
1781

1789–1799
Survives the French Revolution despite her royal ties

1800

1804
Empress Josephine acquires two of her paintings

Empress Josephine

Finishes what critics call the "summation of her career," *Still Life with Lobster*
1817

1818
Anne Vallayer-Coster dies

1820

Look *and Compare*

Realism and Abstraction in Still Lifes

The styles of Anne Vallayer-Coster and Mexican artist Rufino Tamayo could hardly be more different. Despite their differences, both artists use formal elements, such as balance, overlapping, and repetition of shape and color to help them create the arresting still lifes they are known for.

A still-life artist often gets inspiration from common objects in her or his environment.

Vallayer-Coster

For Vallayer-Coster, reproducing reality was the goal. She was skilled at capturing the effect of light on any texture, from the glint of a hammered copper horn to the luxurious sheen of red and green velvet. Her likenesses are so exact you can even read the notes on sheet music she painted. Throughout her long career she chose to paint subjects such as foods of all kinds, animals from the hunt, and lavish floral arrangements.

Tamayo

Rufino Tamayo (1899–1991) was not interested in portraying his subjects realistically. He was more interested in working with the formal elements of art, such as color, texture, and line. Tamayo used bright colors to paint his still lifes. He also painted animals and people. Born in the western Mexican state of Oaxaca, Tamayo became interested in pre-Columbian art at a young age. Many of his early works combine the European styles of Cubism and Surrealism with the flat shapes and straightforward perspective of Mexican folk art. Tamayo's style evolved as he got older. In his later works, he used vivid, robust colors to create powerful, abstract artworks.

Anne Vallayer-Coster. *The Symbols of Music,* 1770. Oil on canvas, 34 ⅓ by 45 ¼ inches. Musée du Louvre, Paris.

Rufino Tamayo. *Watermelons,* 1941. Oil on canvas. Private collection.

Compare & Contrast

- How are the two artworks similar? How do they differ?

- Rufino Tamayo said that "Art is a way of expression that has to be understood by everyone, everywhere." How does each of the artworks fulfill this ideal?

Lesson 6

The Power of Landscapes

A stretch of desert, a mountain view, an expanse of forest seen from a clearing—these glimpses of natural scenery are known as **landscapes.** Artists are drawn to landscapes for different reasons. Some want to show the details of a scene so accurately that you could find the spot where they placed their easel. Others use landscapes to express moods and feelings. Still others want to capture the sweep of a **panorama,** a wide, open view of a large, outdoor area.

Landscape painting captured the American imagination during the nineteenth century. This was the Romantic period, a time when artists, musicians, poets, and playwrights emphasized drama and emotion in their works. The limitless, unspoiled vistas of the American West inspired Romantic landscape artists such as Albert Bierstadt (1830–1902). Bierstadt, born in Germany, made small paintings as he traveled through the West. Then he returned to his New York studio and transformed the small paintings into enormous, detailed artworks. Bierstadt often used atmospheric perspective in his landscapes, but he was not always true to the view. He changed details of the landscape and applied color to reinforce the feeling of awe and grandeur. Look at Bierstadt's painting below. How do you think American pioneers would have responded to a painting like this?

Albert Bierstadt.
The Rocky Mountains, Lander's Peak, 1863. Oil on canvas, 73 by 120 inches. The Metropolitan Museum of Art, New York.

What technique did the artist use to show depth and space in this landscape painting?

William H. Johnson. *Harbor, Lofoten, Norway,* 1937. Smithsonian American Art Museum, Washington, D.C.

The Landscape of the Spirit

Not all landscape paintings are realistic, even if they are based on a real place. American painter William H. Johnson (1901–1970) traveled extensively throughout Europe. He painted the landscape above during a trip to Norway. He used bold, vibrant colors to show the rugged hills, the ocean, and the sky. "My aim," Johnson once said, "is to express in a natural way what I feel, what is in me, both rhythmically and spiritually. . . ." Do you think this painting reflects his aim? Explain why or why not.

Sketchbook Journal

Make sketches of the sky at different times of the day, using colored pencils. Pay particular attention to sunsets. What colors stand out? What happens to the colors of objects around you as the sun sets? Label your sketches with the location and the time of day.

Georgia O'Keeffe. Purple Hills Ghost Ranch-2/Purple Hills No. II, 1934. Oil on canvas, 16 ¼ by 30 ¼ inches. Georgia O'Keeffe Museum, Santa Fe, NM.

How does O'Keeffe's use of color differ from that in atmospheric perspective?

American artist Georgia O'Keeffe (1887–1986) painted these desert hills near her home in New Mexico. The creases and folds in the landscape appear almost human in form. Notice these details as you study the painting:

- The artist limited her palette to tints and shades of red, green, and blue.
- The hills in the background are darker than those in the foreground, opposite of the technique of atmospheric perspective.

The Purpose of Painting

When she first began painting, in the early 1900s, O'Keeffe worked in the realistic style that was popular at the time. But she quickly abandoned realism for a new way of expression. O'Keeffe came to believe that the purpose of painting was to create artworks that reflected the artist's own ideas and feelings. Using this idea as a guide, she began to develop the style she has become known for. O'Keeffe is best known for her paintings of rocks, mountains, bones, and other natural forms. Look back at O'Keeffe's painting, *From the Plains 1,* on page 45. What similarities does it share with *Purple Hills No. II?* How are the two paintings different?

Technique Tip

Crisp Edges

Use masking tape to keep a crisp, white edge on your painting or drawing. Lightly press each length of tape against your clothing to make it a little less sticky. Then tape all four edges of your blank paper. Use the back of a fingernail to press the tape to the paper. When you are done with your artwork, remove the tape to reveal a clean border.

Make a Landscape Postcard

Use what you have learned to create a landscape postcard that conveys a mood or feeling.

Materials

✓ Sketchbook Journal or sketch paper
✓ white cardstock or posterboard
✓ pencil and eraser
✓ tempera or watercolor paint
✓ small paintbrushes and a water container
✓ markers, rulers, scissors ⚠

1 Choose a landscape that you have drawn or create a new one. Cut two postcard-size rectangles from cardstock or posterboard.

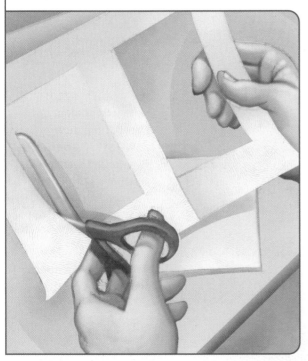

2 Lightly draw the landscape on each of the rectangles. Add paint to express a mood or feeling.

3 When your landscapes are dry, add a message to one, address it, and mail it to a friend. Keep the other for your portfolio.

Review and Reflect

- Is your landscape real or imagined? Did you paint it realistically or abstractly?
- Which elements of art and principles of design stand out the most?
- What mood does your landscape convey? How do the colors and painting style you chose contribute to that mood?
- What is most appealing about the landscapes you painted? Explain.

Lesson 7

Expressions in Cityscapes

A **cityscape** is an artwork showing a scene of city life, such as sidewalks crowded with people; streets busy with cars, buses, and taxis. Cities and the areas around them make up the urban environment. With more people living in towns and cities, the urban environment is increasingly important, not only to the people who live there, but also as a subject for art.

Street Scene, Autumn by Sidney Goodman (1936–) is an example of a cityscape. The artist combined many of the elements of an urban environment—buildings, a public plaza, and crowds of people. He used the techniques of perspective and overlapping to give the illusion of space and distance. Look at how much information the artist gives you with the details in this painting. The color of the trees tells you it is fall. But it is only the beginning of fall because the trees in the background are still green. The clothing says it is not too cold yet. The foreground appears littered with debris, and a big red trash dumpster stands in the middle of the plaza. All the people seem to be men. Do you think the artist painted an actual city scene or do you think he added parts of it from his imagination to make a point?

Sidney Goodman.
Street Scene, Autumn,
1974–1977. Oil on canvas,
78 3/4 by 117 1/2 inches.
© Virginia Museum of
Fine Arts, Richmond,
VA. Gift of Sydney and
Frances Lewis.

How did the artist show
depth in this cityscape?

Lois Mailou Jones. *Pont Louis Philippe, Paris,* 1958.
The Corcoran Gallery of Art, Washington, D.C.

Expressing Feelings in Cityscapes

American artist Lois Mailou Jones (1905–1998) enjoyed Paris. Her love of the city and its views is expressed in the painting above. Notice the wide brush strokes of blue tints that make up the sky and the watery rhythm created by the patches of reflected color in the river. The buildings seem to sway ever so slightly as they recede into the background on the left. On the right, the artist hints at the buildings beyond with shapes blurred by atmospheric perspective. How does this cityscape compare with *Street Scene, Autumn*? Which city would you most like to visit? Why?

Sketchbook Journal

Make sketches of buildings from different perspectives. Draw buildings from their foundations looking up, and draw them from their roofs looking down. Notice how changing perspective gives your drawings a different mood.

John Marin. *Lower Manhattan (Composing Derived from Top of Woolworth),* 1922. Watercolor and charcoal with paper cutout, 21 5/8 by 26 7/8 inches. Museum of Modern Art, New York.

Why do you think the artist chose to paint this cityscape in an abstract style?

American artist John Marin (1870–1953) captured the energy and chaos of a big city in this artwork without using the exact likenesses of buildings or cityscapes. As you examine the artwork, look for these details:

- Marin attached a star-like paper cutout to the watercolor with thread. Recall that when materials are combined this way, the work is described as mixed media.
- There are no people in Marin's painting. He preferred to focus on the buildings and structures that make up a city.
- The variety of lines Marin used creates a sense of rhythm and motion.

Energy and Chaos

Marin was almost forty years old before he decided to dedicate himself to fine art. Before that, he worked in the office of an architect. His interest in architecture shows in his artwork. When Marin looked at the buildings in New York City, he could almost feel the huge buildings pushing and pulling against each other. He used his art "to express graphically what a great city is doing." Do you think he succeeded with the artwork above? Why or why not?

Technique Tip

Pastel Clean-up

Pastels are pure pigment with very little binder, so they create dust as you drag them across your paper. Use an easel when you work with pastels. Tape your paper to a drawing board, and set it on the easel ledge. Place a damp paper towel on the ledge beneath the paper. Your pastel dust will fall onto the damp paper towel as you work. When you are done, fold it up and throw it away.

Studio 7

Draw a Cityscape

Use what you have learned to create an abstract composition that captures the energy of a very large city.

Materials

- ✓ photographs or videos featuring cities and buildings
- ✓ 12" × 18" white paper
- ✓ pencils and a ruler
- ✓ crayons or pastels
- ✓ colored markers
- ✓ spray fixative (optional) ⚠

1 Study various photographs or videos of city skylines. Pay attention to structures such as bridges, skyscrapers, towers, and overpasses.

2 Use pastels or crayons to draw a real or imagined cityscape. Simplify or alter each of the elements to create an abstract composition.

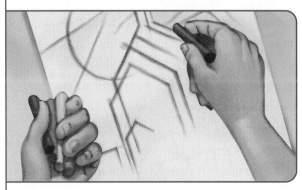

3 Add details with markers to create interest and depth. If you use chalk pastels, spray your work with fixative.

Review and Reflect

- What elements of a large city did you include in your cityscape?
- How did you use the elements of art to simplify or alter the objects?
- How do the colors you used contribute to the overall composition?
- Does your abstract composition capture the energy of a big city? Explain.

Expressions in Fantasy Art

Visualize a world where anything is possible. Rocks float. Watches melt. People are made of birdcages and apples. This is the world of the Surrealists, artists who combine dream and fantasy in surprising and sometimes shocking images. But the Surrealists were not the first to make fantasy art. Artists have used images from their imaginations for centuries.

Belgian Surrealist painter René Magritte (1898–1967) is known for combining fantasy, comedy, and mystery in his artworks. Magritte created a detailed world that defies reality. His style and his range of imagery, including apples, men in bowler hats, castles, rocks, and the sea, make his images instantly recognizable. Look at *The Castle of the Pyrenees* at the right. Magritte has portrayed the ocean and sky with almost photographic realism. The intense blue of the sky fades as it meets the horizon. The blue of the ocean at the horizon gradually changes to green as it reaches the foreground. And between the sky and the ocean floats a castle atop a massive boulder that seems to defy gravity. Impossible, but Magritte makes it appear real.

Many artists use computer technology to create fantasy artworks. But Magritte used oil paints to achieve the same realism. This artwork is an example of his skill at observing the environment, which he then expressed in a fantastic way.

René Magritte. *The Castle of the Pyrenees.* Oil on canvas. Israel Museum, Jerusalem, Israel.

What principle of reality is challenged in this Surrealist painting?

Rudolf Hausner. *Adam rational*, 1975. Color serigraph, 53 x 65 cm. Galerie 10, Vienna, Austria.

Speaking Rationally

Austrian artist Rudolf Hausner (1914-1994) used dreamlike imagery in his serigraph *Adam rational.* He divided the work into two parts. On the left, a man's head is depicted using exaggerated facial features. His eyes glare out of the canvas, fixed on the viewer. On the right, a sphere-like object "floats" above a transparent geometric structure. Look closely at the objects in the painting. Do you think the artist had an intended meaning or did he simply want to spark the viewer's own imagination? Why do you think so?

Notice how Hausner used the elements of art and principles of design. His combination of lines, shapes, and colors provides unity and a sense of rhythm in the different sections. Value and shading give form and a realistic quality to the objects and the human figure. Where do you notice patterns?

Sketchbook Journal

Exercise your imagination with a fantasy sketch. Think of an idea you want to express. Choose four or five objects or people to draw that will help express your idea. Create a sketch by combining the objects in an unusual way. Change their scale, color, or some other important aspect.

Technology *and Expression*

Karin Kuhlmann. *Cascade,* 1997. Computer-generated 3-D scene, digitally edited.

Why might the artist have chosen a computer as her medium for this artwork?

Does this look like a place you have visited? German artist Karin Kuhlmann (1948–) used computer technology and software to create this fantasy scene. Notice these details as you study the artwork:

- The effects used in the background are similar to those of atmospheric perspective.
- The tints and shades of the cool colors in the water creates the illusion of movement.
- The stepped rock formation in the foreground is repeated from a different viewpoint in the middle ground.

Three-dimensional Effects

Computer drawing and painting programs offer artists a variety of tools with which to create three-dimensional effects. Kuhlmann used these tools in different software programs to create *Cascade.* Notice how she created the illusion of form, space, and texture in the artwork. The spheres or bubbles appear to be transparent and reflect the scene below. Their smooth, shiny texture and less-than-perfect shape help the viewer imagine them as actual bubbles floating through the air. The rocks appear rough in contrast. The inclusion of the chair and its size in relation to other objects add to the artwork's fantasy expression.

Technique Tip

Tie It Together

When you are creating a collage, consider adding unusual elements to bind objects together. For example, use a needle and thread to sew images together. Or, make a needle and thread out of a stick and some twine to make a cruder seam. Use ribbon or fine copper wire to bind elements together. Do not be afraid to experiment.

Studio 8

Create Computer Fantasy Art

Use what you have learned to create a fantastic mixed-media collage using a computer, software, and other media.

Materials

✓ magazines, scissors ⚠
✓ computer, paint software, scanner, and printer or 12" × 18" white paper
✓ paint, brushes, and rinsing water
✓ colored pencils and markers
✓ glue stick or other adhesive

1 Examine magazines for photographs you can use in your collage. Cut out enough images to fill a 12" × 18" space.

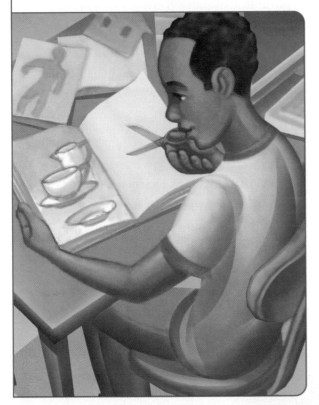

2 Scan your collection into a computer. Use software to combine the images in fantastic ways, or glue the images to white paper.

3 If using a computer, print out your composition. Add other media to your collage to enhance the sense of fantasy.

Review and Reflect

• What images did you include in your collage? How are they combined?
• How does your choice of media contribute to the fantasy effect?
• What meaning might a viewer get from your collage?
• What comments do you think Magritte or Kuhlmann might have about your fantasy collage?

Portfolio *Project*

Create Self-Portraits in Three Styles

Francis Bacon. *Self-Portrait,* 1976. Pastel on canvas. Musée Cantini, Marseille, France.

Plan

British painter Francis Bacon (1909–1992) was self-taught. He developed a powerful personal style and explored painful emotions in his artwork. His images of nightmarish creatures and screaming faces brought him recognition and respect. Bacon had the ability to capture a person's likeness with smeared paint and unnatural colors. Look at his self-portrait on this page. Despite the distortions he introduced, the image is clearly the artist's own face.

- What media did Bacon use in this self-portrait? How would you characterize its style?
- What emotion can you read on the artist's face? How do the colors and the style of the painting contribute to or detract from that emotion?
- What emotion would you like to portray in a self-portrait? How could you convey that emotion in different styles?

Use what you have learned to create three self-portraits that express a single emotion in three different styles and three different media.

Sketchbook Journal

Write down as many emotions, such as anger and surprise, as you can name. Look at your face closely in a mirror without showing any emotion, and then begin making faces that show those emotions. Observe your features closely. Make quick sketches of each of the faces you make.

Materials

- ✓ mirror
- ✓ newsprint
- ✓ 3 sheets of 12" × 18" heavy white drawing paper
- ✓ various media, such as pencils, pastels, acrylic, tempera paint, watercolor, charcoal, and colored pencils
- ✓ various tools, such as a computer, scanner, and paint software

Create

1 Look at the sketchbook drawings you made. Choose the three emotions to portray in three self-portraits. Set your mirror up where you can see yourself as you draw.

2 Draw each self-portrait in a different style, such as realistic, surrealistic, or abstract. Pick different media for each self-portrait to enhance the style and emotion you are expressing.

3 Add a secondary element, such as a landscape in the background, an animal at your feet, or a still life on a table, that add meaning to each self-portrait.

4 As you work, keep in mind the emotion you are expressing. Choose colors that reinforce each emotion, or colors that contradict it.

Reflect

- What emotion did you choose to express in each of your self-portraits? What styles did you use to support this mood?
- Why did you choose the colors you used in each of the artworks?
- What did you discover about making self-portraits? What does each self-portrait say about you?
- What problems did you encounter while completing your artwork? How did you solve them?

193

Unit 4 *Review*

Vocabulary Review

A Match each art term below with its definition.

cityscape	Surrealism
features	style
non-objective	portrait
mixed media	still life
panorama	landscape

1. a wide, unbroken view of a natural outdoor scene
2. an artwork that represents a person, a group, or an animal
3. art movement in which artists combined fantasy and reality
4. an artistic representation of a city
5. artwork featuring inanimate objects, such as food or flowers
6. components of the body, such as eyes or ears
7. an artist's characteristic manner of visual expression
8. art that has no recognizable subject matter
9. technique of combining more than one material in a work of art
10. work of art showing trees, sky, mountains, or other outdoor scenery

Artists and Their Art

B Each work of art listed in the box appears in this unit. Match each artwork with its description below.

Harbor, Lofoten, Norway
The Castle of the Pyrenees
Pont Louis Philippe, Paris
Purple Hills No. II
Arrangement in Grey and Black
Head of a Young Girl

1. ___, by Lois Mailou Jones, shows rhythm created by the reflected colors of a cityscape.
2. William H. Johnson used simplified shapes and bold, swirling colors to express his emotions in ___.
3. Georgia O'Keeffe expressed her thoughts and feelings about the New Mexico landscape in ___.
4. René Magritte defies gravity in his Surrealist painting ___.
5. ___ is a delicate, realistic portrait by Mary Cassatt.
6. James Whistler painted a portrait of his mother against a wall and called it ___.

James Whistler

Georgia O'Keeffe

Respond to Art

C Look at these two versions of *El Coleccionista.* Match each art term below with the letter in the illustration of Gonzalo Cienfuegos Browne's painting.

Gonzalo Cienfuegos Browne. *El Coleccionista (The Collector),* 1991. Oil on canvas. © Kactus Foto, Santiago, Chile.

Art Terms

1. shade
2. frontal view
3. still life
4. rhythm

Unit 4 *Review*

Write About Art

Analytical Paragraphs

D Look back at the artworks in this unit. Choose one that intrigued you and made you wonder what the artist was saying. Analyze the artwork and decide what you believe to be the idea behind it. Develop three arguments to support your analysis by explaining how the artist used the elements of art or the principles of design to reinforce the idea. Back yourself up with research from the library or the Internet. Copy the chart below and use it to organize your thoughts before writing.

Work of Art, and the Idea Behind It
_____

_____

Argument 1
    visual evidence _____
    factual reinforcement_____

Argument 2
    visual evidence _____
    factual reinforcement_____

Argument 3
    visual evidence _____
    factual reinforcement _____

Your Studio Work

E Answer these questions in your Sketchbook Journal or on a separate sheet of paper.

1. Which style of art in this unit did you find most intriguing?
2. Which do you think is closest to your own personal style?
3. In what new ways did you use landscapes, cityscapes, still lifes, portraits, and animals in your artworks?
4. What subject most inspired you to create your own works of art?
5. Of all the artworks you created in this unit, which do you think was the most successful? Why?

Put It All Together

Giuseppe Arcimboldo. *Spring*, 1573. Oil on canvas. Musée du Louvre, Paris.

F Discuss or write about Giuseppe Arcimboldo's work of art *Spring* using the four steps below for viewing artwork critically.

1. **Describe** What does this painting show? What elements make up the figure? What styles and subjects from this unit do you recognize in this work of art? What media has the artist used?

2. **Analyze** How do the flowers and vegetables Arcimboldo chose reinforce the title of the artwork? Why do you think the artist arranged them in the figure of a person? How did he manage to make plants look like human features?

3. **Interpret** Why do you think Surrealists like Salvador Dali admired the work of this sixteenth-century painter? What do you think was Arcimboldo's reason for painting this artwork?

4. **Judge** Has the artist successfully communicated his ideas to the viewer? Why or why not? Do all the elements in the painting work together to convey an idea? Is this a successful work of art? Why or why not?

Giuseppe Arcimboldo's realistic self-portrait gives little indication of his sense of humor.

Giuseppe Arcimboldo. *Self-Portrait of Arcimboldo,* 1575. Pen and blue pencil on paper, 9 by 6 inches. National Gallery, Prague, Czech Republic.

"Arcimboldo amused his peers and his boss, the Emperor Maximilian of Austria, with his bizarre symbolic paintings that distorted and made fun of the popular art of his time."

Artist unknown, Mayan. *A Ruler Dressed As Chac-Xib-Chac and the Holmul Dancer,* ca. A.D. 600–800. Ceramic with traces of paint, height 9 3/8 inches. The Kimbell Art Museum, Fort Worth, TX.

Unit 5
Art Through the Ages

Throughout history, artists have found creative ways to visually express their ideas to the world. Studying art history means learning about artists from the past and the struggles they faced in order to express their ideas. We are often encouraged and inspired by the stories of the artists who came before us.

We learn about these artists and their styles from the art itself and from **art historians.** They study artists and the contributions that those artists make to a culture. In this unit, you will read about the art and artists of Europe, the Mediterranean countries, and parts of the Middle East. You will read about art from Egypt, China, and Africa. You will also read about **pre-Columbian art,** the art that evolved in Mexico, Central America, and South America before Columbus encountered the New World. This history will help enrich your own works of art as you complete the studios.

Artist unknown, Mayan. *Head of a Warrior,* ca. A.D. 200–850.

About *the Artist*

The Mayan civilization thrived in the Western Hemisphere between A.D. 250 and A.D. 900. Much of Mayan art reflects the importance of religion and nature in Mayan life. Turn to pages 220–223 to read more about this culture and the art that survived it.

Lesson 1
Prehistoric Beginnings

Scientists believe that the human culture developed during the Stone Age, an enormous span of time that began about 2.5 million years ago and ended about 4,000 years ago. At some point during that time span, people began carving images out of bone, wood, or soft stone and painting images on cave walls. These images were almost always animals. Only rarely did the earliest human beings depict themselves.

Very early Stone Age people were nomadic and lived by hunting animals as they migrated. They relied heavily on animals for food, clothes, and the raw materials for weapons and tools. Deposits found in prehistoric caves indicate that reindeer was the major source of meat.

Although images of reindeer appear almost as rarely as images of people in cave paintings, prehistoric artists did use reindeer antlers as a carving medium. Look at the image of the carving on this page. The Stone Age artist carved the image of a bison from a reindeer antler. Notice how the form of the bison follows the curve of the antler. The bison's head is thrown back toward its tail, as if it were trying to brush away a fly with its tongue. Why might the artist have chosen to carve a sculpture of a bison?

Artist unknown. *Paleolithic Representation of a Bison,* 15,000–9000 B.C.

Architect unknown. *Stonehenge*, ca. 3100 B.C. Wiltshire, England.

Centuries of scavenging builders have dismantled much of Stonehenge. Some of the stones used to build Stonehenge came from mountains 240 miles away.

Circle of Stones

Around 3100 B.C., a group of Stone Age people began creating Stonehenge. What started as a circular ditch twenty feet wide and up to seven feet deep ended as a great stone circle on the plains of southern England. The massive stone circle, made of four-ton stone pillars topped with curved stone lintels, or crosspieces, was added eleven hundred years later. The artisans who put the enormous stones together fit the joints with the precision of woodworkers. Theories for Stonehenge's purpose abound, but no one knows for sure what it was used for or why it was built.

Sketchbook Journal

Research some of the animals that lived during the time of the prehistoric cave paintings, such as bison, reindeer, mammoths, and horses. Make sketches of the animals based on your findings. Note any similarities and differences in the animals' physical structures.

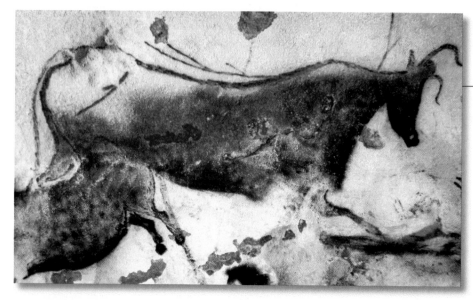

Artist unknown. *Hall of the Bulls,* 15,000–13,000 B.C. Lascaux, France.

What is the subject of this fifteen-thousand-year-old painting?

Art is a form of communication. The cave paintings at Lascaux, which you also saw on page 172, are proof of that statement. Look at the image above. Someone who lived approximately fifteen thousand years ago has communicated through an image that can be appreciated and understood. As you look at the painting, notice these details:

- The horns on its head identify the animal as a bull.
- Its shape is outlined and then partially filled with color.

Fading Glory

The Stone Age paintings of Lascaux were discovered in 1940 by four teenage boys exploring in France. The cave contains several halls whose walls and ceilings are covered with images. At the time they were discovered, all of the paintings were in near perfect condition. The cave was opened to the public for fifteen years, but was closed because the once-vivid colors began to fade. Tourists can now visit a partial replica of the cave or look at the paintings online.

Technique Tip

Line Quality in Acrylic

Acrylic paint is a versatile medium. You can use it to create many different looks, depending on what you add to it. To get a flowing, inky line, add water until the paint reaches a slightly thicker-than-ink consistency. Then load a round brush and vary the pressure in your stroke. Practice making lines on a separate sheet of paper before you try it on your stone.

Studio 1

Paint an Animal Scene on Stone

Use what you have learned to paint prehistoric animals on a flat stone.

Materials

✓ newsprint and pencil
✓ a flat, slightly rough stone, at least 7" wide, or a terra-cotta or limestone quarry tile
✓ black or brown acrylic paint
✓ round paintbrushes and a container with rinsing water
✓ umber, sienna, and ocher chalk pastels
✓ a hog bristle paintbrush or other stiff paintbrush

1 Select one or more animals that lived during the Stone Age. Draw a composition with several animals on newsprint.

2 Draw the outline of your composition onto your stone or tile. Paint flowing black or dark brown lines to outline each animal. Let it dry.

3 Add color and the illusion of form with chalk pastels. Rub the pastel over the stone. Work the color into the stone with a bristle brush.

Review and Reflect

- Describe the Stone Age animals you included in your composition.
- What elements did you use to show the animals' form?
- What significance did those animals have to prehistoric society? How did you show that in your painting?
- How does your painting resemble a Lascaux cave painting? How does it differ?

Lesson 2

Ancient Egypt

The architectural monuments, sculptures, paintings, and decorative arts of ancient Egypt tell of the society's political and social systems. These artworks sometimes served as messages from the powerful rulers to the people. They tell of the names and triumphs of ancient Egyptian queens and kings, or pharaohs. The names of the artists who created them, however, are often unknown.

The glories of the pharaohs and wealthy citizens were often inscribed on the walls of their tombs in **hieroglyphics,** a system of writing composed entirely of pictures. This writing system includes more than seven hundred symbols, such as those shown below. These and other artworks provide information about the lifestyles and history of the ancient Egyptian culture.

The waves of *N* come from water.

M looks like an owl.

The hieroglyph for the *B* sound looks like a foot.

The symbol for the *D* sound resembles a hand.

Hieroglyphic symbols usually represent particular sounds or groups of sounds.

Artist unknown. *Great Sphinx and the Pyramid of Khafre.* Giza, Egypt.

Workers in Giza began building the Sphinx, a portrait sculpture of Egyptian King Khafre, in about 2575 B.C.

Architect unknown. *Temple of Amon Ra, Hypostyle Hall,* 1530 B.C. Karnak, Egypt.

Under the Pillars

The hypostyle hall in the Egyptian Temple of Amon is a marvel of the ancient world. Hypostyle, which means "under pillars," describes the hall's construction. The structure is built of massive pillars that support giant slabs of stone, which used to support the roof. Enormous by itself, the hall is part of a much larger temple compound. Building began in about the fifteenth century B.C. Art added over hundreds of years shows the changing fortunes of the Egyptian Empire. Sculpture carved in low relief in the room shows the story of how two Egyptian rulers led their armies to victory in Palestine and in Syria.

Research

Learn to write your name using Egyptian hieroglyphs. Go online or to your local library to find out about the Egyptian hieroglyphic symbols. Use your findings to "write" your name as an Egyptian scribe might have written it. What might these hieroglyphs represent today? What symbols might you use to create your own hieroglyphs?

Artist unknown, Egyptian. *Wall Painting From Tomb of Nebamun at Thebes,* ca. 1350 B.C. Fresco on dry plaster, height 32 inches. The British Museum, London.

How realistic is the scene depicted above?

Hunting scenes were commonly found on the walls of ancient Egyptian tombs. The artist or artists of the paintings in the Tomb of Nebamun included precise details to reflect the textures of the animals. Each of the paintings in the tomb shows an aspect of the life of Nebamun, an official in the Egyptian government. The scene above shows Nebamun hunting with his wife and daughter. Look for these details:

- Like most Egyptian paintings, the figures appear flat and two dimensional.

- A cat with a bird in its mouth balances on two bent reed stems. The reeds are papyrus, from which the Egyptians made paper.
- Even though the party is hunting birds, a goose stands on the prow of the boat.

Symbols in Egyptian Art

Unlikely details like these lead art historians to speculate that the painting has symbolic meaning. Other details reinforce this idea. The cat's eye is gilded, decorated with gold leaf. The flounder-looking fish below the boat is a tilapia, which is associated with new life. And it is unlikely that a hunting party of three would use a boat so small. What symbolic meaning do you think the artist was trying to convey in this work?

Technique Tip

Paper
The Egyptians used paper made from the inner stem of the water plant papyrus. The inner material, called pith, is laid at right angles, and then dried in the sun. The result is a gently textured paper whose slightly uneven surface adds interest to a work. If you cannot find papyrus, try using any other handmade or roughly-textured paper.

Studio 2

Paint an Egyptian Scene

Use what you have learned to create a symbolic scene from your life in the ancient Egyptian style.

Materials

✓ rice paper, papyrus, or watercolor paper
✓ pencil
✓ paint
✓ paintbrushes and a container with rinsing water

1 Brainstorm ideas for a scene from your life. Think of objects you could include that would serve as symbols of your life.

2 Draw the scene on paper. Use Egyptian elements such as profiles and animals. Scale each person to show his or her importance.

3 Add color to your scene with watercolors. Refer to Egyptian paintings to be sure your color scheme is appropriate.

Review and Reflect

- Describe what is happening in the scene you painted.
- How do the colors and views you used reflect the Egyptian style?
- What symbols did you include? What do they represent?
- Would a viewer understand the symbolic meaning of your work? Explain.

Lesson 3

Ancient Greece

The ancient Greek culture flourished from about 1200 B.C. to about 323 B.C. This culture would come to influence the Western world longer and more profoundly than any other. Ancient Greece is often considered the birthplace of many aspects of Western tradition. The arts and government of Western culture are patterned after the ancient Greeks. And much of the artwork in this book has its foundation in the artistic traditions of ancient Greece.

For the Greeks, art was the visual expression of individual feelings and ideas. This was a new conception of the role of the artist. Because the Greeks believed this, we know the names of the architects and sculptors associated with one of the well-known artistic achievements of ancient Greece. The Parthenon was designed by the architects Ictinus and Callicrates, who oversaw its construction from 447–432 B.C. The style of the art and architecture of this structure is called the **Classical style.**

The temple was dedicated to the goddess Athena. The sculptor Phidias oversaw the carvings. The *Birth of Athena* is shown in one **pediment,** the triangular structures that support the roof and provide space for sculptures in high relief. Athena's battle with the ocean god Poseidon is shown in the other.

Ictinus and Callicrates, architects. *Parthenon,* ca. 447–432 B.C. Marble, approximately 101 by 229 by 49 feet. Athens, Greece.

The Parthenon used to house a massive gold statue of Athena by Phidias.

Artist unknown. *Birth of Athena, Reconstruction of the Parthenon East Pediment.* The British Museum, London.

Notice how the high-relief figures were carved to fit in the triangular shape of the pediment.

Benjamin Latrobe: original architect, Charles Bulfinch and Thomas Walter: additional architects, *U.S. Capitol Building*, 1793–1868, Washington, D.C.

Building on the Capitol began in 1793, but the dome was completed during the Civil War.

Thomas Jefferson, architect. *Monticello,* 1769. Charlottesville, VA.

Thomas Jefferson designed his home and many of the items in it.

A New Classicism

The Greek belief in the worth of the individual expressed itself in an early form of democracy, the Greek city-states. This form of democracy was the seed that would flower more than two thousand years later in the United States. Is it any wonder, then, that many early American buildings were also inspired by those of ancient Greece? Two of the best-known examples of neo-classical architecture are shown on this page, the Capitol Building in Washington, D.C., and Thomas Jefferson's home at Monticello, Virginia. What elements can you identify in each building that were inspired by the architecture of ancient Greece?

Research

Many of the public buildings in Washington, D.C., were inspired by ancient Greek and Roman architecture. Go online or to your library to research buildings in the United States capital. Choose one, and write two paragraphs about its design. Include sketches of the building styles with your writing.

Greek Figures *in Architecture*

Artist unknown. *Poseidon, Apollo and Artemis*, 440 B.C. Section of the East frieze of the Parthenon. Marble, height 43 inches.

How would you describe the relief style used in this frieze?

The figures above are part of a **frieze,** a band of sculpture that runs along the top of a building. This one is 525 feet long, and it runs along the top of a room inside the Parthenon. Notice these details:

- Bodies are turned at different angles, giving them a natural appearance.
- The figures are carved in high relief; they project from the surface but are not free of it.
- Each figure is shown in standard proportion to the others, giving each one equal importance.

A Family Affair

The figures in the section of the frieze shown here represent the Greek gods Poseidon, Apollo, and Artemis. Poseidon was the violent god of the sea. Though he lost his battle with Athena, Poseidon was still worshipped in the countryside around the Parthenon. Apollo was so proud that only his father and mother could stand to be with him. He made humans aware of their guilt, and then absolved them of it. He also was the god of crops and was associated with the sun. Artemis, Apollo's twin, was the goddess of the hunt. To celebrate this goddess, ancient Greek maidens dressed as nymphs, or nature goddesses, and danced.

Technique Tip

Whites in Watercolor

The traditional way to have white in a watercolor painting is to not paint areas intended to be white. If you get color on white areas, wet the area with clean water. Let it sit thirty seconds, and then blot with a clean paper towel. Repeat until color is gone. It may not come all the way out, since some colors stain paper.

Studio 3

Create an Architectural Frieze

Create a design for a Greek-style architectural frieze that tells a story about you, your family, or your community.

Materials

- ✓ newsprint
- ✓ pencil or vine charcoal
- ✓ 4 sheets of heavy 12" × 18" white paper
- ✓ watercolor paints
- ✓ paintbrushes and water container
- ✓ ruler

1 Draw your ideas on newsprint. When you are satisfied, draw a six-inch rectangular band across each sheet of white paper.

2 Transfer your narrative frieze design from newsprint to the white paper panels.

3 Paint the scenes in watercolor. Use shading techniques to show the scenes in relief.

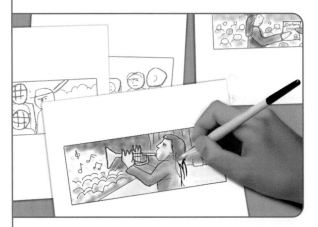

Review and Reflect

- What does your Greek frieze show?
- How do the objects and figures relate to one another to show unity in your frieze?
- How did you tell a visual story?
- Would someone understand the basic story from your frieze design? Explain.

Lesson 4

Ancient Rome

Not far from Greece, ancient Romans were building an empire based in present-day Italy. In about 200 B.C., Rome began to expand its empire. All of Europe fell under Rome's sway: the painted caves of France; Egypt and the Sphinx; England and Stonehenge; and even the Parthenon in Greece. Skilled Greek artists and architects worked on many Roman projects. As a result, as Rome spread, so did the ideas and images of ancient Greece.

Expanding Roman cities required huge amounts of water. Romans built massive aqueducts to carry water long distances. These structures were enormous, symmetrically proportioned engineering marvels. The aqueduct shown below spans the River Gard to take water to the French town of Nîmes. This structure, built out of enormous masonry blocks, has survived more than two thousand years. It owes much of its strength to its arches. The curve of an arch can carry much more weight above it than the flat surface of a beam. An extended arch or a series of arches that form a curved ceiling is called a barrel vault. Both the arch and the barrel vault were known to the Egyptians. But it was the Romans who made the most of the forms, using them in bridges, temples, and aqueducts.

Architect unknown, Roman. *Pont du Gard,* Nîmes, France.

Masons let stones jut from the surface to hold scaffolding for later repairs.

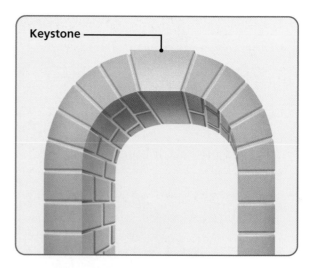

The last stone to be placed in an arch is the keystone. Until it is set, the bottom of the arch must be supported. A continuous series of arches forms a barrel vault.

Architect unknown. *Colosseum*, ca. A.D. 70–80. Stone, concrete, and marble, approximately 620 by 513 by 158 feet. Rome, Italy.

In the Colosseum

Citizens in crowded Roman cities had an immense appetite for grisly entertainment. Spectators packed stadiums across the empire to watch slaves fight to the death in gladiatorial battles. Early stadiums were dug into hillsides. The most massive stadium was Rome's freestanding *Colosseum*, which could hold fifty thousand spectators. Notice the pattern created by the arches. Why might the architect have used the arch so repeatedly?

All that is left now of the huge arena is a ruin. The marble seats and intricate decorations that once graced it were stolen long ago. It was restored somewhat in the 1990s, and in 2000, a theatre group staged a series of plays in the structure. They were the first performances held there in more than fifteen hundred years.

Visual Culture

Look at the buildings and structures at your school and in your town. What elements from Greek and Roman architecture can you identify? Take photographs of Greek and Roman details, or draw them in your Sketchbook Journal. Label each image with the building it comes from and its style.

Artist unknown, Roman. *Bust of Euripides,* date unknown. Marble. Private collection.

What details suggest these are portraits of real people?

Artist unknown, Roman. *Head of Agrippina the Elder,* 2nd century. Marble, height 14 inches. Musée du Louvre, Paris.

Ancient Romans created remarkably realistic portrait sculptures. Not only do the portraits above look like the individuals they portray, but they also offer a glimpse into their personalities. Look for these details:

- The smile lines around the eyes and the slight upturn in the mouth make Euripides seem friendly but perhaps a little worried.
- Wavy and curved lines around her face and down her neck define the hair of Agrippina the Elder. She appears seriously deep in thought or contemplation.

Making the Past Present

As in other areas, Roman sculpture borrowed heavily from the Greek. In fact, many of the well-known artists of the ancient Roman era were themselves Greek. Even so, sculptures like the portraits shown here truly express the Roman spirit. They reflect the Roman preference for the ordinary over the heroic. Each wrinkle, crease, and feature is faithfully copied, making these seem like people you might know. Sculptures like these help bring the history of ancient Rome alive.

Technique Tip

Empty Your Head

To fire a three-dimensional clay portrait without having it explode, you must hollow it out until the walls are about three-fourths of an inch thick throughout. Begin by hollowing out the neck from the bottom. To get further into the head, carefully cut off the back with a wire tool. Carve out the excess clay. Score the cut edges and reattach the back of the head with slip.

Studio 4

Sculpt a Roman-Style Portrait

Use what you have learned to sculpt a portrait in the Roman style. Choose a person that you admire as your subject, such as a family member or historical figure.

Materials

- ✓ photographs of your subject
- ✓ 5" × 7" block of clay, plus extra
- ✓ clay tools
- ✓ acrylic paint, tempera paint, or clay glaze
- ✓ paintbrushes and water container

1 Collect photos of the person you have chosen. Try to get views from all sides of the person's head, including the top.

2 Use your photographs as a reference to sculpt a three-dimensional portrait of your selected subject's head from the block of clay.

3 When you are done, carefully hollow out the neck and head and allow it to dry completely before firing. Finish with paint or clay glaze.

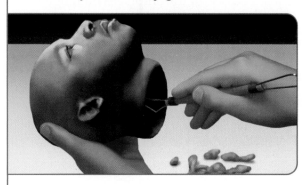

Review and Reflect

- Whose portrait did you sculpt?
- What elements of your portrait reflect the Roman style?
- How does the style affect others' reactions to the portrait?
- Which parts of your sculpted portrait most resemble the person it is based on? Which parts could you improve?

Lesson 5
Art of the Middle Ages

In A.D. 410, Rome was overthrown by the Visigoths from the north. Soon the discoveries and advances made by the Greeks and Romans in science and art were replaced with the teachings of the new Christian church. The focus of art and learning was no longer on the individual or the natural world, but on religion. Italian scholars called this time period the **Middle Ages** to separate the years between the ancient cultures and the Renaissance that revived them.

The Middle Ages, also called the Medieval period, lasted from about A.D. 400 to about A.D. 1300. Because of the emphasis on religion, the church building naturally became the

focus for architectural innovation. Some of the most elaborate churches were **cathedrals,** a type of church where a bishop has his official seat. Architects tried to express a sense of spiritual awe in soaring yet delicate structures. They treated the stone like lace—carving, piercing, and shaping it until it seemed as airy as the space it enclosed. Renaissance writers coined the term **Gothic** to describe this extremely decorative type of architecture. As admirers of simplicity and order, they meant the term as a criticism.

Various architects. *Chartres Cathedral,* A.D. 1028–1215. Chartres, France.

Various architects. *Reims Cathedral,* A.D. 1211–1260. Champagne-Ardenne, France.

Architects used supporting arches called flying buttresses to prevent buildings from collapsing.

This magnificent French cathedral was restored after bombs damaged it in World War I.

Artist unknown. *Letter Page from Book of Kells*, A.D. 800. Manuscript illumination. Trinity College, Dublin, Ireland.

Medieval Illuminations

Many medieval manuscripts, or books, also focused largely on religion. The pages were often adorned with elaborate letters and illustrations created by illuminators. These artists used rich colors and gold or silver leaf in their intricate designs. The addition of the colorful details made the pages "light up."

The *Book of Kells* is a religious book written by Irish monks around A.D. 800. It is remarkable for its illuminations, illustrations as luminous as stained-glass windows. The Latin text is accompanied by illuminations of different sizes. They often feature spirals and curves that coil and interlace. Figures of animals, humans, and fanciful creatures are also common. Each illustration and design in the *Book of Kells* is original; none of the patterns or combinations are repeated.

Visual Culture

The distinctive interwoven designs created by the ancient Celts of Ireland may be more popular today than they were in their own time. Celtic knot designs appear on rings, bracelets, pillows, wall hangings, and greeting cards. Look for images that feature Celtic designs. Make a list of each one you find and include a sketch if possible.

217

Interlace *Illuminations*

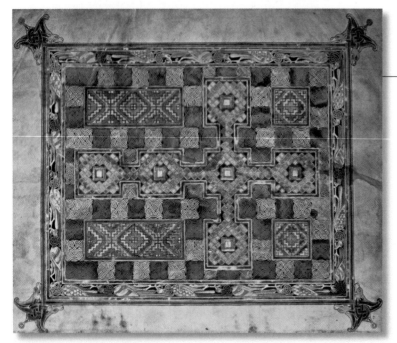

Artist unknown. *Lindisfarne Gospels: Carpet Page with Cross Introducing St. Jerome's Letter to Pope Damascus,* ca. A.D. 710–720. The British Museum, London.

What images can you identify in this design?

The illumination above was made about the same time and in the same style as the *Book of Kells*. It comes from the *Lindisfarne Gospels*, a book written to honor St. Cuthbert. This former shepherd survived the plague and became head of the Lindisfarne Abbey. The swirling, interlocking design is called an **interlace.** As you examine it, look for these details:

- Many different geometric shapes and lines repeat to form patterns.
- The organic shapes of plants and birds are woven among the geometric shapes and lines.

Hiberno-Saxon Style

This style of art is the result of the combination of two ancient traditions. Irish monks who sailed to England in A.D. 635 took with them designs from their ancient Celtic ancestors. They combined these decorative swirls, knots, and spirals with the animal forms used by the Anglo-Saxons who were living in England when the Irish, also called Hibernians, arrived. This combination is called Hiberno-Saxon style.

Technique Tip

Visual Resources

In any attempt to draw a plant, an animal, or an ancient style of design, it is helpful to have reference photos. Even if your design is abstract, reference photos can provide visual information or spark an idea. Go to your school library for books and magazines, or go online and print out useful images from the Internet.

Studio 5

Create an Interlace Design

Create an illuminated page with an interlace design that features a letter of the alphabet surrounded by a Celtic border.

Materials

- ✓ newsprint
- ✓ white construction paper
- ✓ pencil, eraser
- ✓ watercolors, brushes, and rinsing water
- ✓ fine-tipped markers
- ✓ ruler
- ✓ metallic ink pens

1 Select a letter. Draw it large on a sheet of newsprint. Draw an interlace design that includes plants and animals. Add a border of interwoven Celtic knots.

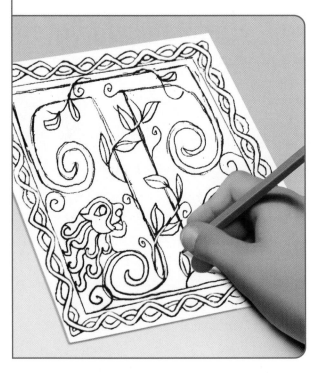

2 Use a brown watercolor wash on the white paper to simulate age. When it dries, transfer your design to the "aged" paper.

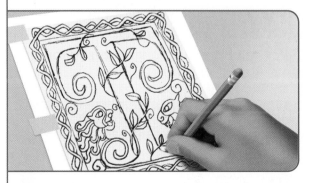

3 Add color with markers and watercolors. Keep your lines crisp and your colors bright.

Review and Reflect

- Describe the parts of your illumination design.
- How do the lines, shapes, and colors you used work together to create an interlace design?
- Are your animals and plants realistic or do they look more abstract?
- How does your illumination resemble the Hiberno-Saxon style?

Meet *the Artist*

The Maya

The art of the ancient Maya is a record of gods and rulers, ritual and daily life. Much of what is known today about the ancient Mayan culture comes from their art. Their complex and beautiful work offers a glimpse into the lives and beliefs of a sophisticated civilization. Before Christopher Columbus ever left the ports of Spain, the Maya began to abandon their great cities and vanish back into the jungle.

Artist unknown, Mayan. *Head of a Warrior,* ca. A.D. 200–850.

"On the road to the city of San Pedro, in the first town within the province of Honduras, called Copán, are certain ruins and vestiges of a great population, and of superb edifices, of . . . skill and splendor. . . ."

—DIEGO GARCÍA DE PALACIO, 1576, FROM THE EARLIEST SURVIVING DESCRIPTION OF THE MAYAN CITY OF COPÁN

Art in the Cities of Stone

For more than two thousand years, Mayan civilization flourished in southern Mexico, Belize, Guatemala, and parts of Honduras and El Salvador. The civilization reached its height of power and artistic and scientific achievements from about A.D. 250 to A.D. 900, a span called the Classic period.

Art was an essential part of Mayan life, and it was everywhere. Rulers and nobles hired artists to carve their faces in stone, model their portraits in plaster, paint them on stone walls, and write about their exploits in the elegant picture-words called hieroglyphs. This art adorned palaces, temples, and tombs. Artists carved intricate images into objects made of jade, shell, and bone. Remarkably, all this work was created without the use of metal tools. Instead they used obsidian, a hard volcanic stone that could be sharpened to a razor edge.

Vanished Civilization

No one knows why, but after about A.D. 900, Mayan civilization began to decline rapidly. Without the extraordinary works of art they left behind, the names of the great Mayan kings and queens, their beliefs, and their ceremonies would have disappeared.

Talk About It

Look back at the sculpture on page 198. This ruler wears a headdress associated with the god of war and religious rituals. Why might an artist have made this image?

The Maya in History

2600 B.C.

2575 B.C.
Fourth Dynasty begins in Egypt; construction on Great Pyramids starts soon after

1500 B.C.

Maya ruins at Tikal

People first settle in the Copán Valley, Honduras
1100 B.C.

Tikal, Guatemala, first settled
600 B.C.

509 B.C.
Roman Republic founded

400 B.C.

A.D. 410
Visigoths sack Rome

A.D. 250
Classic period of the Maya begins

A.D. 700

Classic period of the Maya ends
A.D. 900

Columbus arrives in the New World
A.D. 1492

Maya first encounter Europeans
A.D. 1511

Spanish conqueror Hernán Cortés

Spanish conquest begins; Aztec capital of Tenochtitlán falls to the Spanish
A.D. 1521

A.D. 1697
The last independent Mayan kingdom falls to the Spanish

A.D. 1800

Look *and Compare*

Two Temples, Two Worlds Apart

The two temples on the next page were built about six hundred years and half a world apart. Yet they have striking similarities. Both are made of stone and covered with intricate relief sculptures. Both are part of complex ancient cities. And both give us glimpses of a rich and complex way of life long vanished from Earth.

The ancient Maya once flourished in present-day Mexico, Guatemala, and Belize.

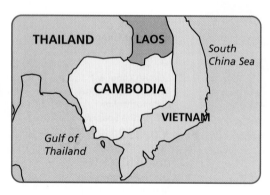

The Khmer empire occupied a vast territory in what is now Cambodia, Vietnam, Laos, and Thailand.

The Maya in the Yucatán

Chichén Itzá was founded about A.D. 500, and *La Casa de las Monjas (The Nunnery)* was one of the first buildings constructed there. Look for the stylized faces carved in the stones at the right edge of the Mayan building. Two of the curved stones that stick out are noses. The faces represent Chac, the Mayan god of rain.

The city began to diminish about A.D. 1194, and by the time the Spanish arrived in the next century, Chichén Itzá was abandoned.

The Khmer in Southeast Asia

Angkor was the capital of the vast Khmer empire in Cambodia from about A.D. 800 to about A.D. 1400. It was the largest, most prosperous kingdom in the history of Southeast Asia. Rulers used the country's riches to build enormous structures to glorify themselves and the capital. Borrowing religious ideas from India, builders arranged the city like a symbolic universe. Neak Pean sits in the middle of a specially built pond that historians think may represent the lake at the center of the universe, according to the Khmer. The small temple, built in the late 1100s, is covered with relief sculptures carved from the soft sandstone. The city was abandoned in A.D. 1431 after an invasion.

Architect unknown, Mayan. *La Casa de las Monjas (The Nunnery),* ca. A.D. 500. Chichén Itzá, Mexico.

Architect unknown, Cambodian. *Neak Pean Shrine,* A.D. 1181–1219. Angkor, Cambodia.

Compare & Contrast

- How do the buildings differ and how are they similar?

- "Without an architecture of our own we have no soul of our own civilization." How do these temples reflect American architect Frank Lloyd Wright's statement?

223

Lesson 6

The Renaissance

Renaissance means "rebirth." For the artists and thinkers of the Renaissance, the fourteenth and fifteenth centuries were a rebirth of civilization and culture. The rediscovery of the ancient Roman empire awakened interest in classical ideals of beauty and thought. Knowledge in astronomy, mathematics, and physics grew by leaps and bounds as European countries competed to lay claim to previously unexplored areas of the world. These advances also served as inspiration for artistic expression.

The Catholic Church retained vast power during the Renaissance. Often the Church was the source of work for an artist. This patronage, coupled with bold scientific and artistic thought, spurred artists to create prominent works of art for cathedrals. One of those works of art is *David*, by Italian sculptor Michelangelo Buonarroti (1475–1564). This large-scale sculpture was commissioned by the city of Florence to adorn its cathedral.

Michelangelo knew the rules of anatomy and proportion. But in his sculpture of the biblical slayer of the giant called Goliath, Michelangelo broke those rules for dramatic effect. By making them larger, the artist draws attention to the subject's hands and head. David's massive head, with its forceful and determined expression, has become a symbol of the spirit of the Renaissance.

Michelangelo Buonarroti. (Detail) *David*, A.D. 1501–1504. Marble, height 13.5 feet. Galleria dell'Accademia, Florence, Italy.

What do you notice about the proportion of David's hand in relation to his head?

Overcoming Challenges

Women of the Renaissance received little opportunity or encouragement to pursue their artistic talents. But Italian painter Sofonisba Anguissola (ca. 1532–1625) rose above those challenges to become a well-known artist. Encouraged by her father and educated as a painter, Anguissola was later employed as the court portraitist for Philip II of Spain. Her realistic portraits, such as the one shown here, suggest that she painted what she saw rather than flattering her subjects.

Learning to See

Renaissance artist and scientist Leonardo da Vinci (1452–1519) had little formal education. He relied on his observation skills. To better understand how the human body functions, for example, he made drawings from dissected human cadavers. To better understand the natural world, he made drawings of everything in it: rocks, trees, water, animals, landscapes. How does the portrait, *Ginevra Benci,* reflect Leonardo's quest for *saper vedere,* knowing how to see?

Sofonisba Anguissola. *Alessandro Farnese, Duke of Parma,* ca. 1561. National Gallery of Ireland, Dublin, Ireland.

Leonardo da Vinci. *Ginevra Benci,* ca. 1474. Oil on panel, 16 13/16 by 14 9/16 inches. National Gallery of Art, Washington, D.C.

Sketchbook Journal

For the next seven days, take your Sketchbook Journal and pencil with you wherever you go. Make sketches constantly. Draw all kinds of things you come across: an empty paper cup, a tree, a television set. Try to perfect your direct observation skills as you draw.

Ghiberti. *Baptistery Doors,* 1452. Bronze and gold plate, height 17 feet. Florence Cathedral, Florence, Italy.

On what kind of building would these doors be appropriate?

Ghiberti. (Detail) *The Fall of Jericho,* Baptistery Doors, 1452.

Lorenzo Ghiberti (ca. 1378–1455) designed these massive bronze doors for a church in Italy. Each panel is a relief sculpture inspired by stories from the Bible. Ghiberti wanted to make the reliefs so detailed and lifelike that they would seem like paintings. Look for these details:

- Ghiberti indicates space with linear perspective and overlapping.
- The panels are surrounded by a border of sculpted portraits.

The Gates of Paradise

Ghiberti produced the doors in response to a competition. The contest was held in the city of Florence, the thriving center of Italian Renaissance art. The city council selected Ghiberti to decorate the great bronze doors of Florence Cathedral's baptistery, the part of a church where baptisms are performed. It took Ghiberti more than twenty years to complete and install the work. The doors, cast in bronze and painted with gold, became known as the Gates of Paradise.

Technique Tip

Ink Washes

When you are working with ink washes, it is handy to have several small containers, three for each color you are using. Spice jars or medicine bottles work well. Add two tablespoons of water to each container. Drip in ink to create containers of light, medium, and dark values of each color you use. Paint from these containers to control your values.

Studio 6

Design a Door-front Relief

Use what you have learned to design a set of doors for a large public building in the Renaissance style.

Materials

- ✓ 1 large sheet of heavy white drawing or watercolor paper
- ✓ brown and black ink or watercolor
- ✓ paintbrushes and a container with rinsing water
- ✓ extra small containers to hold different values of ink washes (optional)

1 Choose a public building. Consider the types of activities that occur in the building and the people who use it.

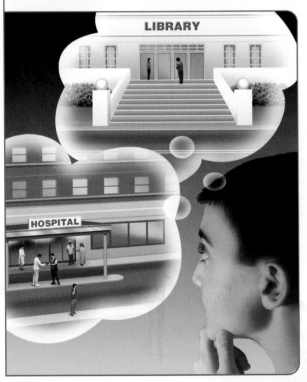

2 On a large sheet of paper, draw the outline for a set of doors. Lightly draw images into the door's panels and borders.

3 Use washes of dark brown and black ink to create the illusion of a relief. Leave the highlights white.

Review and Reflect

- What images did you include in your design?
- How did you use value to help give the appearance of a relief sculpture?
- How would your doors change the overall effect of the building you chose?
- What, if anything, would you change about your door design? Explain.

Lesson 7
Art of the Americas

As the power of the Maya began to decline, two other empires were gaining power in the Americas. By A.D. 1500, when the Maya were all but gone, the empires of the Aztec in Mexico and the Inca in Peru had become vast and populous centers of power. But they met their doom at the hands of Renaissance Europe. Through war and disease, European conquerors destroyed both of these glittering empires.

Beneath the busy streets of modern Mexico City have been found the remains of the magnificent Aztec capital of Tenochtitlán. Founded in A.D. 1325, the city grew to cover five miles and support 200,000 people. At its height in A.D. 1519, it ruled over six million people in five hundred states.

The city was built on an island in Lake Texcoco, and at its height, it was a thriving urban center of palaces, markets, and pyramids. At its center stood the Great Pyramid, which honored Huitzilopochtli. According to Aztec myth, Huitzilopochtli led them to found the city at that site. The temple honors elements of nature, too, and stone serpents and frogs adorn the stairways and walls.

One Aztec deity, Quetzalcóatl, is honored at the Temple of Quetzalcóatl. Carvings from this temple are shown in the image on this page. The carvings that look like animals wearing ruffled collars are depictions of the Feathered Serpent, Quetzalcóatl, himself.

Architect unknown, Aztec. *Temple of Quetzalcóatl,* ca. A.D. 800. Near Mexico City, Mexico.

Aztec emperor Montezuma at first mistook the Spanish conqueror Hernán Cortés for this feathery god.

Architect unknown, Inca. *Ruins at Machu Picchu,* ca. A.D. 1450. Machu Picchu, Peru.

The Inca

When the Spaniards reached Peru, the Inca were expecting them. Their system of relay runners, who could carry a message 150 miles in a day, had already sounded the alarm. High in the mountains the invaders found cities hewn of stones fit together so closely that the blade of a knife still cannot squeeze between them. Homes, temples, and pyramids were carved with intricate designs in relief. The Inca were highly skilled at working metal as well as creating portrait vessels like the stirrup pots on pages 160 and 162. But they could not match the Spaniards' military power. The Spanish arrived in A.D. 1532. By 1535, the Inca empire had fallen.

Research

The Maya, Aztec, Teotihuacán, and Inca cultures all used animal forms in their art. Choose one of these cultures and research the way it viewed and represented different animals. Create a chart that includes an image of the animal and a description of its significance to the culture.

Animals *in Aztec Art*

Artist unknown, Aztec. *Vessel in the shape of a Monkey,* A.D. 1325–1521. Obsidian, 5 7/8 by 5 7/8 inches. National Museum of Anthropology, Mexico City, Mexico.

How does this vessel reflect a type of relief sculpture?

Animals were frequently used by the Aztec as subjects for sculpture and pottery. Like the portrait pots of the Moche, this animal pot is called an effigy vessel. As you study it, notice these details:

• The monkey holds its tail, which circles the rim of the pot and projects in front like a handle.
• The monkey's arms, head, tail, and feet project from the surface of the pot.
• The polished surface creates a smooth, shiny texture.

Monkey Business

This pot is made of **obsidian,** a volcanic glass that is slightly harder than ordinary window glass. The interior of the pot was most likely hollowed out by a skilled artist using drills made of bamboo. The image of a monkey holding its tail is common in pre-Columbian art, art made before Christopher Columbus arrived in the New World in A.D. 1492. Historians speculate about the meaning of monkey vessels like this one. Some believe the Aztec saw monkeys as the creators of the arts. Others believe that, according to the Aztec, monkeys represent the wind god, who blows life into all things. How do you think vessels like this might have been used?

Technique Tip

The Inside Scoop

One way to create a hollow papier-mâché form is to wad up newspapers, tape them into shape, cover the shape with plastic wrap, and apply papier mâché over it. When it is dry, cut the form open and pull out the crumpled newspapers. Or, use an object such as a balloon as your interior support. Then when the papier mâché is dry, deflate the balloon.

Studio 7

Create a Pre-Columbian Animal Vessel

Research the animals of a pre-Columbian culture. Create a papier-mâché vessel in the form of an animal that has a mythological meaning to that culture.

Materials

✓ newsprint and pencil
✓ papier-mâché paste or liquid starch
✓ newspaper, in pages and in strips
✓ masking tape
✓ plastic wrap, or 1 or more balloons (optional)
✓ tempera or acrylic paint, paintbrushes
✓ adhesive

1 Choose an animal form for a pre-Columbian style container. Draw your ideas on newsprint.

2 Wad up newspapers and tape them into shape, or use a balloon as your interior structure. Apply papier mâché to the form.

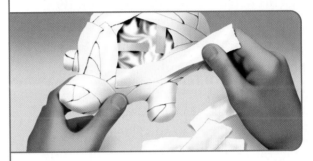

3 When your form is dry, cut it open and remove the interior support. Reattach cut edges. Finish the form with tempera or acrylic paint.

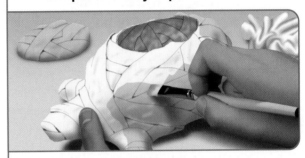

Review and Reflect

- Describe the form and colors in your vessel.
- How does form reveal the animal you chose?
- What meaning might your vessel represent to a pre-Columbian culture? How might it have been used by this culture?
- What did you find most difficult about creating a papier-mâché vessel? How did you solve the problems you encountered?

The Art of China

The art of China has a long history. Its culture and artistic traditions are almost as old as those of Egypt. But China's Classic periods of art began in about A.D. 600, as Egypt and Western Europe were settling into the Middle Ages. Chinese artists began to be influenced by Taoism. This religion, with its emphasis on the harmony of nature, has inspired both Eastern and Western works of art.

The *Great Wall of China* stands as a marvel of Chinese architecture. The wall began as a bulwark, or wall of defense against invaders, to protect the state of Chu. From about 600 to 300 B.C., similar walls were built by neighboring states. In about the third century B.C., the states became united and individual walls were connected. Later dynasties added to the wall until it snaked its way over about forty-five hundred miles of mountains and valleys.

The image of the *Great Wall of China* below shows how animals, both real and imaginary, played an important role in Chinese art and architecture. Notice how similar the animals that adorn this portion of the wall are to the Aztecs' Feathered Serpent, Quetzalcóatl, which you saw on page 228. The head and the eyes are remarkably similar. What could account for the similarities between carvings separated by hundreds of years and thousands of miles?

Architects unknown, Chinese. *Great Wall of China,* ca. 700 B.C.–A.D. 1640. Various materials, approximately 4,500 miles long. Northeastern China.

Artist unknown, Chinese. *Guardian Lion,*
A.D. 618–907. Marble with traces of color,
11 ¾ by 9 ¾ inches. Nelson-Atkins Museum
of Art, Kansas City, MO. Purchase: Nelson
Trust. Photo by Robert Newcombe.

Lion Tales

The prosperous years of the T'ang
dynasty supported a rich tradition of art and
literature. From A.D. 618 to 907, as the Maya
reached the peak of their power in Mexico
and Central America, the emperors of the
T'ang expanded China farther west than
ever before. Music and poetry reached new
heights of expression as well as popularity.
The lion above is an example of T'ang
sculpture. Notice how stylized its features
are. Lions are not native to China. Chinese
artists based their lion sculptures on stories
and descriptions from travelers.

Sketchbook Journal

**Think of an animal you have
heard about but have never
seen, not even in pictures. Look
up the name of the animal
in a collegiate dictionary. Pick
a different animal if there is
an illustration. Draw a picture
of the animal based on the
dictionary definition only.
Then find a photograph online.**

Wang Hui. *Autumn Landscape,* 16th–17th century. Ink on paper. Musée des Arts Asiatiques-Guimet, Paris.

How did the artist create a sense of depth in this painting?

Chinese landscapes often reflect the Taoist emphasis on nature. Notice in the landscape above, how the colors of the artist's muted palette combine with the asymmetrically balanced composition to create a sense of harmony. Chinese artist Wang Hui (1632–1717) used techniques such as aerial perspective and overlapping to

show mountains receding into the distance along the shore. As you look at the artwork, notice these details:

- The values are darker in the foreground and lighter in the background.
- The mountains in the foreground appear larger than those in the background.

Calligraphy

Chinese landscapes frequently combine painting and writing. The delicate and detailed designs are most often created with ink on paper or silk. To the Chinese, their flowing form of writing with a brush, called **calligraphy,** is as much an art form as painting. Where do you notice calligraphy in *Autumn Landscape?* Just as in landscape painting, the main inspiration for Chinese calligraphy is the harmony of nature.

Technique Tip

A Permanent Record

Many of the inks you write with are not permanent. They will fade over time. To get rich black lines that will not fade, use India ink. In traditional mixtures it is made of carbon called lampblack, produced from non-electric lamps. It is also compressed into wettable cakes. In this form it is called Japanese or Chinese ink.

Paint a Chinese Landscape

Use what you have learned about Taoism's emphasis on nature and harmony to paint a Chinese landscape scroll.

Materials

- ✓ white craft paper
- ✓ pencil
- ✓ watercolors and India ink
- ✓ paintbrushes and a container with rinsing water
- ✓ wooden dowels and glue

1 Cut the paper to 12" by 18". Draw your landscape in pencil. Leave a one-inch border on the top and bottom edges.

2 Use watercolor to add subtle hues to your landscape. Use India ink and delicate calligraphic lines to sign your name vertically.

3 Paint the borders with a decorative Chinese design. When it is dry, glue the dowels to the back on the top and bottom.

Review and Reflect

- Describe your landscape and the colors you chose.
- How do the elements of art work together to unify your painting?
- How do the colors and the composition reinforce the mood of your painting?
- How well does your painting reflect the Chinese landscape style? How does it reflect the Taoist idea of harmony?

Lesson 9
Art from Africa

The striking and powerful art of Africa has inspired artists throughout the world. At the beginning of the twentieth century, for example, European artists like Picasso and Braque drew inspiration from geometric designs in African sculpture to create Cubism. Africa's art is as varied as the many cultures that have arisen on the vast African continent. It displays an elegance of form born of the techniques and skills of the African artists.

The masks below reflect the variety in African art. Masks have many different purposes and forms. They can represent specific ancestors or spirits. Some cultures believe that masks can serve as messengers to the gods. They can also conceal the identities of those wearing the masks. Notice how the artists have created contrast in the masks with texture and color. What similarities do you notice?

The Yoruba of West Africa considered the Nigerian city of Ife to be the birthplace of humanity. From the eleventh to the fifteenth century, the Ife culture flourished. Sculptors created portrait heads with such personality and detail that they seem almost to breathe. Look at the example below. It is made of **terra cotta,** a reddish-brown clay. Ife sculptors also used brass, which is a combination of copper and zinc, or **bronze,** which is a combination copper and tin, to cast their sculptures.

Artists unknown, African. *Tribal Masks,* various dates. National Museum of African Art, Smithsonian Institution, Washington, D.C.

Artist unknown, Akan culture. *Terra-cotta Head,* date unknown. Anspach Collection, New York.

Architect unknown,
African. *Conical Tower*,
ca. 1500. Stone, 33 by
16 feet. Great Zimbabwe,
Zimbabwe (Rhodesia).

Stone City

In southern Africa lie the ruins of the
Iron Age society known as Great Zimbabwe.
At its peak from A.D. 1100 to 1500, it was
home to about 15,000 Bantu-speaking Shona
people. In Bantu, *Zimbabwe* means "stone
houses." The name reflects the city's
buildings. Skilled masons fit huge granite
boulders and blocks into walls up to 20 feet
thick. The tower above is part of the Great
Enclosure. It is surrounded by a stone wall
that is 820 feet around and 36 feet tall. The
tower itself is made of solid rock; it is not
hollow. How might the Shona have used it?

Sketchbook Journal

**Visualize a city you would have
ruled as head of an empire
in the year A.D. 1100. Draw
a design for your personal
imperial city of stone. Include
all the buildings necessary to
support fifteen thousand
happy citizens—and one wise
and benevolent ruler: you.**

237

Symbolic *Plaques*

Artist unknown, Benin culture. *Plaque,* 17th century. Bronze, 14 ¾ by 15 ½ inches. Nelson-Atkins Museum of Art, Kansas City, MO. Purchase: Nelson Trust. Photo by Jamison Miller.

Which figure in this composition is most important and how can you tell?

Plaques, such as the above, are flat plates, slabs, or tablets that are engraved or cast and used as memorials or for decoration. This plaque was created to decorate the sprawling palace complex in the West African city of Benin. Artists used the size of the people on the plaque to indicate their status. Notice these details:

- The figure in the middle is largest. The attendants to the right and left are either slightly smaller or much smaller.
- The clothing each figure wears is a symbol of his or her status.

Lost Wax

Artists made hundreds of plaques like this one in the sixteenth and seventeenth centuries using a process called **lost wax casting.** With this method, artists can cast metals such as brass or bronze. First, a sculpture is made of wax and then covered with a heat-resistant clay mold. When the clay mold is fired, the wax melts away and is lost, which is how it gets its name. The wax is replaced by hot, liquid metal. When the metal hardens, the mold is removed to reveal the metal sculpture.

Technique Tip

The Midas Touch

If you want to give your sculpture the illusion that it is made of metal, you can apply metallic paint in the form of a paste, but you need to use a light touch. Apply the paste sparingly with a finger wrapped in two layers of cloth. Apply it only to the high points of your sculpture. This simulates an aged metal that is shiny only where it has been rubbed.

Create a Personal Plaque

Using what you have learned about the art of Africa for inspiration, design a plaque with personal meaning.

Materials

- ✓ 12" × 14" sheet of cardboard and cardboard pieces
- ✓ glue and utility knife or scissors ⚠
- ✓ miscellaneous found objects
- ✓ tempera or acrylic paint, paintbrush
- ✓ metallic paint paste and cotton cloth

1 Cut cardboard into the shapes of objects that have a special meaning to you. Glue the objects onto the cardboard sheet.

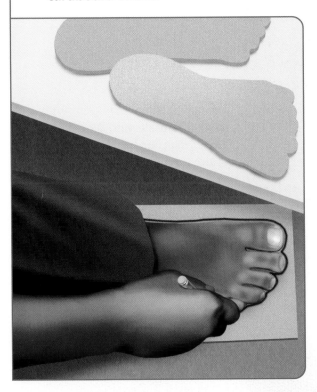

2 Add texture and detail by attaching found objects such as cord, beads, or wood. Let your plaque dry.

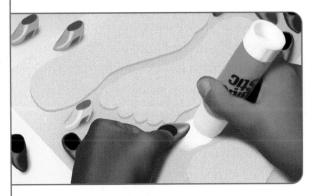

3 Paint your plaque black and let it dry. Use metallic paint to create the illusion that the plaque is bronze or brass.

Review and Reflect

- What shapes and objects did you include in your plaque?
- How did the addition of metal paint enhance or detract from the plaque?
- How does the arrangement of objects reflect your personal meaning?
- Would the meaning of your plaque be clear to a viewer who does not know you? Why or why not?

Lesson 10

Op Art

In the middle of the last century, Western artists, especially in the United States, began to experiment with a branch of abstract art called *optical art*. The techniques of **Op Art,** as it is popularly known, are based on the fact that the eye can be fooled. Op Artists realized that by repeating elements of art, such as lines and shapes, to form a pattern, they could create an illusion of depth and movement.

American Op Artist Richard Anuszkiewicz (1930–) often uses geometric shapes in bright colors to create the illusion of movement on a canvas. In *Glory Red*, the artist created optical sensations using gradual changes in hue and value. The flat surface of the canvas seems to keep shifting, sometimes bending inward and sometimes bowing outward. The squares appear to float above the surface and be part of it at the same time. The effect gets stronger near the center, where the contrast between the red and green colors is strongest. How does repetition unify this composition?

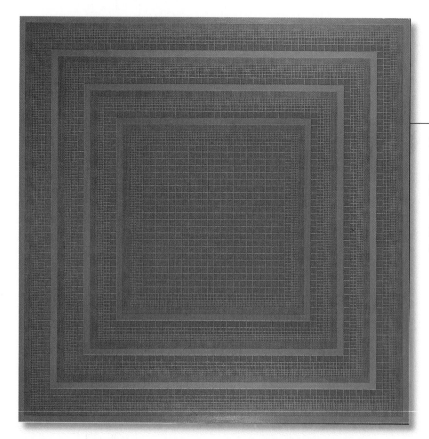

Richard Anuskiewicz. *Glory Red,* 1967. Collection of the artist. © Richard Anuskiewicz licensed by VAGA, New York.

How does the artist's use of color help create an optical illusion?

Lucas Samaras. *Mirrored Room,*
1966. Mirrors on wooden frame,
8 by 8 by 10 feet. Albright-Knox
Art Gallery, Buffalo, NY.

How is this installation an
example of Op Art?

Illusion in Three Dimensions

Most Op Art is two-dimensional, but
Greek-American artist Lucas Samaras (1936–)
created optical illusions in three dimensions.
In the installation above, Samaras lined every
surface in the room with mirrors, including
a chair and table. The mirrors make the
walls, the ceiling, and even the floor seem
to disappear. Viewers can step inside and
experience the dizzying sensation of floating
in space. Can you visualize how your image
might become fragmented in a room like
this? What might the artist be saying with
this installation?

Sketchbook Journal

**Practice making optical
illusions by drawing parallel
lines very close together.
Experiment with the effects
you can create by changing
the contour of the lines.
Create different illusions by
repeating geometric shapes
that gradually increase and
decrease in size.**

Optical *Illusions*

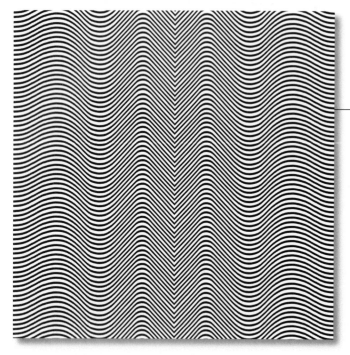

What optical illusion is created by this work of art?

Look at the artwork on this page for a minute and then notice these details:

- The lines ripple at the center of the paper, making the paper seem as if it has been folded or bent.
- If you look at it for a while, the image seems to vibrate because the lines are placed so closely together.

The Eye, Not the I

You have seen how artists use their paintings, sculptures, or computer art to express the way they feel or to offer insight into the subject of their artwork. This is not the case with Op Artists. Op Artists are not interested in representing anything realistic, and they do not want to express personal emotions through their artwork. In fact, they try to take personal expression out of

their art-making process. After arriving at an idea, many Op Artists let assistants use mechanical methods to produce the work of art. How do you think this artistic process affects the meaning of the final work of art?

Technique Tip

Tools of the Trade

Precision is an important part of Op Art. All the lines must be smooth and uniform. To get this type of mechanical perfection, use tools such as a ruler, compass, protractor, French curve, and a fine-point pen. These tools, plus a little bit of patience, will help you get the precision you need.

Studio 10

Create an Op Art Drawing

Use what you have learned to create an Op Art drawing.

Materials

- ✓ white paper
- ✓ scissors ⚠
- ✓ fine-tipped black ink pen
- ✓ glue stick
- ✓ black construction paper
- ✓ ruler, French curve, or other tools (optional)

1 Divide a sheet of white paper into at least eight pieces, like a jigsaw puzzle. Cut the pieces apart with scissors.

2 Draw a curving line through the center of each piece. Create the illusion of depth by drawing lines parallel to the first line.

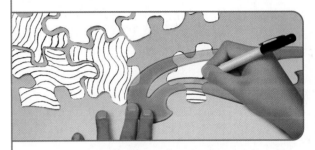

3 Mount the pieces on a single sheet of black construction paper. Leave a one-eighth inch space between each puzzle piece.

Review and Reflect

- Describe the lines you used to create your Op Art drawing.
- How does the arrangement of lines in your drawing affect the viewer's optical perception of it?
- What effect does the puzzle-like arrangement of pieces have on your work of art?
- How could your artwork convey a sense of depth or movement more effectively? Explain.

Create a Pop Art Meal

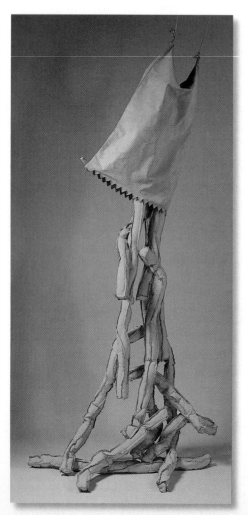

Claes Oldenburg. *Shoestring Potatoes Spilling From a Bag,* 1966. Canvas, kapok, glue and acrylic, 108 by 46 by 42 inches. Collection Walker Art Center, Minneapolis, MN. Gift of the T. B. Walker Foundation, 1966.

Plan

If you are looking at Claes Oldenburg's fries as a side order, you had better have a big appetite and an iron stomach. His nine-foot-tall potatoes are made of canvas and stuffed with kapok, the silky fibers of the ceiba tree. This work of art, along with Oldenburg's artworks on pages 29 and 74, are examples of **Pop Art.** Pop Art, which flourished during the 1960s, uses common objects of popular culture as subjects. It offers a critical and often amusing commentary on various facets of modern life.

- Notice how the scale of the fries is not of standard proportion. How does the scale of the sculpture affect its meaning?
- How could you combine different items of food to create a commentary on modern American life?

Use what you have learned to create a Pop Art place setting, complete with food, that comments on life in modern America.

Sketchbook Journal

Write a list of all the foods you associate with the United States. Beside each item of food, write the country it came from originally. Make a separate list of adjectives that describe Americans' attitudes toward food. Keep these lists in mind as you brainstorm ideas for your Pop Art place setting.

Materials

- ✓ newsprint and pencil
- ✓ construction paper and scissors ⓢ
- ✓ papier-mâché paste and strips
- ✓ self-hardening clay
- ✓ acrylic paint, paintbrushes
- ✓ markers
- ✓ glue

Create

1 Draw ideas for a table place setting, including a place mat, utensils, food, and a place card. Cut your place mat from construction paper and decorate it with markers.

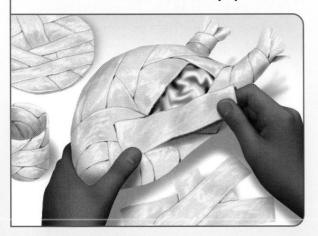

2 Using papier-mâché materials, create your three-dimensional plate and glass. Create some of the food for your meal as well, choosing items whose forms lend themselves to papier mâché.

3 Use self-hardening clay for smaller items such as olives or peas, or curvier items such as a fork or spoon. After the clay and papier-mâché items are dry, paint them realistically.

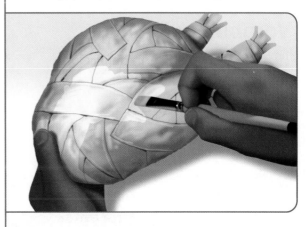

4 Use illuminated lettering or calligraphy to decorate the place card. When all the parts are finished, display the setting at a table. If available, use a tablecloth and centerpiece.

Reflect

- What items of food did you include in your Pop Art meal?
- How did you combine the objects to create a commentary on American life?
- What problems did you encounter while completing your artwork? How did you solve them?
- Would a viewer understand your view of American life after seeing your Pop Art sculpture? Explain.

245

Unit 5 *Review*

Vocabulary Review

A Match each art term below with its definition.

bronze	plaque
calligraphy	hieroglyphics
Pop Art	Op Art
pediment	Gothic
interlace	terra cotta

1. art that creates the illusion of movement and depth by tricking the eye
2. reddish-brown clay
3. square or rectangular relief sculpture that can be attached to a wall or column
4. a flowing style of writing often created with a brush
5. ornate style of architecture that flourished during the Middle Ages
6. design that features curving lines interwoven with images of animals, people, and plants
7. an alloy of copper and tin
8. art that incorporates the images of everyday objects to make a point about modern culture
9. picture writing
10. triangular structure that supports a roof

Artists and Their Art

B Each work of art listed in the box appears in this unit. Match each artwork with its description below.

Terra-cotta Head
Great Sphinx
Stonehenge
David
Guardian Lion
Parthenon

1. ___ is an enormous ancient Egyptian portrait sculpture.
2. The design of many U.S. buildings was inspired by buildings in ancient Greece, such as the ___.
3. ___ by Michelangelo has come to symbolize the ideals of the Renaissance.
4. From the eleventh to fifteenth centuries, artists in western Africa made startlingly lifelike heads of terra cotta and bronze, such as ___.
5. ___ in England is made of huge blocks of stone set in a circle.
6. Chinese artists had to rely on descriptions given by travelers to make sculptures such as ___.

Respond to Art

C Look at *Mosaic of Female Musicians* from the Mogao Grottoes in China. In a class discussion or on a sheet of paper, match each art term below with examples from the mosaic.

Artist unknown, Chinese. *Mosaic of Female Musicians,* A.D. 366–1366. Mogao Grottoes, Dunhuang, China.

Art Terms

1. tint
2. calligraphy
3. overlapping
4. shade
5. rhythm
6. neutral color
7. foreground
8. organic shape

Unit 5 *Review*

Write About Art

Persuasive Paragraph

D Look back at the artworks you saw in this unit. Choose one to write about in a persuasive paragraph. In your paragraph, convince others of the importance of preserving this and other artworks. Copy the chart below and use it for prewriting. Use the completed chart to help you organize your writing. Revise your draft for organization, supporting sentences, and transitions. Check for correct usage, spelling, capitalization, and punctuation errors.

(Artwork Title)

Reason for Preservation	Possible Results if Destroyed

Concluding Sentence:

Your Studio Work

E Answer these questions in your Sketchbook Journal or on a separate sheet of paper.

1. Which era of art history inspired you most to create artwork of your own? Why?
2. What culture from this unit did you most enjoy reading about? What aspects interested you most?
3. What problems did you encounter as you experimented with the art of the historical eras in this unit? How did you solve the problems you encountered?
4. Of the artworks you created in this unit, which was most successful? What makes it a success?

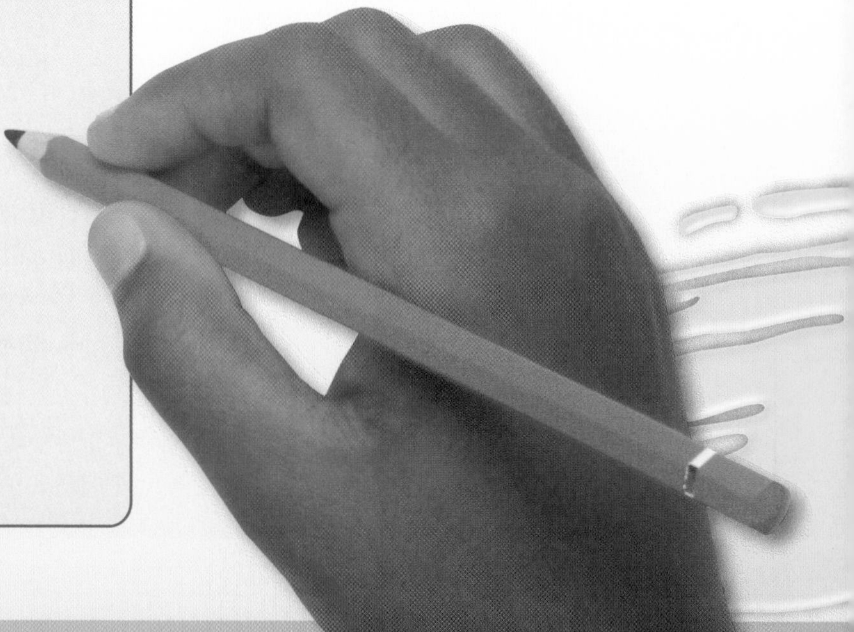

Put It All Together

Pablo Picasso. *Dancer*, 1907. Burstein Collection.

F Discuss or write about Pablo Picasso's painting *Dancer* using the four steps below for viewing artwork critically.

1. **Describe** What is the subject of this work of art? What kinds of colors did the artist use?

2. **Analyze** How can you tell what this abstract figure represents? How did Picasso use lines and color to show the figure? What type of balance does the painting show?

3. **Interpret** What is the mood of this painting? What elements contribute to this mood? What do you think the artist is trying to say with this artwork?

4. **Judge** Spanish artist Pablo Picasso (1881–1973) was inspired by the art of Africa when he first saw it in about 1905. He drew on the elegant and simplified forms of African sculpture as he began to create innovative, abstracted works. Judging from this painting and the information you have read in this unit, how do you think this painting reflects Picasso's interest in African art? How does Picasso's quote below remind you of landscape art from China?

"The hidden harmony is better than the obvious."

—PABLO PICASSO

The art of Pablo Picasso was very influential among artists of the twentieth century.

Harold Cohen. *Meeting on Gauguin's Beach,* 1988. Computer-drawn image hand-painted with oil on canvas, 90 by 68 inches. Collection of Gordon and Gwen Bell.

Unit 6

Careers in Art

Artists work in many industries doing things you might not expect. An artist designed the cow on your milk carton, and the bus you took to school. Artists created the visual effects in the most recent monster movie, and the monster too.

If you choose a career in art, you would put together a collection of your artwork, or **portfolio,** to show prospective employers or buyers. You could work in the **applied arts,** the functional branch of art that includes architecture and costume design, or you could work in **fine arts,** which include drawing, painting, and sculpting. Fine artists create artworks for sale in galleries. They make art for the main purpose of expressing themselves visually.

In this unit you will learn that if you like to draw, paint, or sculpt, or if you just like to be around fine art, you can find a challenging and satisfying career. You also will have an opportunity to practice some of the skills artists in these careers use every day.

About *the Artist*

Hoping to better understand how artists paint, British artist **Harold Cohen** set out in the 1970s to model the painting process on computer. Instead, Cohen "taught" his computer how to paint. Learn more about this pioneer in art and artificial intelligence on page 272.

251

Lesson 1

Computer Artist

Compared to other art media, such as charcoal and oil paint, the computer is new and extraordinarily versatile. An artist can use it to draw and color a two-dimensional work of art. It can be programmed to project images or to control a mechanical drawing arm. Or it can give motion to an entire sculpture. Artists are still only beginning to explore the breadth of art they can create with the help of a computer.

While a graphic artist uses a computer to design images for business use, a **computer artist** uses a computer to create art that is a personal expression. Both begin with the same equipment: computer hardware and software. The **hardware** includes the box and everything in it, such as the wiring, the circuits, and the drives, as well as the keyboard and cables and other equipment that goes with a computer. The **software** is the computer program that makes all that equipment run. There are software programs that allow the user to combine drawing, painting, images, and text in a single document. Other software lets you manipulate a photograph's **pixels,** the dots that form the onscreen image. Another kind of software, called **computer-aided design (CAD) software,** allows artists, architects, engineers, and others to create precise two- and three-dimensional drawings.

The artist used a computer to combine two Leonardo da Vinci artworks, a self-portrait and the *Mona Lisa.*

Joel Slayton. *Markface*, 1981. Computer-enhanced Polaroid print, 68 by 40 inches. © Joel Slayton.

Common Elements, New Art

Most artists see the computer as more than just a tool, because it can be programmed to be any one tool, or many tools at once. For example, an artist can capture a person's portrait with a video camera, then change it on the computer screen by adding text and manipulating the image itself. Notice how, in the image above, the artist created balance, emphasis, and unity. The artist also created a pattern of pixels on the figure's shadow on the left and used repetition by copying the area in the middle of the face. What effect does the artist's use of contrast have on the artwork?

Research

Research the different ways artists have used computers. Create a chart in your Sketchbook Journal to record your research. Include the name of each computer artist, their birth and death dates, nationality, and a brief description of the way the artist used computers to create works of art.

Lillian Schwartz. *Leonardo Morphed to the Mona Lisa,* adapted from "The Art Historian's Computer" in *Scientific American,* April 1995, p. 106. © 1995, Lillian F. Schwartz. All rights reserved.

The artwork above is an example of **morphing,** a technique for gradually changing one image into another. To understand how the image changes, isolate one feature and examine the way it changes from frame to frame. Look at the lips in each frame, for example, and notice these details:

- The expression of the mouth changes from a slight frown in the drawing to a slight smile in the painting.
- The shape of the lips stays almost the same from one frame to the other.

Using Math in Art

Computers help artists morph two-dimensional and three-dimensional images. Software programs let the user specify points on the original image, and link them to corresponding points on the final image. Then the computer uses a mathematical formula to gradually change one image into the other. But if you do not have a computer to morph an image, you can draw each frame.

Technique Tip

Saving Is Good

When using a computer program to manipulate a digital photograph, make sure you work on a copy of your scanned or downloaded image, rather than on the original. When you are happy with a version, save a copy with a new name and keep going. Try more effects, and then save another new copy. That way you can pick the images you want to keep.

Create a Computer-Generated Self-Portrait

Use what you have learned to create a self-portrait with a computer.

Materials

- ✓ digital camera or film camera and scanner
- ✓ computer
- ✓ image manipulation software
- ✓ glue stick or two-sided tape
- ✓ posterboard
- ✓ water-based colored markers

1 Photograph yourself from the shoulders up. Load or scan your photograph into the computer and open it in your software program.

2 Try unusual colors, reverse or repeat your image, or change the angles of your face. Use a pen or paintbrush tool to add lines of color.

3 Print your portrait and attach it to posterboard. Use markers to add designs on the posterboard that extend the background.

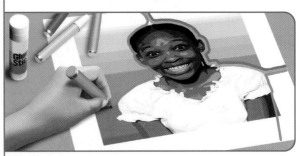

Review and Reflect

- How did you get the photograph into your computer? What software did you use to manipulate the image?
- How did you change the image in the computer?
- Why did you make those changes? How did they affect the mood of the photo?
- Does the background you added on the posterboard enhance your work of art? Explain.

Animator

Think about the animated cartoons you have seen on film or on TV. Who are your favorite characters? What is it that makes them memorable? Behind each of those characters is an animator—or more likely, a team of animators. The job of an **animator** is to bring a character to life by drawing the figure in motion either by hand or on a computer.

An **animation** artist makes still pictures seem to move by creating a series of slightly different images. Each of these images is called a **frame.** Some artists draw each image, or part of it, on transparent acetate, called a **cel.** The images are then photographed and transferred to film. Many of the animations made this way were inspired by cartoon strips or fairy tales.

Modern computer animation has cut much of the repetition out of that difficult and time-consuming process. Computer software programs allow computer animators to draw, color, and shade on screen. Some animators begin with hand-drawn character illustrations. They then scan the images into a computer to create the animation. This technique saves countless hours of hand-drawing each movement of the characters.

Another animation method is called **stop action,** or stop motion, in which a still model is photographed, moved slightly, and photographed again until each motion is captured. A Russian art student was one of the first to use this method in 1912. He used dolls and bugs as his models.

Hanna Barbera Studios. *Cartoon Animation Still.* © Hanna Barbera Studios.

Eddie Pittman. *Legends of the Night Sky: Orion,* 2002. Four-color animation still. © 2003 Audio Visual Imagineering.

The four-color animation above began as line drawings of the character.

Eddie Pittman. *Legends of the Night Sky: Orion,* 2002. Character illustrations. © 2003 Audio Visual Imagineering.

Characterization

An animation studio employs hundreds of artists to make an animated film. A visual-development artist works with others to create the look of an animated film and its characters. A layout artist designs the background in which the characters move. The background painter then paints it. But it is the animators who give characters their personality. They can do it with pen and paint, or they can be Computer Generated Imagery (CGI) animators. These artists create characters on computer. To make a character interesting and memorable, an animator gives each character a unique way of speaking, moving, and acting.

Deborah Blau. *Storyboard for TV Commercial,* 1989. Markers on layout paper, mounted on storyboard matte, 15 by 20 inches. © Deborah Blau.

Action Speaks Louder

Storyboard artists must be adept at communicating plot through action. Whether the artist draws each frame by hand or uses a storyboarding program, the storyboard is the map of the production.

A storyboard does not include every frame in the film, however. Instead, it depicts each scene and what is essential in that scene. Under each drawing is often a written description of the scene, along with a description of the mood and setting in that scene. Other information on the storyboard can include type of shot, description of scene and action, camera angles, and cuts.

A storyboard artist creates the drawings that show the sequence of scenes and actions in an animation. Each episode of a series has a **storyboard** that determines the angles used and the pacing of each scene. Storyboards are also used in the production of movies, music videos, and Web pages.

Some storyboards, such as the one above by Deborah Blau, are created to show the scenes for a TV commercial. Each frame of this storyboard shows a scene involving a henhouse. Notice how the images show the progression of the commercial, from the first frame to the last. The once quiet henhouse suddenly becomes a flurry of egg-producing hens.

Technique Tip

Act Out

To be an animator, you have to be part actor too. While you are working out the movements you want to draw, get into those positions yourself. Understanding how you are balanced and where your weight is will help you translate your position into your character's body.

Studio 2

Create a Storyboard

Use the characters you drew in your Sketchbook Journal to create a storyboard for the climactic scene of an animated feature.

Materials

✓ paper
✓ pencils and water-based markers
✓ white drawing paper

1 Brainstorm ideas for a scene using your characters. Write down each major action and any dialogue you want to include.

2 Divide a sheet of paper into the number of frames you will need.

3 Fill each frame of your storyboard with drawings that show the action.

Review and Reflect

* Describe the scene you chose to show in your storyboard.
* How do the images you chose enhance the drama of the scene?
* How did this activity change the way you think about telling a story through animation?
* Do you think your finished storyboard would make an interesting scene? Explain.

Lesson 3
Special Effects Artist

What do you do if you are a movie director and you need to show a tornado ripping through a town? Or you need a cockpit fire at thirty thousand feet, or a herd of stampeding dinosaurs? Call a special effects artist and no one gets hurt. **Special effects artists** are masters with multimedia. They combine sound, text, images, and animation to create creatures and situations that would be impossible, or at least unwise, in the real world.

You have seen actors do amazing things in movies. They can fly through a darkened city or watch from a lifeboat as a massive ocean liner sinks in the distance. One way that special effects artists create these kinds of images is by filming actors against a blue background called a **blue screen.** The scenery, like the darkened city or the vast ocean, is supplied in the form of a **matte painting,** a background painted on glass or created with a computer. Special effects artists combine the two images into one. This process, called **compositing,** is done by burning or recording the combined images onto a single piece of film by using either photographic or computer equipment. The goal is to make it appear as though the image had never been separate.

Judith Crow. *Titanic,* 1997. TM and Copyright © 20th Century Fox Film Corp. All rights reserved. Courtesy Everett Collection.

Titanic had more than 450 special effects shots.

All the extra work that goes into a movie like this is expensive. *Spider-Man* cost an estimated $140 million to make and employed 200 visual effects artists.

Getting Into Sync

Movies like *Spider-Man* use a motion control camera to achieve certain special effects. This type of camera is controlled by a computer. It can be programmed to move in exactly the same way, repeatedly. This control gives special-effects artists the ability to shoot different elements of a scene in precisely the same way. As a result, individual images fit together when they are combined in the composite image. In *Spider-Man*, the visual effects team had an additional challenge: moving between shots of the actor, the stunt double who takes the place of the actor in difficult or dangerous scenes, and the CGI digital Spidey.

Sketchbook Journal

Design some backgrounds you would use for the climactic scene of an animated feature film. Use the characters and scene you created in Studio 2 or think up new ones. Draw a variety of views of the interiors and exteriors. Add drama by choosing unusual perspectives or using high contrast.

Doug Trumbull. *Star Trek, The Movie.* Courtesy Everett Collection.

Special effects artists create objects in different ways. A whole world of materials is open to an artist who wants to create a model of even the most fantastic objects. The Starship Enterprise, for example, was modeled to scale with plastic molded around a metal frame, and then painted. Notice these details:

- The images are composites, uniting the ship and the background in one frame.
- The ship looks realistic, once placed with its star-filled background.

Other Movie Jobs

If you want to work in the movies, but not with special effects, there are other jobs that require art skills. Directors, cinematographers, art directors, and set designers all contribute to the final outcome of a film. The director shapes a film by guiding it from script to screen. The art director designs the look of the film. Set designers make miniature and full-sized sets, and draw outdoor and indoor scenes. The cinematographer works with the photographer so that each shot in the film contributes to the overall effect.

Technique Tip

Cutting with a Utility Knife

Do not rush or press too hard. Make several passes with the blade rather than trying to make a cut in a single pass. Keep your blade sharp by replacing it regularly. A dull blade is more dangerous than a sharp one. If you can, use small clamps to hold the wood while you cut it.

Studio 3

Create a Model

Use what you have learned to create the model of a vehicle for a movie that is set one hundred years in the future.

Materials

- ✓ newsprint
- ✓ pencil
- ✓ balsa wood
- ✓ utility knife ⚠
- ✓ found objects, such as bottle tops, toy wheels, and pieces of plastic
- ✓ glue and wire

1 Visualize how the world might be in one hundred years. Draw designs for a vehicle that people would use in your future world.

2 Use your sketches as a guide. As you work, keep in mind the mood of the setting you imagined.

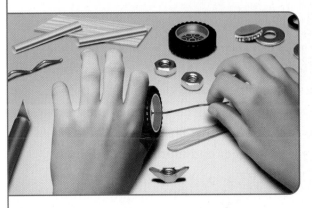

3 Combine found objects with objects you construct. Attach all the pieces securely.

Review and Reflect

- Describe your world of the future and the type of vehicle you chose to create.
- How did the setting you imagined affect the materials used to make your vehicle?
- How did the materials you had to work with affect the design?
- What would you do differently if you were to make another model?

Architect

Have you ever thought about designing homes or office buildings—planning the rooms and spaces and the way they would look? Perhaps you should consider being an architect. Architects design homes, office buildings, and other structures. And as cities get bigger and more crowded, many architects have become **urban designers.** They are interested in the design of entire cities, from the layout of roads and parks to the preservation of the natural environment.

Architects consider three things when designing a structure: the way a building looks, what people do in it, and how it is made. The relationship between those elements has changed over the centuries. At the beginning of the twentieth century, Bauhaus was the cutting-edge style.

Bauhaus was an art, architecture, and design school founded in Germany in 1919. Bauhaus influenced all areas of art. In architecture, the Bauhaus influence was evident in the simplified forms. It also focused on the purpose of the building and the use of industrial materials, like glass, steel, and chrome. Bauhaus was part of the larger Modern architecture movement.

Emerging at the beginning of the twentieth century, architects of the Modern style thought buildings should not use elements taken from other time periods. **Postmodern** architects, who came along in the 1960s, disagreed. They created buildings that combined elements of many different architectural styles.

Bauhaus buildings tend to be unadorned boxes of glass, steel, and concrete.

Mies van der Rohe. *Seagram Building,* 1954–1958, New York. Ezra Stoller, © Esto. All rights reserved.

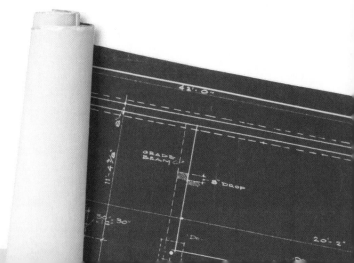

Rebecca Binder. *Information Computer Sciences/Engineering Research Facility,* 1991. University of California, Irvine (Phase III). Photograph courtesy of Mary Ann Sullivan, Bluffton College, Bluffton, OH.

Design Considerations

When designing a building, an architect first considers who will use the building. The rooms in a hospital are arranged in a different way than the rooms in an office building because people use them for different purposes. Architects consider the way traffic will flow and what workspaces are necessary. They also plan the lighting, heating, and cooling for a structure. Look at the building above. Would you want to work in this building? Why or why not?

Sketchbook Journal

Think of a structure you would like to design. Make notes in your Sketchbook Journal about what kind of structure it is and how it would be used. Use diagrams to work out ideas for traffic flow and arrangement of rooms. Draw the exterior of the building, blending styles from different periods.

Ricardo Legorreta Vilchis. *San Antonio Library,* 1999. San Antonio, TX.

Architecture for Everyone

There is still disagreement about an exact definition of Postmodern style. It began as a reaction against the Modern movement, which some people believed to be stale and boring. Modern architects created efficient designs without decoration, but Postmodern architects added extravagant color and exaggerated detail.

Postmodernists celebrate not only fine art and architecture but also pop culture. They include pop culture references as well as historical references in their designs. Postmodernism is often referred to as a populist style—a style for the people.

The Postmodern architect of this building used light, color, water, humor, and conscience in his design. He wanted visitors to admire the interesting architecture of the library, but also to want to stay and read. The two elements that tie the design together reflect the qualities of Postmodern design:

- Strong, simple, geometric shapes
- Bright, intense colors

Do you think the architect used these same Postmodern elements on the library's interior? Why or why not?

Technique Tip

Creating Texture

You can create the illusion of texture using colored pencils to simulate the building materials you might use in a structure. A sharp point has a very different effect than a dull one. Try pressing lightly with the tip of your pencil and then gradually press harder. Lean your pencil to the side and use the long part of the point. Layer colors to create depth.

Studio 4

Design a Postmodern Facade

Use what you have learned about Postmodern architectural styles to create a unique building facade that is whimsical and surprising.

Materials

- ✓ pencil and 18" × 22" white paper
- ✓ ruler and protractor
- ✓ ink and colored pencils
- ✓ watercolors, brushes, and water
- ✓ black posterboard or heavy paper
- ✓ glue stick

1 Decide if your design will be for the exterior of a private home or a public building. Conduct research to get ideas.

2 Design on white paper. Use a variety of media to show building materials, such as brick and stone.

3 Mount your work on black posterboard, leaving a two-inch border.

Review and Reflect

- Describe the size, shape, and use of your building facade.
- Describe some of the Postmodern elements you used in your design.
- What types of materials would your building be made of?
- Would you enjoy using the building you designed? Explain.

Costume Designer

Calvin Southwell. *Fashion Design #4.* Photo by Andres Aquino, FashionSyndicatePress.com.

Imagine a movie set in the Middle Ages. The scene is inside a dank stone castle. A long table is set with pewter mugs and plates piled high with steaming food. The guests arrive, each dressed splendidly in blue jeans and T-shirts. Wait. What is going on? Somebody forgot the costumes, the clothing characteristic of the time period. **Costume designers** help bring a story to life. Their well-researched and designed costumes help a play or film seem more authentic.

Large theater companies have costume designers and wardrobe masters on staff. Smaller companies often use freelance designers. Film and television studios have their own costume departments.

Costume designers need an excellent grasp of color, texture, and style. They gain some of this knowledge through the study of art history. They often use paintings and sculptures of earlier artists in their research. The more accurate the costume is to the period, the more effective it will be with audiences and the actor who wears it.

Knowledge of fabrics is also an important part of costume design. If the play or movie is set in modern times, the fabric choices are fairly simple. A play or movie set in the Middle Ages may prove more difficult since many of today's fabrics were not available during that period. Each aspect of a costume's design makes it an important tool in helping tell a visual story.

Virginia Yazzie-Ballenger. *Turquoise Dress Design.* Photograph © 2000 by LeRoy De Jolie, Navajo photographer.

In the Name of Fashion

Academy Award-winning costume designer Edith Head (1897–1981) once said, "What a costume designer does is a cross between magic and camouflage. We create the illusion of changing the actors into what they are not. We ask the public to believe that every time they see a performer on the screen, he's become a different person." Some of her designs inspired trends in everyday fashions.

The designs of other costume designers also affect trends in retail design. Consumers clamor for clothing similar to the garments they have seen stars wear on television or in the movies. Celebrities generate millions of dollars for the fashion industry this way.

Visual Culture

Look through several fashion magazines and examine how people and their clothing are presented. Study items in both editorial (the part designed by the magazine staff) and advertising (space that is paid for). How are they similar? How do they differ? Make notes about what you find.

Lois De Armond. *Celtic Warrior,* character and costume. Designed and illustrated by Lois De Armond.

To create historically accurate costumes, designers use their art history research as well as research on fashion history. History is helpful even if the story is set in the future. Costume designers often take ideas from the past to create the fashions of the future. Notice these details in the costume above:

- The curving linear patterns on the jacket, belts, and cape are inspired by designs made by the Celts, who lived in Europe from about 700 B.C. to A.D. 100.
- The use of the Celtic design and the limited palette of colors create unity.

The Process

To create costumes for a production, the designer first reads the play or script and consults with the director and scenic designer. He or she then makes rough sketches of all the costumes. When the director approves them, the costume designer searches for appropriate fabrics. After the cast is chosen, the costume designer finalizes the costume drawings. Experienced cutters, drapers, and fitters can then begin to make the designs a reality.

Technique Tip

Fashion in Art

Costume designers often turn to paintings and sculptures to find out how people dressed in different periods throughout history. You can do the same thing by visiting virtual museums on the Web. A quick way to find historically accurate images is to use a search engine. Use keywords such as *Renaissance* (or other time period), *painting,* and *museum*.

Studio 5

Design a Costume

Use what you have learned to design a costume for a Renaissance fair.

Materials

✓ paper
✓ pencils
✓ watercolors and water-based markers
✓ brushes and a container with water
✓ pen and India ink

1 **Research Renaissance-era clothing. Choose a character to portray, such as a noble or a peasant, and make notes about their dress.**

2 **Use pencil to lightly draw your costume design. Check that your details are historically accurate.**

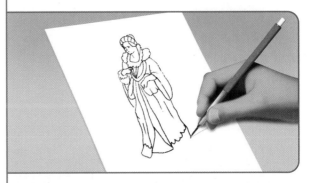

3 **Use watercolors to show the texture and color of the fabrics in your design. When it dries, outline your drawing with India ink.**

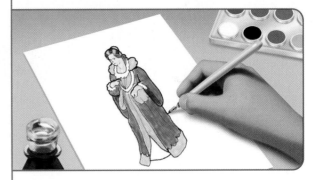

Review and Reflect

- What kind of costume did you design?
- What was most difficult about designing a historically accurate costume?
- What would you do differently next time?
- Would your costume be comfortable to wear in your climate? How do you think the original Renaissance wearer felt about his or her clothes?

Meet *the Artist*

Harold Cohen

Harold Cohen was one of Britain's leading abstract artists when he began learning to program computers. Although museums around the world still display his abstract work, Cohen is best known for transforming the computer from a mere processor of art into a machine that can make paintings in much the same way a human can.

Harold Cohen demonstrates AARON's drawing and painting "skills."

"If what AARON is making is not art, what is it exactly, and in what ways, other than its origin, does it differ from the 'real thing'?"—HAROLD COHEN

A Permanent Sabbatical

Tired of the London art world in the late 1960s, Cohen moved to California. He met a graduate student in the Music Department who showed him some of the basic concepts of programming. Cohen used his new skills to solve a problem he had been working on for years. He wanted to understand the process that artists use when they paint a picture.

The Birth of AARON

Cohen wrote a computer program to model the process that artists use when painting. His first version, called AARON, could create only simple shapes without perspective or spatial relationships. Cohen has since refined both his software and his hardware. AARON can now paint and add shading to its drawings of people and objects.

To teach a computer to draw people in their environments, Cohen wrote software describing the way people look and move and setting rules for the physical world. He included a random-number generator to determine each action the computer will take. As a result, each drawing or painting AARON makes is unique.

AARON does not just take human direction to create an image designed by a human. Instead, Cohen has created a computer that acts like an artist.

Talk About It

Look back at *Meeting on Gauguin's Beach* on page 250. It was drawn by AARON and painted by Cohen. Is it a successful work of art? Why or why not?

The Life of Harold Cohen

1928 —————— 1928
Harold Cohen is born

1945

1966
Cohen represents the United Kingdom as an abstract painter at the Venice Bienale

While a visiting professor at UCSD, Cohen meets a graduate student, who teaches him to program

1962

1968 —————

1973 —————
Artificial Intelligence Laboratory of Stanford University invites Cohen to be Guest Scholar

Tate Gallery in London hosts demonstration of AARON as it draws

1979

1983 —————

1985 —————
Cohen represents the United States at the World's Fair in Japan

World's Fair, Japan

1995
Exhibits AARON's first painting at the Computer Museum in Boston

1996

Cohen at Computer Museum exhibit

273

Look *and Compare*

The Medium and the Message

Even though they are so different, both of the images on page 275 can be described as computer art. It is that flexibility that attracts artists to the medium. There is much speculation about the future direction of art made with computers. Some still question whether computer art is art at all. But no matter how it is made, it is the finished product by which the viewer decides if it is art or merely lines on paper.

Computer Artist

The artwork at the top of page 275 looks like a traditional oil-on-canvas painting, inspired, perhaps, by the bright colors of Matisse. But this painting actually was made by Harold Cohen's computer, AARON. The program, not Cohen, made each of the decisions about how to arrange shapes and apply color. Do you think the painting looks like it was made by a computer? The program is designed to imitate the process that a painter goes through when making a work of art. Does that mean the computer is creating art? If it is creating art, does that make the computer an artist?

Computer Art

Drawing in Time was created using a computer as a tool. It was the artist, Sonia Landy Sheridan, who made each of the decisions about how to manipulate the image. Sheridan works with computers because she appreciates the range of things she can do with them. She often uses software to incorporate photography, drawing, morphing, and colorizing into one image. What point do you think the artist is making with this image?

Harold Cohen. *Untitled,* 1995. AARON-generated, ink on paper, 36 by 48 inches. Private collection.

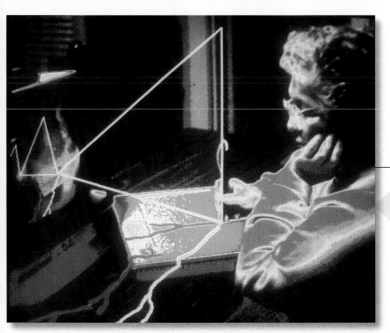

Sonia Landy Sheridan. *Drawing in Time,* 1982. Ektachrome print, computer generated with black-and-white video, 16 ⅝ by 27 inches. © Sonia Sheridan.

Compare & Contrast

- Which image seems more like "computer art"? Why?

- Harold Cohen said, "Art to some degree has always been a commentary on the nature of art itself." How do these artworks reflect that idea?

Lesson 6

Product Designer

The style of the fork you eat with, the chair you sit on, and the bicycle you ride each began in the mind of an artist. Product designers use the elements of art and the principles of design to create things people can use. Door knobs, automobiles, toys, computers, furniture, lamps, and toothbrushes all were created by an industrial designer to make life more efficient, attractive, and fun.

Product designers are a kind of industrial designer, the creative people who design the products, machines, and equipment used by modern society. They determine how a product's use, or **function,** will be reflected in its form, or height, width, and depth. For example, look at the design of the containers to the right. The designer created a simple yet striking form that could serve a variety of functions.

Product designers combine artistic talent with many other skills. They research the way a product is used, understand customers' needs, and then consider marketing, materials, and production methods to create the most functional, appealing, and sellable design.

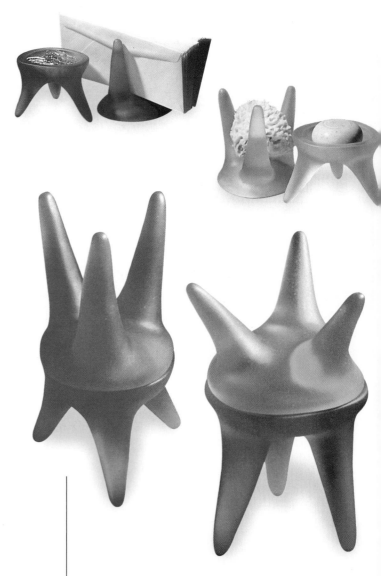

Roberto Zanon and Satomi Yoshida. *Urchin Container,* 1996. Resin. Benza, Inc., Italy.

Why do you think the designer chose these colors?

Bridget Means and Giovanni Pellone. *Folding Trash Can,* 1996. Recycled cardboard, for Zago. Benza, Inc., U.S.A.

Choosing Materials

Product designers come up with designs for new products and redesign old products as well. They consider not only the look and function of the product but also the materials used to make it. A successful design incorporates materials that last the life of the product.

Look at the *Folding Trash Can* designs above. What are they made from? Is this a good choice of materials for the products? The designer has included photographs of urban images, such as a fire hydrant, a manhole cover, and a trash can. How do these images enhance the design?

Think of products that you use on a daily basis, such as a pen, a toothbrush, and a drinking glass. Consider how the shape and form of each product, and the materials from which it is made, affect your use of it.

Visual Culture

Look around you for product designs that appeal to you. Make sketches, take photographs, or cut photos from magazines. What catches your eye about the design? Does it function properly? Is it innovative? Make notes on your photographs or drawings about what you think is successful and what could be improved.

277

Design *for Everyday Products*

Laurene Leon Boym. *Cloud Nine Bathroom Accessories,* 1999. Benza, Inc., U.S.A.

Sometimes the form of a product is inspired by more than its mere function. Look at the products above and notice these details:

- The name of the product includes the words *cloud nine.*
- The outline of each form suggests a stylized cloud.
- The products' forms and color provide a unifying theme.

Hurry Up and Buy

Many products, including health and hygiene products, are part of a trend in the design industry called *artificially accelerated obsolescence.* This means designers try to come up with designs so appealing that customers will replace their old products before they are worn out. The trend started in the fashion industry, where it is now common for consumers to wear items of clothing for just one season. It is behavior like this that prompted the term *throwaway society* to describe the United States and other industrialized countries.

Technique Tip

Protect Your Clothes

Dye can stain your hands and your clothes. When you are working with dye, wear rubber gloves and a smock or rubber apron. If you are using the hot-dying method on a stove, be sure to continually stir the items you are dyeing. If you quit, the items will settle and dye will not reach each surface evenly. The result will be a patchy dye job.

Design an Everyday Product

Use what you have learned to create an everyday product using a common form.

Materials

- ✓ newsprint and paper
- ✓ various items, such as foam balls, cones, and squares; wooden dowels and craft sticks; plastic kitchen utensils; and cardboard
- ✓ tape and glue
- ✓ ink, dye, or acrylic paint
- ✓ brushes, paper towels, and water
- ✓ pencil

1 Think of a common form and brainstorm ideas for new ways to use it. Choose the idea you think would sell best and draw it.

2 Work from your sketch to create a model of the form. Use whatever materials will make your model look most authentic.

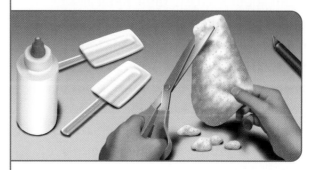

3 Use acrylic paint, ink, or dye to add color to your product. Be sure to use a color scheme that you think will help your product sell.

Review and Reflect

- Describe the purpose of your product. How did you make it?
- How did you choose the colors you used? How do the colors make your product more appealing?
- How is your product an improvement over similar products?
- Does your model look authentic? Do you think your product would sell? Explain.

Lesson 7

Furniture Designer

From about 3000 B.C. until about 1940, chairs did not change very much. A thirty-five hundred-year-old Egyptian stool looks and functions pretty much like a sixty-five-year-old American stool. But new materials like plastics and new methods of production have given designers more flexibility—literally. The new materials let **furniture designers** create chairs, desks, tables, sofas, and other furniture forms that were not possible a century ago. These alternatives fit right in with Postmodernism.

The basic purposes of furniture have remained the same. Furniture design, the way the furniture looks, has varied from elaborately decorated to unadorned and simple. The **decorative design** of the nineteenth century was still popular at the beginning of the twentieth century. It began to change with designers incorporating flowers, leaves, and the twisting lines of vines into furniture and graphic design. Thus, a new style, known as **Art Nouveau,** was born.

Bauhaus ideas began creeping into furniture designs in the 1930s. After World War II, people were able to afford more furniture, and they also moved around more often. So furniture became smaller and easier to move and carry.

Lawrence Alma-Tadema, designer. *Armchair,* ca. 1884. Mahogany with veneered inlaid decoration. Made by Norman Johnstone. Victoria and Albert Museum, London.

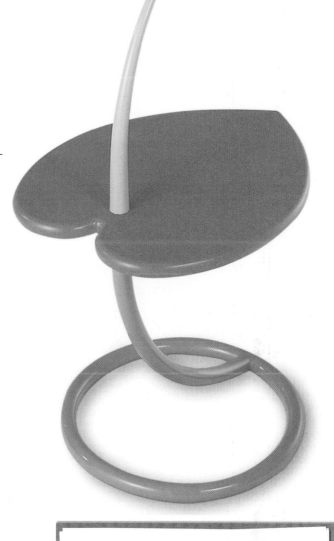

Masanori Umeda. *Anthurium Table,* 1990.
Designed for Edra, Italy.

Color, Form, and Humor

As in architecture, the Modern furniture
of the first half of the twentieth century
featured streamlined forms mass-produced
from Industrial-age materials. Postmodern
furniture designers reacted to what they saw
as the bleak Modern forms by introducing
bright colors and a hint of humor to their
designs. Look at the table above. It was
inspired by the heart-shaped form of a
tropical flower called an anthurium. Why
do you think the designer chose to model
his table after a flower? What elements
make the table Postmodern?

Sketchbook Journal

Draw a design for a
Postmodern rug that combines
design motifs from different
eras. For example, you could
combine themes from ancient
Egypt with those from modern
popular culture, such as a fast
food chain or a musical group.
Use markers to add color to
your design.

Masanori Umeda. *Getsuen Chair,* 1990. Designed for Edra, Italy.

Finding a Market

Like other commercial designers, furniture designers research the ways their products will be used and their customers' needs. They combine this information with their knowledge of materials and production methods to create a piece of furniture that is attractive and that they think will sell well. Who do you think would be most likely to buy a chair like this?

Look at the bold flower form of the chair above. What kind of flower do you think inspired it? Like a sculpture, the chair uses elements such as balance, repetition, rhythm, color, and form to create unity. Even the material the artist chose contributes to the overall form, giving the finished work soft, plump curves. Notice these details:

- The form of the chair is symmetrically balanced on either side of a vertical center line.
- The repeated forms of the petals create a rhythm within the chair's design.
- The chair's color and form reflect a Postmodern design.

Technique Tip

Building with Cardboard

Cardboard is a sturdy building material for models, but remember, it is essentially a type of thick paper. If it gets wet, it will be weaker. A flat cardboard surface that has been bent or creased will not be as sturdy as one that is flat. Also, for furniture legs and struts, try creating tubes from the cardboard. The structure will be much more sturdy that way.

Studio 7

Design a Chair with a Natural Form

Use what you have learned to create a chair model with a form that is inspired by nature.

Materials

- ✓ newsprint, pencil, colored markers
- ✓ glue, tape, scissors ⚠
- ✓ sheets of corrugated cardboard and cardboard tubes
- ✓ other supplies, such as papier-mâché materials, cloth, foam, twine, raffia, or beads
- ✓ acrylic or tempera paint
- ✓ brushes, water container

1 **Make several sketches of designs for a Postmodern chair with a natural form. Indicate your color choices with colored marker.**

2 **Fold or cut the cardboard to construct the basic form of the chair. Add other materials for texture and interest.**

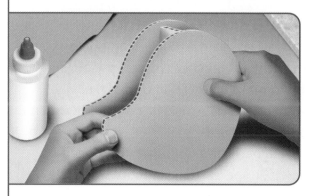

3 **Add color and pattern with paint or other materials, such as beads and raffia.**

Review and Reflect

- Describe the design and form of your chair.
- How do the elements of art you used add interest to your chair design?
- Where in a house could your chair be used? Why? In what ways could your chair be described as Postmodern?
- What color(s) would you paint a room in which you placed your chair? Why?

Lesson 8

Installation Artist

Artists in the 1960s started looking for a way to create art that could not be commodified. In other words, they did not want to make objects that could be easily bought and sold. Artists began to experiment with **installations,** works of art composed of multiple parts and designed for a specific space. The space can be indoors, such as a museum, or outdoors, such as a field or a park. The parts can be anything: paintings, video, sculpture, or found objects. Whatever the artist needs to communicate a message can be used as an element in an installation.

The photograph below shows an indoor installation. What is the subject of the installation? What point do you think the artist was trying to make?

Outdoor installations can be massive and difficult to assemble. Bulgarian-born American artist Christo (1935–) is known for his enormous outdoor installations. He often uses hundreds of assistants in these projects. Christo's installations have included enormous sheets of fabric stretched between poles in a Colorado canyon. Other artists of outdoor installations may use natural materials such as sand to create sculptures on a beach. Works like these are often seen by people who do not go to museums, exposing a new segment of the population to fine art.

COLLECTANEA

Renee Green. *Import/Export Funk Office,* 1992. Collection of the Museum of Contemporary Art, Los Angeles, CA. Gift of Wilhelm and Gabi Schürmann. Photo by Andrea Stappert.

How long do you think it took the artist to set up this installation?

Dan Flavin. *Greens Crossing Greens (to Piet Mondrian who lacked green),* 1966. Fluorescent light fixtures with green lamps: 2 and 4 feet, 53 by 230 ¼ by 147 inches overall. Solomon R. Guggenheim Museum, New York.

Forever or a Day

Look at the installation above. The artist used florescent light fixtures with green bulbs to cast a glow on every surface in the room. The glow of the lamps contrasts with the green light that fills the room. Although this installation is a permanent part of a museum collection, some installations are temporary.

If an installation lasts only a short time, a record of it must be made. Since future historians will not be able to view a temporary installation to study it, as they can with a painting or sculpture, this record will be very important. Why might an artist choose to create a temporary, rather than a permanent, installation?

Sketchbook Journal

Think of an emotion you could express in an installation. Would it be more appropriate indoors or out? Make a series of sketches to explore your ideas. Include the surroundings in your drawings to give a more accurate idea of how the finished work would relate to its environment.

David Hammons. *Skillets in the Closet,* 1988. Installation. Collection of the California African American Foundation. Courtesy of the California African American Museum, Los Angeles, CA.

One reason an installation can be effective is because it gives the artist an opportunity to place ordinary objects in a new context. An artist can emphasize an object by removing it from its everyday use, making the viewer think about it in a new way. *Skillets in the Closet* features a common household tool. Notice these details as you study the installation:

- Both the cabinet and the skillets have been isolated from their usual kitchen setting.
- The skillets are made of cast iron and look like they have been well used.

Ideas and Emotions

Like other artists, installation artists use their artwork to communicate political ideas, explore current issues, or express personal emotions. By combining everyday objects in an unusual setting, an artist can convey a variety of ideas and emotions. What do you think the artist was trying to convey in this installation?

Technique Tip

Simulating Texture

Reproducing a texture like marble requires practice. Apply a base coat of paint. Stipple a color onto the dried base coat, and manipulate the pattern with a brush. Use a smaller brush to stipple two other related colors. Create veins in a fourth color. To learn more, go online or to the library and research faux painting.

Design an Installation

Use what you have learned to design a model of an installation that conveys an emotion.

Materials

- ✓ corrugated cardboard sheets
- ✓ glue
- ✓ scissors or a utility knife ⚠
- ✓ various found objects
- ✓ acrylic paint, brushes, and a container with water

1 Decide on an outdoor or indoor installation. Gather the materials you will need, keeping in mind the emotion you are interpreting.

2 Create the artwork's surroundings out of cardboard. Paint it to resemble the place where you would show your installation.

3 Finish the model using the materials you gathered. Paint it to represent the materials you would use in the full-scale installation.

Review and Reflect

- What objects or shapes and forms did you use in your model?
- How do the objects you chose work together to reflect an emotion?
- What other elements of your installation help convey the emotion you chose?
- Do you think other people would understand the reference to emotion in your installation? Why or why not?

Portfolio *Project*

Create an Art Careers Exhibit

Exhibit spaces are designed to showcase artworks and to offer information to visitors.

Plan

Artists in each art career have exhibited their artwork at one time or another. They may have shown it in local or national galleries. Or perhaps it was displayed for prospective employers. Exhibiting their artwork helps make others aware of the artists' talents and skills. It also offers visitors an opportunity to observe and appreciate visual art and to learn more about the processes involved in its creation. As you plan for an exhibit, ask yourself the following questions:

- What setting or space would best showcase the artwork? How should the exhibit be arranged?
- What would attract viewers to the exhibit space? How will viewers interact with the exhibit? What information should they know?
- How can the elements of art and principles of design be used to plan the exhibit space?

Use what you have learned about visual art to create an exhibit showcasing careers in art. Work with your teacher and classmates to find an appropriate location in your school or community.

Sketchbook Journal

Plan a layout for exhibiting each art career. Decide how each career would best be featured. Draw the location layout and include display areas. Consider how visitors will navigate through the area. Work with classmates to combine the best features of each student's sketch into a final plan.

Materials

✓ Unit 6 artwork from your portfolio
✓ 8 ½" × 11" white paper and a pen
✓ colored construction paper
✓ cardboard or cardboard boxes (optional)
✓ tempera paint and brushes (optional)
✓ scissors ⚠
✓ tape, glue, and glue stick
✓ exhibit location layout sketch

Create

1 Select one of your artworks from this unit that reflects an art career that interests you. Write a description of the creative process you used to make the artwork. Include your name, the artwork title, and why you chose the career you did.

2 Conduct research on the career. Write a brief, informative description of the career and what opportunities it offers. Combine your research with that of classmates who chose the same career. Work together to design your display.

3 Use cardboard or boxes to create displays for three-dimensional artworks. Mount two-dimensional artworks, the career description, and your process summary on colored construction paper.

4 Use your layout sketches as a guide to arrange your area of the exhibit. Consider how lighting in the exhibit location can best showcase the artworks. Mount the artworks and information materials on the wall or displays.

Reflect

- Describe your display area of the exhibit.
- What elements of art and principles of design did you use to arrange your display?
- What message does your display give about the art career you chose?
- Do you think your exhibit display will encourage others to choose the art career you did? Explain.

Unit 6 *Review*

Vocabulary Review

A Match each art term below with its definition.

> stop action   Art Nouveau
> installation   storyboard
> morphing   compositing
> software   applied art
> Bauhaus   hardware

1. functional arts, such as architecture and furniture design
2. style in which artists were inspired by the forms of flowers, leaves, and vines
3. computer programs
4. combining two or more images onto a single piece of film
5. art made for a specific indoor or outdoor space
6. a series of drawings that show the action in a proposed film
7. the physical components of a computer
8. a form of animation in which models are photographed, moved, and then photographed again, repeatedly
9. influential German school of art and design
10. the technique of gradually changing one thing into another

Artists and Their Careers

B Each art-related profession listed in the box appears in this unit. Match each job title with its description below.

> *special effects artist*
> *product designer*
> *architect*
> *computer artist*
> *costume designer*
> *animator*

1. designs buildings
2. gives movement to an object or drawing
3. creates designs for objects people use every day
4. conducts research into historic styles of dress and designs clothes for actors
5. creates unlikely or impossible images and sounds for motion pictures
6. uses computers to make works of art that express personal feelings and ideas

Respond to Art

C Look at each of the four photographs representing art careers. Then choose the art term below that best matches the letters in each photograph.

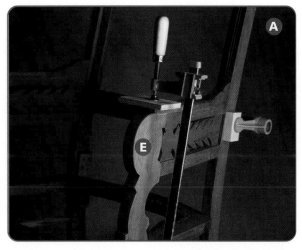

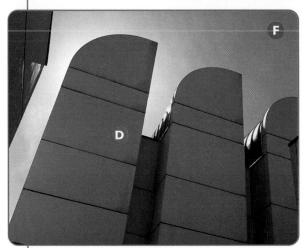

Art Terms

1. fashion
2. Bauhaus
3. furniture designer
4. costume designer
5. animator
6. decorative design
7. frame
8. architect

Unit 6 *Review*

Write About Art

Persuasive Paragraphs

D Review the jobs and careers you read about in this unit. Choose one career you might like to try. Write three paragraphs about what the job entails and why you think you would enjoy doing it. Describe the parts of the job you think you would be best at and the ones you think you may not like. Copy the chart below and use it to organize your thoughts before you start writing.

Job Title:

_____

Job Description:

_____

_____

_____

Pros: | Cons:

Your Studio Work

E Answer these questions in your Sketchbook Journal or on a separate sheet of paper.

1. Which of the projects in this unit did you find most enjoyable to complete? What about it did you find most rewarding?
2. What challenges did you face as you worked on each of the Studios? How did you solve the problems you encountered?
3. Which of the projects inspired you to find out more about a particular career? Why?
4. Which of the skills used in this unit were you best at? Which job would you be best suited for? Explain.

Put It All Together

Julie Taymor. *Ostrich,* from *The Lion King,* 1997.
Photo © Joan Marcus.

F **Julie Taymor designed this bird costume for *The Lion King* on Broadway. Discuss or write about Taymor's design using the four steps below for viewing artwork critically.**

1. **Describe** What shapes and colors can you identify in this costume? What materials has the designer used? What is the scale of the bird? How can you tell?
2. **Analyze** Are the color choices realistic? How has the designer suggested the bird's tail and body feathers? How are the feathers on the head made? How do you think the bird is able to move?
3. **Interpret** Why do you think the designer chose to portray a real bird with shapes and colors like these? How do you think the bird's design affects the way it moves across the stage?
4. **Judge** Read Julie Taymor's quote below. How does this costume reflect her attitude toward her materials? How do you think this costume would look as part of a stage performance? What other types of costumes can you imagine would accompany this one?

Taymor made her materials into the flightless star of the Broadway stage.

"You play with the materials you have and use your imagination to make them into something else."

—JULIE TAYMOR

293

Elements *of Art*

The elements of art are the basic parts and symbols of an artwork.

Line

A **line** is a continuous mark made by a moving point. Lines vary in width, length, direction, color, and degree of curve. Artists use line in many ways, for example, to define a space, create a pattern, or show movement.

Ando Hiroshige. *Fuji from Sagami River.*

Fernand Léger.
Disks, 1918.

Shape

A **shape** is an enclosed area of space, often defined by line. Shapes are two-dimensional, or flat, but can be made to look like solid three-dimensional objects. Some shapes are geometric, such as a rectangle or circle. Others are organic, having an irregular outline.

Form

A **form** is an object with three dimensions—height, width, and depth. Like shapes, forms can be geometric or organic.

Deborah Butterfield.
Riot, 1990.

Space

Space is the area around, above, between, inside, or below objects. Positive space is the area occupied by an object. Negative space is the empty area surrounding objects. Artists vary positive and negative space to imply size and distance.

Grant Wood. *Stone City,* ca. 1930.

Value

Value refers to the lightness or darkness of a color. A light value, such as light pink, is a tint. A dark value, such as dark red, is a shade. Artists show transitions between different values to create depth or suggest a mood.

Mary Williamson. *Stick Pond,* 1993. Pencil. Gallery Contemporanea, Jacksonville, FL.

Anonymous, Chile, Inca. *Fez style hat with alternating step-volute design,* ca. 1530–1570.

Color

Color is the appearance of an object created by the characteristic of light it reflects and absorbs. A red object, for example, reflects red light and absorbs all other colors.

Texture

Texture refers to the way a surface feels to the touch (tactile texture) or how it appears through the sense of vision (visual texture). Artists work one or both types of texture into their artworks to help viewers understand a surface quality.

Wassily Kandinsky. *Fragment of Composition II,* 1910.

Principles *of Design*

The principles of design are guidelines that artists use to organize the elements of art in a composition.

Balance

Balance refers to the way the elements of art are arranged to create a sense of stability and equal visual weight. An artwork has balance if no one part visually overpowers another.

Claes Oldenburg. *Clothespin*, 1976.

Artist unknown, Aztec. *Pendant representing the sun.*

Proportion

Proportion refers to the relationship between the parts of an artwork to each other and to the whole. An artist painting a portrait, for example, may keep in mind the size relationship of the nose to the face.

Emphasis

Emphasis in an artwork is the sense of importance given to any one part of the composition. Artists add emphasis when they want to draw attention to a certain object or idea.

Marc Chagall. *The Farm, the Village (La Ferme, le Village)*, 1954–1962.

Pattern

Pattern is the repeated use of an element, such as line, shape, or color.

Artist unknown, Asante People, Ghana. (Detail) *Woman's Kente cloth,* mid-20th century.

Rhythm

Rhythm is a sense of movement in a composition created by the regular repetition of an element. Rhythm in an artwork can appear vibrant and active or calm.

José Cuneo. *Ranchos Orilleros,* 1932.

Unity

Unity is the quality of wholeness achieved when the separate parts of an artwork work well together. An artwork with unity often shows repeated elements, such as the frequent use of a shape.

Henri Matisse. *Harmony in Red (The Red Room),* 1908.

Variety

Variety refers to the combination of different elements in an artwork. Artists energize their compositions by varying patterns, shapes, and colors. They strive to strike a balance between unity and variety.

René Magritte. *Title Unknown (The Horsewoman),* 1922.

Think Safety

Read these safety rules and be sure to follow them when you create artworks.

1. Keep art materials away from your face to prevent eye irritation and skin rashes.

2. Do not breathe chalk dust or art sprays. These materials can be harmful to your lungs.

3. If you are allergic to an art material, notify your teacher before the project begins.

4. If you experience an allergic reaction to any art materials, stop using the materials immediately and notify your teacher.

5. Read the labels on art materials and look for the word *nontoxic*. This label tells you the materials are safe to use.

6. If you use a sharp-pointed object, such as a clay tool or scissors, point it away from your body. Point these objects away from other students, as well.

7. If you spill paint or other art materials on the floor, clean it up right away. It is unsafe to walk on a wet or cluttered floor.

8. Use only *new* meat trays and egg cartons as art materials. Used ones may carry harmful bacteria.

9. After you finish an artwork, wash your hands with soap and water.

Technique Handbook

Drawing with Crayon and Oil Pastels

1 Use the tip of a crayon or edge of the oil pastel to make a variety of lines, such as straight, curved, wavy, and cross-hatched. Draw short lines or dots of different colors side-by-side to create an Impressionist effect.

2 Peel the paper off the crayon or oil pastel and use the side to draw thick lines. Break the tool in half to reduce line width.

3 Press down firmly for bright colors. Press lightly for soft colors. Mix colors by putting one on top of another and blending them with your fingers or a tissue. Add a small amount of black to make a darker shade. Shade forms gradually from dark to light.

Drawing with Chalk Pastels

1 Use the tip of the chalk pastel to make a variety of lines. Practice drawing vertical, horizontal, and diagonal lines. Create broken lines by periodically lifting the chalk from the page.

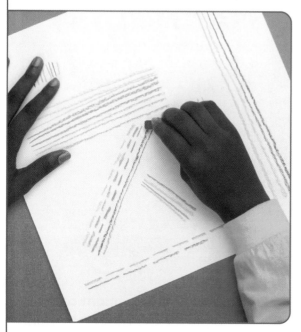

2 Use the side of the chalk to draw thick lines. Apply varying degrees of pressure to increase or decrease line quality.

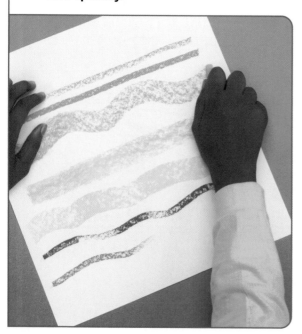

3 Mix colors by putting one color on top of another. Blend colors with a tissue, shading stump, or tortillon.

4 Use a kneaded eraser or an eraser of similar quality to add highlights.

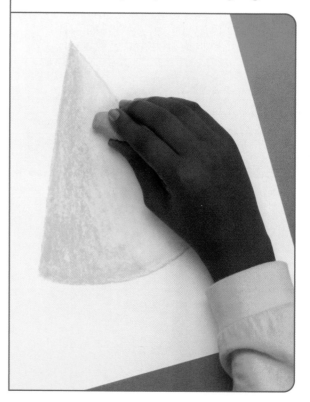

Drawing with Pen and Ink

1 Select a pen and drawing paper. Technical pens have different sized tips, or nibs, which allow you to draw lines of varying width. Ballpoint pens create crisp, clean lines. Choose smooth paper when working with ink. Rough paper can absorb ink quickly and give your drawing an uneven look.

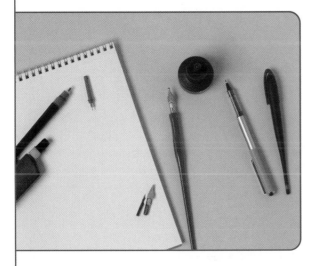

2 Draw your design in pencil first. To create circles, use a compass and a pencil, or use patterns of circles cut from posterboard. Then go over the lines with a pen. Work from one side of the paper to the other to avoid smearing ink.

3 Shade forms with one or more of the following methods:

- Use a ruler to draw a series of parallel lines that get closer together. These lines will create a light-to-dark effect.

- Try cross-hatching. Draw parallel lines. Then add a layer of lines going the other way. Space the lines out or draw them close together for light and dark areas.

- Use the stippling method. Draw points or dots with the tip of the pen. Gradually add more dots to create darker values.

Creating a Contour Drawing

1 Place your drawing tool at the top of the paper and draw the contour lines of an object. Draw slowly to record the inside and outside folds, wrinkles, and creases as you see them. To create a continuous line, keep your hand and forearm in fluid motion and do not lift the drawing tool from the paper.

2 To create a blind contour drawing, cover your drawing paper with another sheet of paper and do not watch your progress. To create a modified contour drawing, allow yourself to look at the drawing from time to time to correct proportions.

Creating a Gesture Drawing

1 Notice the movement, pose, shape, weight, and form of a figure, preferably in action. Draw the figure using quick, rhythmic, scribbling sketches for one to three minutes. Draw geometric shapes to quickly capture the different forms that make up the human figure, such as an oval for the head and a cylinder shape for the neck.

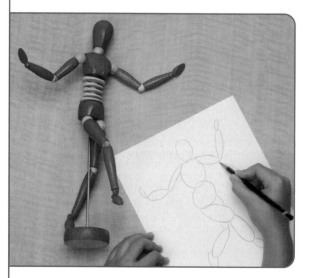

2 Add details by showing dark areas, light areas, and gesture lines that contour around parts of a figure in action. Draw on large newsprint with charcoals, pastels, chalks, felt-tip pens, and other drawing media.

Making a Papier-Mâché Mask

1 Create the armature, or framework, for the mask. Cut out the shape of the mask from tagboard, posterboard, or another pliable material.

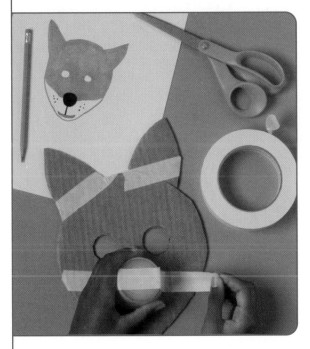

2 Glue or tape pieces of scrap cardboard, newspaper, or foam core to the armature to make the facial features stand out from the surface.

3 Tear and soak newspaper strips and/or paper towels in papier-mâché paste. Apply the strips, one over the other, to build up the surface of the armature, allowing each layer to dry. Add paper towels as the final two or three layers for a smooth surface. Use soft tissue paper soaked in papier-mâché paste to form eyes, eyebrows, and other features.

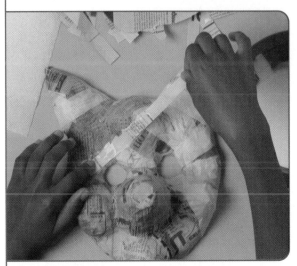

4 Allow the papier mâché to dry before applying paint. For best results, use acrylic-based paint. Or apply a water-soluble sealant to the dry surface for tempera paint. Add final details with yarn, raffia, beads, metallic foils, or other found objects.

Painting with Tempera or Acrylic Paint

1 To mix a tint, begin with white paint and add a dot of colored paint. Continue adding color until you get the tint you want. To mix a shade, start with a color. Add a small amount of black paint and mix the two together. Avoid using too much black.

2 Dip the bristles of your paintbrush into the paint. Push down on the paintbrush for thick lines and use the tip for thin lines. Hold the brush at different angles to vary your lines.

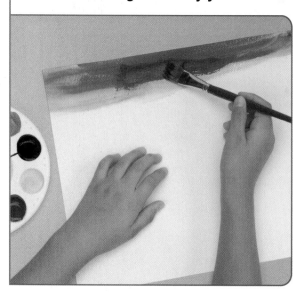

3 Clean your paintbrush every time you switch colors. Dip the brush in water and wipe it on the side of the water container. Blot the brush on a paper towel before charging with the next color.

4 When finished, wash your paintbrush with warm, soapy water. Rinse the brush and blot it on a towel. Put the paintbrush into a jar, bristles up.

Painting with Watercolor

1 Prepare paints by brushing a large drop of water onto each color of paint. For best results, use watercolor paper for your compositions.

2 Practice mixing colors as they appear on the color wheel. Begin with a light color, such as yellow, and add a small amount of a darker color, such as blue. To create tints, add water. Water allows the white paper to show through the paint. To create shades, add a dot of black.

3 Plan a white space in your composition by creating a resist with a white crayon or white oil pastel. Then use a wet-wash to create sky and ground areas. Wet a broad brush and paint over your paper with clear water. Charge your brush with a color and pull the brush horizontally across the top. Work your way down to the horizon line without recharging your brush. Rinse the brush and repeat with a second color. Lift your paper vertically to allow the wet wash to blend.

4 Allow your wet wash to dry before you paint details, such as boats, rafts, a dock, or birds. Use watercolor paints, crayons, or oil pastels for the details. When the painting is dry, create highlights by scraping some paint away with a scraping tool.

Making a Monoprint

1 Cover a sheet of paper or a hard, slick surface with acrylic paint. Use a pencil or pen to draw a design into the paint.

2 Place a sheet of clean paper on top of your design. Smooth it down gently with your hands. Carefully peel the paper off, known as "pulling the print," and let the paint dry.

Making a Relief Print

1 Use a pencil to draw a design on material such as a slab of clay or a clean meat tray. Cover a roller, or brayer, with water-based printers' ink or acrylic paint. Roll the ink or paint evenly over the design.

2 Place a clean sheet of paper on top of your design. Rub the paper gently with your hands. Carefully pull the print and let the ink or paint dry.

Making a Stamp Print

1 Cut a shape from a material such as cardboard or a clean meat tray. Attach a piece of twisted masking tape to the back of the shape to create a handle.

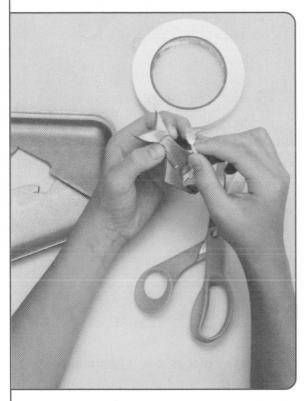

2 Use a brayer to roll a thin layer of printing ink or acrylic paint onto a printing tray or other flat surface.

3 Dip the face of the printing block or stamp into the ink or acrylic paint. Carefully, but firmly, press the stamp onto a sheet of paper. Lift the stamp to see the print.

Making a Collage

1 Decide on an idea or theme for your collage. Then collect what you will need. Cut out and tear shapes from colored papers and fabrics.

2 Arrange the paper and fabric pieces on a sheet of construction paper. Move them around until you find an arrangement that you like. Be sure to fill the construction paper background.

3 Glue the pieces, one at a time, to the background. Add found objects to create texture and enhance your design.

Working with Clay

Setup

When working with clay, cover your desk or work area with a plastic mat or canvas. Prepare any unwedged clay by wedging it. To wedge clay, take a large lump of it and thump it down on the work surface. Press the clay with the palms of your hands, turn it over, and press into it again. Keep pressing the clay until it has no air bubbles.

Forming a Pinch Pot

1 Make a small ball of clay and place it in the palm of your hand.

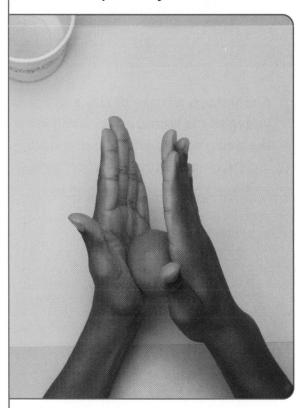

2 Press your thumb into the middle of the ball. Pinch it with your fingers.

3 Start pinching at the bottom and then move up and out. Keep turning the ball as you pinch.

Using the Slab Method

1 Use a rolling pin to roll out a piece of wedged clay between two sticks. Roll the clay until it is approximately one-half inch thick.

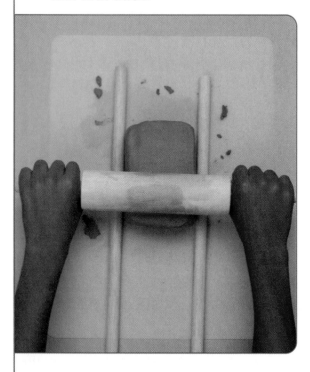

2 Cut out slabs for the bottom and sides of a container using a plastic knife.

3 Use a moist toothbrush, toothpick, or plastic fork to create score marks. These rough grooves make it easier to join one piece of clay to another.

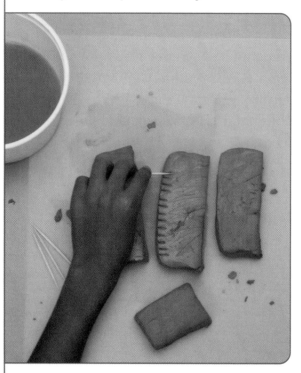

4 Apply slip, a mixture of clay and water, to the scored edges. Then join the slab pieces together and smooth any irregular places with your fingers.

Using the Coil Method

1 Begin with a flat and round slab as the base. Score the edges of your base.

2 Make a coil, or rope, of clay by rolling the clay back and forth between your hands and the work surface. Start rolling in the middle and move toward the edges.

3 Score each coil and apply slip to the coils and base.

4 Wind the coils into a form. Cut extra coils into pieces to form handles and other parts for your form. Score them and apply slip before you press them in place.

Making a Repoussé

1 Cut a sheet of metal foil made of aluminum or copper. Place tape around the edges of the metal for safety.

2 Draw a design on paper that will fit the size of the foil.

3 Place the foil on a soft pad, such as an old magazine or stack of newspapers. Use a blunt pencil to transfer your drawing to the foil.

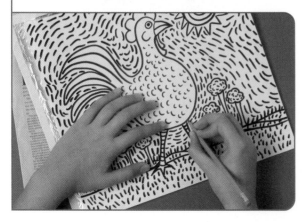

4 Remove the paper design and deepen the outline in the foil using craft sticks or the eraser end of a pencil.

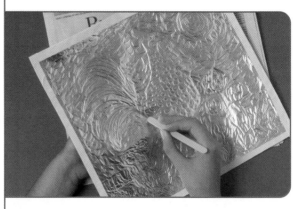

5 Turn the foil over and deepen the other shapes to make them stand out from the front side.

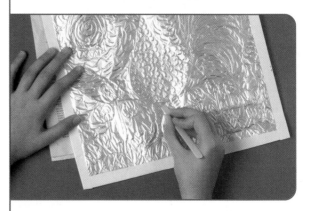

6 Brush waterproof ink or black shoe polish over the foil design. When the ink is dry, lightly buff, or rub, the raised surfaces with steel wool or a dry paper towel. Mount your repoussé on wood or heavy cardboard. Use acrylic spray to protect the artwork.

Weaving

1 Cut a piece of cardboard to make a square or rectangular loom. Use a ruler to draw lines one-half inch from the top and from the bottom. Then make a mark every one-fourth inch or so along the lines. Draw slanted lines from the edge of the cardboard to the marks. Cut along the slanted lines to make "teeth."

2 Next, create a warp. Make a loop in one end of a piece of yarn. Hook the loop around the first "tooth" at the top of the loom. Then take the yarn down to the bottom of the loom. Hook it around the first "tooth" there. Take the yarn back up to the second "tooth" at the top, hook it, and so on. Keep wrapping until the loom is filled with warp threads, or vertical lines of yarn.

3 Finally, weave the weft. Tie yarn through a hole in a narrow craft stick. Start at the bottom center of the loom. Weave toward one edge by going over and under the warp threads. When you get to the last thread, loop the craft stick around it and start weaving back in the other direction. Keep weaving, over and under, until the loom is covered. Unhook and remove the weaving from the loom. Tie any loose end pieces.

Making Stitchery

1 Select a needle. A crewel needle, used for embroidery, is short and has a long eye. A blunt needle, used for weaving, is a big needle with a dull point. A darner is a long needle with a big eye. It is used with thick threads, such as yarn. Never use a sharp needle without the help of an adult.

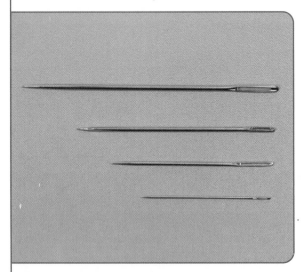

2 Thread the needle by dampening your fingers and pinching one end of the thread to flatten it. Push the flattened end through the eye of the needle and pull it through. Make a knot at the other end to keep the thread from coming through cloth.

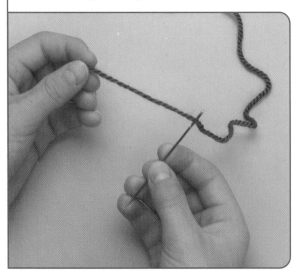

3 Start a stitch on the back of the cloth. Push the needle through and pull the thread up until the knot stops it. Continue pushing and pulling until you have finished your stitching. Finally, push the needle and thread through to the back. Make two small stitches next to each other and push the needle under these two stitches. Pull the thread through, knot it, and cut it off.

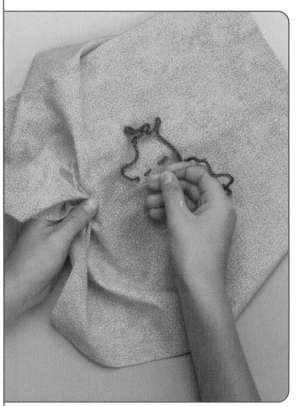

Drawing and Painting on a Computer

1 Select a new document from a drawing or painting software program. Practice using the drawing tools, such as thick and thin lines, shapes, paint, spray, eraser, and fill, as well as the text tool. Shade basic shapes to create forms. Create contour and gesture drawings of objects or a classmate. Fill the screen with your experimental designs.

2 Choose one of your practice designs or create a new design. Using the program's drawing tools, add form, color, texture, and value to your design. A graphics tablet and stylus may be used in place of a mouse. Repeat certain elements of your design. Add a background by scanning a design you created or using the fill and gradient patterns in your software program.

3 Use the text tool to incorporate a phrase or message around the edges, in the foreground or background. Use your imagination to help make your text message stand out.

List *of* Artists *and* Artworks

Unknown Artists

Artists

318

Artworks

Glossary

A

abstract A style of art that does not show a realistic subject. Abstract art usually includes geometric shapes, bold colors, and lines.

actual lines Lines that are real, not imaginary.

additive method A technique for creating a three-dimensional artwork in which materials, such as clay or found objects, are added or assembled.

aerial perspective A technique used to create the illusion of air and space in an artwork. Close-up objects are bright and consist of darker colors; faraway objects and air consist of muted colors and large portions of white. Also known as *atmospheric perspective.*

altered proportion A technique used by an artist to change the size relationship of shapes in an artwork. See *monumental, miniature,* and *exaggerated.*

alternating rhythm Rhythm created in an artwork by repeating two or more elements on a regular, interchanging basis.

analogous [ə na′ lə gəs] Colors that appear next to each other on the color wheel. Analogous colors have one hue in common. For example, blue, blue-green, and blue-violet all contain blue. Also known as *related colors.*

animation The art of creating drawings in a sequence and recording them onto film. When the film is run at high speed, the pictures appear to be in motion.

animator An artist who creates animations by hand or on a computer.

applied art Artworks that are functional. Also known as *utilitarian art.*

aqueduct A channel or conduit built for transporting water from a distant source.

arch A structure with a curved, pointed, or squared upper edge to an opening, and which supports the weight above it. An arch can frame a doorway or it can support a wall or ceiling.

architect An artist who plans and designs buildings and other structures.

architecture The art and science of designing buildings and other structures.

armature [är′ mə chŭr] A skeletal framework or support for a sculpture.

art historians Those who study art history and cultural traditions that relate to art, such as forms of government, religious beliefs, and social activities.

art media The materials used by artists to create artworks.

Art Nouveau [nü vō′] French for "new art," this style of art in the late 1800s and early 1900s, uses exaggerated asymmetrical designs and makes use of undulating forms of all kinds, most notably tendrils, plant stems, flames, waves, and flowing hair.

artwork A term that refers to any artistic object or production.

assemblage [ə sem′ blij] An additive sculpture often made of recycled objects that assume new meaning within the artwork.

assembling A technique for creating an assemblage, in which objects, usually found or recycled objects, are fit together or assembled.

asymmetrical balance [ā sə me′ tri kal] A type of balance in which the two sides of an artwork look equally important even though they are not alike. Also known as *informal balance.*

atmospheric perspective A technique used to create the illusion of air and space in an artwork. Close-up objects are bright and consist of darker colors; faraway objects and air consist of muted colors and large portions of white. Also known as *aerial perspective.*

B

background The part of an artwork that appears the farthest away.

balance The arrangement of the parts of an artwork to give a sense of overall equality in visual weight. Balance can be symmetrical, asymmetrical, or radial. Balance is a principle of design.

barrel vault A semi-cylindrical structure made up of successive arches.

Bauhaus [baů′ haůs] A twentieth century German school of design, art, and architecture. This style used simplified forms and unadorned functionalism. It was influenced by and derived from techniques and materials used in industrial fabrication and manufacturing.

binder A material, such as wax, egg, glue, resin, or oil, that binds together the coloring grains and powder in a pigment.

blending A shading technique that changes the value of a color little by little.

block In printmaking, a piece of flat material, such as wood or metal, with a design on the surface, which is a mirror image of the composition that will appear as a print. The block is used to print the design. See also *plate.* In sculpture, a solid material, such as wood or stone, used for carving.

blue screen A technique used in filmmaking to create special effects. Subjects or actors are filmed against a blue screen. Later, the blue screen is digitally replaced by another background.

blueprint A photographic print used to copy the final drawing of a plan for building something.

bronze A metal alloy made of copper, tin, and other metals, often used in cast sculptures.

C

calligraphy Ornamental writing, done mainly with a pen in the West and with a brush in China and Japan.

caricature [kar⁄ i kə chür] An artwork that exaggerates the features or aspects of a person or object, usually in a humorous way.

carving A subtractive method of sculpting requiring the sculptor to cut or chip away pieces from a block of material, such as wood, stone, or other hard material.

casting A sculpting process in which a liquid, such as molten bronze or liquid plaster, is poured into a heat-proof mold to create a three-dimensional form or an impression.

cathedral A large and important church that is the official seat of a bishop. Many cathedrals reflect a variety of art forms, such as ornate architecture, painted murals, and sculptures.

cel A frame of an animated film that is created by hand on acetate. Before digital and computer technology, cels were drawn and colored by hand.

ceramics The art of making objects from clay and hardening them with fire or extreme heat. Also, artworks made by this process.

cityscape Artwork that gives a view of a city.

Classical style A term applied to art and architecture that exhibit the characteristics of ancient Greek and Roman art, such as proportion, balance, and idealized forms and themes.

collage [kə läzh⁄] An artwork in which the artist glues bits of cut or torn paper, photographs, fabric, or other materials to a flat surface.

color The visual quality of objects caused by the amount of light reflected by them. Color is an element of art. See *hue*.

color scheme A plan for combining colors in a work of art.

complementary Colors that contrast with one another. Complementary colors are opposite one another on the color wheel.

compositing A process by which combined images are burned or recorded onto a single piece of film by using either photographic or computer equipment.

composition The plan, placement, or arrangement of the elements of art in an artwork. Composition may also refer to any work of art.

computer-aided design (CAD) Computer software used in art, architecture, engineering, and manufacturing to assist in two- and three-dimensional drawing.

computer art Artworks created through the use of computer technology as a medium.

computer artist An artist who uses a computer to create artworks that reflect his or her personal expression.

conservator [kən sər′ va tər] A person who works to protect artworks from damage and decay.

contrast The difference between two unlike things, such as a light color and a dark color.

converging lines Actual or implied lines that move toward an intersecting point in space.

cool colors The family of colors that includes greens, blues, and violets. Cool colors bring to mind cool things, places, and feelings.

costume designer An artist who designs clothing, outfits, or disguises that reflect a particular country, historical period, or culture, usually for stage productions and movies.

creative process The process of inventive and imaginative expression through the use of art materials and tools.

cross-hatching A shading technique using lines that cross each other.

Cubism An abstract art style developed by Pablo Picasso and Georges Braque in the twentieth century in which the subject is divided into shapes and forms, which are then recombined so that each part of the subject is shown from a different point of view.

curator A person who does research for a museum. Curators recommend artworks for the museum to consider purchasing. They also select artworks for display from the museum's permanent collection.

D

decorative art Handicrafts that result in beautiful, useful objects. Rug and fabric design, furniture-making, and glassblowing are all decorative arts.

depth The use of the techniques of perspective and overlapping to show deep space on a two-dimensional plane.

design The creative and organized arrangement of lines, shapes, spaces, colors, forms, textures, and other elements in an artwork. Also, the act of planning and arranging the parts of an artwork.

detail A small part of a larger artwork enlarged for closer viewing. Also, a minute or particularly interesting part of an artwork.

diagonal A slanted edge or line.

digital technology Technology which converts visual images into binary code through the use of items such as digital cameras, video and audio recorders, scanners, or computers.

docent A person who gives information and conducts tours in a museum. Many docents are trained volunteers.

dominance A way to show emphasis in an artwork in which one element or object in the composition is visually the strongest or most important part of the work.

E

effigy vessel A vessel or pot, usually made from clay, that shows a likeness or representation of a person.

elements of art The basic parts and symbols of an artwork. The elements of art are line, color, value, shape, texture, form, and space.

elevation A scale drawing that shows one side of a structure.

emphasis [em(p)⁄ fə səs] Importance given to certain objects or areas in an artwork. Color, texture, shape, space, placement, and size can be used to create dominance, contrast, or a focal point. Emphasis is a principle of design.

exhibition A public display of artworks.

Expressionism A style of artwork developed in the twentieth century that expresses a definite or strong mood or feeling through simple designs and brilliant colors.

F

fashion The prevailing style or custom, as in dress or behavior.

feature Any distinct part of the face, such as the nose, mouth, or eyes.

fiber arts Artworks created from yarn, thread, or cloth, such as stitchery and weaving.

fine art Artworks that are created for the sole purpose of being viewed.

floor plan The arrangement of rooms inside a building.

focal point A way to show emphasis in an artwork in which the artist sets an element apart from the others to create a visual center of interest.

foreground The part of an artwork that seems nearest.

form A three-dimensional object, such as a cube or ball, or the representation of a three-dimensional object, defined by contour, height, depth, and width. Form is an element of art.

frame One of a series of images in a filmstrip or animation. Also, a decorative border or support for an artwork.

frieze [frēz] A decorative horizontal band, usually placed along the upper end or top of a wall or building.

function The intended use or purpose for which an object or artwork is created.

furniture designer An artist who designs functional and decorative artworks, such as chairs, desks, tables, beds, and sofas.

G

genre scene [zhän⁄ rə] An artwork that shows a subject or scene from everyday life, such as people living and working. Also called *genre art*.

geometric form A form such as a sphere, cube, or pyramid, whose contours represent a circle, square, and triangle, respectively.

geometric shape Precise, mathematical shapes, such as the circle, square, triangle, oval, and rectangle.

gesture drawing A drawing technique in which artists move a drawing medium, such as a pencil, quickly and freely over a surface to capture the form and actions of a subject.

glaze A mixture of mostly oxides which, when applied to clay and then fired in a kiln, creates a thin, transparent, glossy coating.

Gothic The name given to the style of architecture, painting, and sculpture, which flourished in western Europe, mainly France and England, between the twelfth and fifteenth centuries.

graphic design The art of communicating through images and lettering, mostly for commercial purposes, such as logos, letterheads, packages, advertisements, posters, signs, books, Web pages, and other publications.

H

hardware Computer components, such as monitors, keyboards, central processing units (CPUs), and modems.

hatching A shading technique using thin parallel lines.

hieroglyphics [hī (ə)rə gli′ fiks] A system of writing using symbols or pictures.

horizon line The line created in an artwork by the meeting of sky and ground, usually at the viewer's eye level.

horizontal line In an artwork, a line that runs side-to-side, parallel to the horizon. Horizontal lines appear peaceful and calm.

hue [hyü] Another word for color.

human-made environment A person's or organism's circumstances or surroundings made by humans rather than occurring in nature

I

implied lines Lines that are not real, but suggested by the placement of other lines, shapes, and colors.

indoor space The space inside a house or building.

installation An artwork that is assembled for a specific space for public viewing. Some installations are permanent, while others are temporary.

installation artist An artist who designs and creates permanent or temporary installation artworks for public viewing.

intaglio print [in tal′ yō] A print that results from a technique in which the image to be printed is cut or scratched into a surface or plate.

intensity The brightness or dullness of a hue. A hue mixed with its complement is less intense than the pure color.

interlace A design that includes swirling and interlocking geometric and organic shapes and lines, which often create a pattern.

intermediate color A color that is a mixture of a primary and a secondary color that are next to each other on the color wheel. Blue-green, red-orange, and red-violet are examples of intermediate colors.

L

landscape A drawing or painting that shows an outdoor scene or scenery, such as trees, lakes, mountains, and fields

landscape architecture The art and science of planning and designing functional and attractive outdoor spaces.

landscape designer An artist who uses plants, rocks, trees, and other materials to design and create pleasing and functional outdoor spaces. Also known as a *landscape architect.*

light source A point of illumination for emphasis, contrast, unity, or dramatic effect in an artwork.

line A mark on a surface usually created by a pen, pencil, or brush. Lines vary in width, length, direction, color, and degree of curve, and can be two-dimensional or implied. Line is an element of art.

linear perspective A technique that makes use of actual and implied lines to create the illusion of depth on a two-dimensional surface. If the lines in an artwork created with this technique are extended, they converge at a point on an imaginary line that represents the eye level of the viewer. This point is called the vanishing point.

lithograph A type of print made by drawing a design on a metal or stone plate using a greasy substance. The plate is washed with water and then covered with greasy ink that adheres only to the design and not the wet surface of the plate. The plate is then pressed onto paper.

loom A frame or machine used to hold yarn, or other fibers, for weaving.

lost wax casting A sculpting process in which an artist first produces a sculpture in wax. He or she then creates a mold around the wax, using a heat-resistant material, such as clay. When the mold is heated, the wax melts away, or is lost. The wax is then replaced by hot, liquid metal, such as bronze. Once the metal has hardened, the mold is removed to reveal the sculpture.

M

matte painting [mat] Scenery, such as a darkened city or a vast ocean, painted on glass or created with a computer as a background to replace the blue screen in a film shot.

Medieval period The period of European history that followed the fall of the Western Roman Empire. Also known as the *Middle Ages* or *Dark Ages.*

medium A material used to create artworks, such as clay or paint. The plural of medium is *media.*

Middle Ages The period in European history between the fall of Rome in A.D. 410 to about 1450. Also known as the *Medieval period* and the *Dark Ages.*

middle ground In an artwork, the part between the foreground and the background.

miniature Artworks that are of smaller-than-life proportions.

mixed media Artworks that are created from more than one medium.

modeling A technique using all types of clay, and other additive media, for building up and shaping a sculpture.

monochromatic [mä nə krō ma′ tik] A color scheme that uses different values of a single hue by showing tints and shades of the same hue.

monumental Artworks that are of larger-than-life proportions.

mood The feeling or emotion created in an artwork through the artist's use of the elements of art and principles of design. For example, warm colors may suggest a lively, sunny mood. Cool colors may suggest a peaceful, lonely, or fearful mood.

morphing [mȯrf′ ing] Transforming an image by computer, such as changing from one shape to another.

mural A large artwork, usually a painting, that is applied directly onto or placed on a wall or ceiling, often in public places.

N

natural environment A natural setting that has not been changed by humans.

natural form A form of, relating to, or concerning nature.

negative space The empty space around and between forms or shapes in an artwork.

neutral A word used for black, white, and tints and shades of gray. Some artists use tints and shades of brown as neutrals.

nonobjective A type of art that usually shows color, form, and texture, but has no recognizable subject.

O

obsidian [əb si′ dē ən] A dark, natural glass formed by the cooling of molten lava, and which is slightly harder than window glass.

oil-based paint A paint made from a mixture of colored pigment and linseed oil.

one-point perspective A form of linear perspective in which all lines appear to meet at a single vanishing point on the horizon.

opaque [ō pāk′] The quality of not letting light through; the opposite of transparent.

Op Art A style of art in which artists create the illusion of movement or other optical illusions. Op Art developed in the 1950s.

optical illusion A visually perceived image that is deceptive or misleading.

organic form A "free-form" which has irregular and uneven edges and is often found in nature, such as an apple, a tree, or an animal.

organic shape A "free-form" shape that is irregular and uneven, such as the shape of a leaf, a flower, or a cloud.

outdoor space The space outside of a structure or building; space that is in the open or leading to the open.

overlapping Partly or completely covering one shape or form with another to show space and distance in an artwork.

P

palette [pa′ lət] A flat board on which a painter holds and mixes color.

panorama An unbroken view of an entire surrounding area.

parallel lines Two or more straight lines or edges that are the same distance apart along their whole length.

pastel [pas tel′] A drawing and painting medium in which pigments are mixed with gum and water, and pressed into a dried stick form for use as crayons. Works of art created with this medium are also called pastels.

pattern Repeated colors, lines, shapes, forms, or textures in an artwork. Pattern is a principle of design. Also, a plan or model to be followed when making something.

pediment In classical architecture, a triangular space at the end of a building, formed by the ends of the sloping roof and the cornice. Also, an ornamental feature having this shape.

photographer An artist who uses a camera as his or her medium.

pigment A coloring material made from crushed minerals, plants, or chemicals, usually held together with a binder.

pixel The basic unit of the composition of an image on a television screen, computer monitor, or similar digital display.

plaque A flat plate, slab, or tablet that is engraved or cast and used as a memorial or for decoration.

plate In printmaking, a piece of flat material, such as wood or metal, with a design on the surface. The plate is used to print the design, which is a mirror image of the composition. See also *block*.

pointillism A painting and drawing technique developed by Georges Seurat in the nineteenth century, in which tiny dots of color are applied to the canvas or drawing surface.

Pop Art An art style that developed in England in the 1950s and spread to the United States in the 1960s. The subjects of Pop Art include everyday, popular objects, such as product packages, comic strips, and advertisements.

portfolio A portable container used to hold and organize artworks, especially drawings and paintings. Also, the artworks collected in this container.

portrait A work of art created to show a person, animal, or group of people, usually focusing on the face.

positive space The space that a form or shape occupies in an artwork.

Postmodern Term used to describe the attempt to modify and extend the tradition of modernism with borrowings from the Classical style.

pottery Useful and/or decorative objects, such as vases, bowls, and dishes, that are made of wet clay.

pre-Columbian Art Artworks created in the Americas before Christopher Columbus and other Europeans arrived in the area.

primary color A color that cannot be mixed from other colors, but from which other colors are made. The primary colors are red, yellow, and blue.

principles of design Guidelines that artists use to organize the elements of art in a composition. Unity, variety, emphasis, balance, proportion, pattern, and rhythm are the principles of design.

printmaking The process of transferring an image from an inked surface to another surface to create an artwork.

product designer An artist who designs the products, machines, and equipment manufactured for and used by modern society. Product designers are a type of industrial designer.

profile The side view of a subject.

progressive rhythm Rhythm created in an artwork by showing regular changes in a repeated element, such as a series of circles that progressively increase in size from small to large. The changes may also progress from light to dark, or from bottom to top.

proportion The relation of the parts of an artwork to each other and to the whole with regard to size, placement, and amount. Proportion is a principle of design.

Q

quilt A type of fiber art made from two layers of cloth that are sewn together with a layer of padding or stuffing in between. Also, the process of creating a quilt.

R

radial balance A type of balance in which lines or shapes spread out from a center point.

regular rhythm Rhythm in an artwork created by repeating the same element, such as a shape, without variation.

relief print The technique of printing in which an image raised from a background is inked and printed.

relief sculpture A type of sculpture in which forms project from a background and are meant to be seen from one side.

Renaissance [re nə sän(t)s⁄] The period between the 1300s and 1600s, during which new ideas and technological advances, as well as renewed interest in the classical styles of the Romans and Greeks, laid the foundation for modern art and society.

rhythm The repetition of elements, such as lines, shapes, or colors, that creates a feeling of visual motion in an artwork. Rhythm is a principle of design. In music, rhythm refers to the pattern of a melody.

S

scale The size of an object in relation to an ideal or standard size.

scanner A device used to transfer text or graphics into a computer.

sculpture An artwork made by modeling, carving, casting, or joining materials into a three-dimensional form. Clay, wood, stone, and metal are often used to make sculptures.

seascape An artwork that represents the sea, ocean, or shore.

secondary color A color made by mixing two primary colors. The secondary colors are orange, violet, and green.

shade A color made by adding black to a hue. For example, adding black to green results in dark green. Also, the darkness of a color value. See *value*.

shading A way of showing gradual changes in lightness or darkness in a drawing or painting. Shading helps make a picture look more three-dimensional.

shape A two-dimensional area created by visually connecting actual or implied lines. A shape can be geometric, such as a circle or square, or organic, having an irregular outline. Shape is an element of art.

size relationships A technique that alters the proportions of compositions. The three categories are monumental, miniature, and exaggerated.

slip A soupy mixture of clay and water that acts as glue to join scored pieces of clay.

software Computer applications used for various functions, such as drawing, Web design, editing text, creating graphics, or altering images.

solvent A liquid, such as turpentine or water, used to control the thickness or thinness of paint.

special effects artist An artist who combines sound, text, images, and animation to create unusual or difficult effects for movies and films, using a variety of media.

space The area around, above, between, inside, or below objects. Positive space is the area occupied by an object. Negative space is the empty area surrounding an object. Space is an element of art.

standard proportion That which appears appropriate in height, width, and depth compared to its surroundings. The human body is considered to be the standard by which the size or proportion of other objects is measured.

still life An artwork showing an arrangement of objects that cannot move on their own, such as fruit, foods, bottles, books, or cut flowers.

still photography The art and science of making a picture with a camera and film other than a motion picture or video camera.

stippling A shading technique creating dark values by applying a dot pattern.

stitchery A term for artwork created with a needle, thread or yarn, and cloth, such as a quilt.

stop action A technique for filming animated features in which figures are positioned into place, a frame is shot, and the figures are repositioned for the next frame. The frames are combined, and when played back, the figures appear to move naturally.

storyboard A series of drawings that represents the visual plan for scenes in a video or film production.

study A preparatory drawing, often in preparation for a larger artwork.

style An artist's individual way of expressing his or her ideas. Also, a technique used by a group of artists in a particular time or culture.

subject A person, an animal, an object, or a scene represented in an artwork; the topic of an artwork.

subtractive method A technique used in creating three-dimensional artworks in which materials, such as clay, stone, or plaster, are removed or carved away.

Surrealism [sə rē′ ə li zəm] A style of art developed during the 1920s that emphasizes the expression of the subconscious by combining realistic images and dream like ideas. Many Surrealist artworks contain illusions.

symbol A letter, color, sign, or picture that represents words, messages, or ideas, such as thoughts and feelings. For example, a red heart is often used as a symbol for love.

symmetrical balance [sə me′ tri kəl] A type of balance in which both sides of an artwork look the same or almost the same. Also known as *formal balance.*

T

tactile texture A texture you can feel with your hands, such as rough or smooth. Also known as *actual texture.*

technique The way an artist uses and applies art media and tools to create a certain type of artwork.

tempera paint [tem′ pə rə] A chalky, water-based paint that is thick and opaque. Also known as *poster paint.*

terra cotta [ter ə kä′ tə] Fired clay with no glaze, used for building, architectural ornament, sculpture, and pottery.

tessellation [te sə lā′ shən] A pattern of shapes that fits together in a way that leaves no space in between, as in the artworks of M. C. Escher.

textile An artwork made from cloth or fibers, such as yarn.

texture The way something feels to the touch (actual texture) or how it may look (visual texture). Texture is an element of art.

tint A light value of a color, such as pink, that is created by mixing a hue with white. Also, the lightness of a color value. See *value.*

transparent The quality of letting light pass through; the opposite of opaque.

triptych [trip′ tik] A picture or carving in three panels.

trompe l'oeil [tròmp lə′ ē] A type of painting in which various illusionary devices persuade the viewer that he or she is looking at the actual objects represented.

two-point perspective A form of linear perspective in which all lines appear to meet at either of two vanishing points on the horizon.

U

unity The quality of seeming whole and complete, with all the parts looking right together. Unity is a principle of design.

urban designer An architect who specializes in the planning of a city.

utilitarian Designed for a specific, functional purpose. Also known as *applied art.*

V

value The lightness or darkness of a color. Tints have a light value. Shades have a dark value. Value is an element of art.

vanishing point In linear perspective, the place on the horizon where parallel lines seem to meet or converge.

variety The use or combination of elements of art, such as line, shape, or color, to provide interest in an artwork. Variety is a principle of design.

vertical line In an artwork, a line that runs up and down, such as a flagpole or a giant redwood tree. Vertical lines appear strong and powerful.

vessel A functional and often decorative container, such as a cup, bowl, or vase, used to hold solids or liquids.

video art A work of art that includes moving images recorded on videotape or on optical disc for viewing on television or computer screens.

visual texture The way a surface appears through the sense of vision. For example, the surface of a sculpture may appear shiny or dull. Also known as *simulated texture.*

W

warm colors The family of colors that includes reds, yellows, and oranges. Warm colors bring to mind warm things, places, and feelings.

warp In weaving, the vertical threads attached to the top and bottom of a loom.

water-based paints Water-soluble paints, such as tempera, watercolor, or acrylic, that use different binders and have different qualities.

weaving A process of interlocking thread, yarn, or other fibers to create a fabric, usually on a loom.

Web design Design specializing in the development of a home page on the World Wide Web for a person, group, or organization.

weft In weaving, the threads that cross over and under the warp fibers on a loom.

Index

Acknowledgments

Illustrations

12, 13, 67, 71, 75, 79, 83, 91, 95, 97, 203, 207, 211–212, 215, 219, 227, 231, 235, 239, 243, 245, 255, 259, 236, 267, 271, 279, 283, 287, 289 Jeff Mangiat; 19, 23, 27, 31, 35, 43, 47, 51, 55, 57, 107, 111, 115, 119, 127, 131, 135, 139, 143, 147, 149 Linda Holt Ayriss; 156, 159, 163, 167, 171, 175, 183, 187, 191, 193, Darryl Ligasan

Photographs

Every effort has been made to secure permission and provide appropriate credit for photographic material. The publisher deeply regrets any omission and pledges to correct errors called to its attention in subsequent editions.

Unless otherwise acknowledged, all photographs are the property of Scott Foresman, a division of Pearson Education.

Photo locators denoted as follows: Top (T), Center (C), Bottom (B), Left (L), Right (R), Background (Bkgd).

Cover: (BL) SuperStock, (BR) © Lisa Berkshire/ Illustration Works, Inc./Getty Images, (T) © Chad Weckler/Corbis.

Front Matter

iv © Michael Newman/PhotoEdit; 1 (T) © 2005 The M. C. Escher Foundation, B.V., Baarn, Holland. All rights reserved./Image © 2003 Board of Trustees, National Gallery of Art, Washington, (B) © Réunion des Musées Nationaux/Art Resource, NY; 2 (L) © Claes Oldenburg & Coosje van Bruggen/Photo © Al Michaud/FPG International/Getty Images, (B) © Werner Forman/Art Resource, NY; 3 (T) © Christie's Images/Corbis, (B) Prints & Photographs Division/ Library of Congress; 4 (T) National Portrait Gallery, Smithsonian Institution/Art Resource, NY, (B) © Gianni Dagli Orti/Corbis; 5 © Kevin R. Morris/ Corbis; 6 Fashion Syndicate Press; 7 (T) Laurene Leon

Boym/Benza, Inc., (B) © 2005 Estate of Dan Flavin/ Artists Rights Society (ARS), NY/Solomon R. Guggenheim Museum/Panza Collection, 1991/91.3705/Photograph by David Heald/©The Solomon R. Guggenheim Foundation, NY; 8 (L) National Portrait Gallery, Smithsonian Institution/Art Resource, NY, (B) © Walter Hodges/Corbis; 9 (B) © Bowers Museum of Cultural Art/Corbis; 10 (B) © Sandy Felsenthal/Corbis, (R) © Gunter Marx Photography/Corbis; 11 (B) Getty Images, (T) © Kelly-Mooney Photography/Corbis.

Units 1–6

14 © 2005 Banco de Mexico. Diego Rivera & Frida Kahlo Museums Trust. Av. Cinco de Mayo No. 2, Col. Centro, Del. Cuauhtemoc 06059, Mexico, D.F./Reproduction authorized by the Instituto Nacional de Bellas Artes y Literatura/Art Resource, NY; 15 Bettmann/Corbis; 16 (B) © Time Life Pictures/NASA/Getty Images; 17 (T) © The Newark Museum/Art Resource, NY, (B) © The Museum of Modern Art/Licensed by Scala/Art Resource, NY 18 © Réunion des Musées Nationaux/Art Resource, NY; 20 (CR) Corbis, (BR) © Jim Richardson/Corbis; 21 © Estate of Fernand Léger/Artists Rights Society (ARS), NY/Photo: © Musée National d'Art Moderne, Centres Georges Pompidou, Paris/SuperStock; 22 © 2005 The M. C. Escher Foundation B.V., Baarn, Holland. All rights reserved./Image © 2003 Board of Trustees, National Gallery of Art, Washington; 24 (CR) © Les David Manevitz/SuperStock, (BL) © Siede Preiss/Getty Images, (BC) Getty Images, (BR) Corbis; 25 © Mattioli Collection, Milan/Bridgeman Art Library, London/SuperStock; 26 Delaware Art Museum; 28 Getty Images; 29 (T) © Claes Oldenburg & Coosje van Bruggen/Gift of Mr. and Mrs. Miles Q. Fiterman, 1991/Collection Walker Art Center, Minneapolis, (B) © Culver Pictures, Inc./SuperStock;